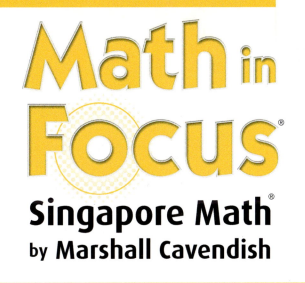

Math in Focus®
Singapore Math®
by Marshall Cavendish

Teacher's Edition
Kindergarten B

Author
Dr. Pamela Sharpe

U.S. Consultants
Andy Clark and Patsy F. Kanter

Marshall Cavendish
Education

U.S. Distributor

**Houghton
Mifflin
Harcourt**

© 2009 Marshall Cavendish International (Singapore) Private Limited
© 2014 Marshall Cavendish Education Pte Ltd

Published by Marshall Cavendish Education
Times Centre, 1 New Industrial Road, Singapore 536196
Customer Service Hotline: (65) 6213 9688
US Office Tel: (1-914) 332 8888 | Fax: (1-914) 332 8882
E-mail: cs@mceducation.com
Website: www.mceducation.com

Distributed by
Houghton Mifflin Harcourt
222 Berkeley Street
Boston, MA 02116
Tel: 617-351-5000
Website: www.hmheducation.com/mathinfocus

First Published 2009

Math in Focus® Kindergarten Teacher's Edition Book B
ISBN 978-0-669-02396-1

Printed in Singapore

8 9 10   1401   22 21 20
4500812213   B C D E

Scope and Sequence Kindergarten–Grade 2

	Kindergarten	Grade 1	Grade 2
Number and Operations			
Sets and Numbers	Use concrete models to create a set with a given number of objects (up to 20).	Use concrete and pictorial models to create a set with a given number of objects (up to 100). Group objects in tens and ones. Numbers up to 100.	Use concrete and pictorial models to create a set with a given number of objects (up to 1,000). Group objects into hundreds, tens, and ones. Group objects into equal sized groups.
	Use cardinal and ordinal numbers.	Use cardinal and ordinal numbers up to 10th.	
Number Representation	Use numbers to represent quantities up to 20.	Use number bonds to represent number combinations. Represent numbers to 100 on a number line.	Use place value models to create equivalent representations of numbers. Represent numbers to 1,000 on a number line.
Count	Count up to 20 objects in a set. Count on and back to 20. Count by 2s and 5s up to 20.	Count to 100. Count by 1s, 2s, 5s, and 10s forward and backward to 100.	Count to 1,000. Count by multiples of ones, tens, and hundreds.
Compare and Order	Compare and order sets and numbers up to 20. Compare and order using the terms *fewer, more, less.*	Compare and order whole numbers to 100. Compare and order using the terms *same, more, fewer, greater than, less than, equal to, greatest, least.*	Compare and order whole numbers to 1,000. Use <, >, = to compare numbers.
Place Value		Use place-value models and place-value charts to represent numbers to 100. Express numbers to 100 in standard and word forms.	Use base-ten models and place-value charts to represent numbers to 1,000. Express numbers to 1,000 in terms of place value. Compose and decompose multi-digit numbers (including expanded form).

	Kindergarten	Grade 1	Grade 2
Number and Operations (continued)			
Fraction Concepts			Connect geometric concepts with unit fractions halves, thirds, and fourths. Understand the relationship between a fraction and a whole. Compare and order halves, thirds, and fourths using bar models.
Decimal Concepts			Use the dollar sign and decimal point.
Money	Identify and relate coin values (penny, nickel, dime, quarter). Count and make coin combinations.	Identify and relate coin values (penny, nickel, dime, quarter). Count and make coin combinations.	Identify $1, $5, $10, $20 bills. Count and make combinations of coins and bills. Compare money amounts.
Whole Number Computation: Addition and Subtraction	Model joining and separating sets. Use +, -, and = to write number sentences for addition and subtraction stories.	Model addition and subtraction situations. Use models, numbers, and symbols for addition and subtraction facts to 20. Use the order, grouping, and zero properties to develop addition and subtraction fact strategies. Add and subtract up to 2-digit numbers with and without regrouping.	Model addition and subtraction with place value. Recall addition and subtraction facts. Use different methods to develop fluency in adding and subtracting multi-digit numbers.
Whole Number Computation: Addition and Subtraction Real-World Problems	Represent addition and subtraction stories.	Formulate addition and subtraction stories. Solve addition and subtraction problems using basic facts.	Solve multi-digit addition and subtraction problems by using a bar model.

	Kindergarten	Grade 1	Grade 2
Number and Operations (continued)			
Whole Number Computation: Multiplication and Division Concepts	Count by 2s and 5s up to 20.	Count by 2s, 5s, and 10s. Adding the same number to multiply. Represent sharing equally and making equal groups.	Multiply and divide with 2, 3, 4, 5, and 10. Represent multiplication as repeated addition. Represent division as repeated subtraction. Use the ×, ÷, and = symbols to represent multiplication and division situations.
Whole Number Computation: Multiplication and Division Real-World Problems			Use bar models to represent multiplication and division situations. Solve multiplication and division fact problems.
Fraction Computation			Add and subtract like fractions.
Decimal Computation		Add and subtract money.	Solve addition and subtraction money problems.
Estimation and Mental Math		Use mental math strategies to add and subtract. Estimate quantity by using referents.	Use mental math strategies to add and subtract. Round to the nearest ten to estimate sums and differences.
Algebra			
Patterns	Describe and extend repeating shape patterns. Count by 2s and 5s. Describe a rule for sorting objects. Find missing terms in repeating patterns.	Identify, describe and extend two- and three-dimensional shape patterns. Skip count by 2s, 5s, and 10s. Identify a rule for sorting objects. Identify and extend growing and repeating patterns. Find missing terms in growing and repeating patterns.	Describe, extend and create two-dimensional shape patterns. Skip count by 2s, 3s, 4s, 5s, and 10s. Identify rules for number patterns. Find missing terms in table patterns.
Properties		Identify 0 as the identity element for addition and subtraction. Use the Associative and Commutative Properties of Addition.	Understand that addition and subtraction are inverse operations. Apply properties of addition. Use the Distributive Property as a multiplication strategy.

	Kindergarten	Grade 1	Grade 2
Algebra (continued)			
Number Theory	Identify odd and even numbers.		
Functional Relationships		Understand the relationships between the numbers in fact families.	Recognize how bar models show the relationship between bar models and number patterns.
Models		Use a variety of concrete, pictorial, and symbolic models for addition and subtraction.	Use a variety of concrete, pictorial, and symbolic models for addition, subtraction, multiplication, and division.
Number Sentences and Equations	Model addition and subtraction stories with addition and subtraction number sentences.	Model addition and subtraction situations by writing addition and subtraction number sentences.	Model multiplication and division situations by writing multiplication and division number sentences. Use bar models and number sentences to represent real-world problems. Determine the value of missing quantities in number sentences.
Equality and Inequality	Understand the meaning of the = sign in number sentences.	Understand the difference between equality and inequality.	Use and create models that demonstrate equality or inequality. Use <, >, and = to write number sentences.
Geometry (continued)			
Size and Position	Understand *big*, *middle sized*, and *small*. Describe and compare objects by position.	Describe position with *left* and *right*. Use positional words to describe location.	
Two-Dimensional Shapes	Identify similarities and differences. Name flat shapes that make up real-world objects. Identify, describe, sort, and classify two-dimensional shapes.	Identify real-world two-dimensional shapes. Identify and describe attributes and properties of two-dimensional shapes.	Identify, describe, sort, and classify two-dimensional shapes.

	Kindergarten	Grade 1	Grade 2
Geometry (continued)			
Two-Dimensional Shapes (continued)	Make flat shape pictures. Compare areas using non-standard units.	Sort and classify two-dimensional shapes. Compose and decompose two-dimensional shapes.	Identify parts of lines and curves. Compose and decompose two-dimensional shapes. Develop foundations for understanding area.
Three-Dimensional Shapes	Name and sort solid shapes. Understand that three-dimensional shapes are made up of two-dimensional shapes. Make shape patterns.	Identify real-world three-dimensional shapes. Identify two-dimensional shapes in three-dimensional shapes. Sort and classify three-dimensional shapes. Recognize shapes from different perspectives. Compose and decompose three-dimensional shapes.	Identify, describe, sort, and classify three-dimensional shapes. Identify surfaces that slide, stack, and roll.
Congruence and Symmetry		Develop initial understanding of congruence and symmetry.	
Measurement			
Length and Distance	Compare lengths and heights using non-standard units. Compare and order lengths (long, short, longest, shortest) Develop a background for measurement using non-standard units.	Compare two lengths by comparing each with a third length (transitivity). Using a start line to measure length. Measure lengths, using non-standard units. Explain the need for equal-length units to measure. Count length units in groups of tens and ones. Compare measurements made using different units. Understand the inverse relationship between the size of a unit and the number of units.	Demonstrate linear measure as an iteration of units. Use rulers to measure length. Measure lengths in meters, centimeters, feet, and inches. Compare and measure lengths using customary and metric units. Demonstrate partitioning and transitivity in relation to length. Solve problems involving estimating, measuring, and computing length.

Scope and Sequence Kindergarten–Grade 2

	Kindergarten	Grade 1	Grade 2
Measurement (continued)			
Weight/Mass	Order objects by weight. Compare weights using non-standard units.	Compare and measure weights using non-standard units. Compare two massess by comparing each with a third mass (transitivity).	Compare and measure masses. Solve mass problems.
Capacity/Volume	Compare capacities.		Measure volume (capacity) in liters. Solve volume problems.
Time	Name and order the days of the week and the months of the year. Compare durations of events.	Identify the days of the week and months of the year. Recognize the correct way to write the date. Tell time to the hour and half hour.	Tell time to five minutes Use A.M. and P.M. Find elapsed time.
Data Analysis			
Classifying and Sorting	Understand similarities and differences in objects and shapes. Sort and classify objects using one or two attributes.	Sort and classify geometric shapes. Sort and classify data in order to make graphs.	Sort and classify two- and three-dimensional shapes by properties. Collect and organize data in picture graphs.
Collect and Organize Data	Organize data for a picture graph.	Collect and organize data in different ways.	Collect, sort, and organize data in different ways.
Represent Data	Represent data in picture graphs.	Represent measurements and data in picture graphs and bar graphs.	Represent data in picture graphs.
Interpret/Analyze Data	Interpret data in tally charts and bar graphs.	Interpret data in picture graphs, tally charts, and bar graphs. Solve problems involving data.	Interpret picture graphs with scales. Solve real-world problems using picture graphs.
Problem Solving			
Build Skills Through Problem Solving	Build skills in addition and subtraction through problem solving.	Build skills in addition, subtraction, and measurement through problem solving.	Build skills in addition, subtraction, multiplication, division, and measurement through problem solving.
Solve Real-World Problems	Solve real-world problems involving addition and subtraction.	Solve real-world problems involving addition and subtraction.	Solve real-world problems involving addition, subtraction, multiplication, division, and measurement.

	Kindergarten	Grade 1	Grade 2
Problem Solving (continued)			
Use Appropriate Strategies and Thinking Skills to Solve Problems		Apply problem-solving strategies in Put on Your Thinking Cap! and Problem Solving activities.	Apply problem-solving strategies in Put on Your Thinking Cap! and Problem Solving activities.
Apply and Explain Problem Solving	Solve real-world problems.	Apply and explain problem solving processes in Put on Your Thinking Cap! and other activities.	Apply and explain problem solving processes in Put on Your Thinking Cap! and other activities.
Reasoning and Proof			
Explore Concepts	Use models to explain reasoning.	Explore concepts more deeply and justify reasoning in Let's Explore and Hands-On activities. Apply Thinking Skills in Put on Your Thinking Cap!, Challenging Practice, and Problem Solving activities.	Explore concepts more deeply and justify reasoning in Let's Explore and Hands-On activities. Apply Thinking Skills in Put on Your Thinking Cap!, Challenging Practice, and Problem Solving activities.
Investigate Mathematical Ideas	Investigate ideas with two-dimensional and three-dimensional shapes.	Further investigate mathematical ideas by completing critical thinking skills activities.	Further investigate mathematical ideas by completing critical thinking skills activities.
Identify, Demonstrate, and Explain Mathematical Proof	Demonstrate that only a few big objects fit into small spaces and many small objects fit into big spaces. Describe, sort, and classify two- and three dimensional shapes. Interpret data in tally charts and bar graphs. Identify and extend repeating shape patterns.	Explore transitivity by comparing lengths and weights of three different objects. Identify and describe attributes and properties of two- and three dimensional shapes. Interpret picture graphs, tally charts, and bar graphs. Identify and extend growing number patterns and repeating shape patterns.	Demonstrate the inverse relationship between the size of a unit and the number of units. Identify, describe, sort, and classify two- and three dimensional shapes. Interpret picture graphs with scales. Identify rules for number patterns.
Use a Variety of Reasoning Skills	Sort and classify using attributes. Identify similarities and differences.	Recognize shapes from different perspectives. Use the Commutative and Associative Properties and tens and ones to solve two-digit addition and subtraction problems.	Identify surfaces that slide, stack, and roll. Explore the inverse relationship between addition and subtraction.

	Kindergarten	Grade 1	Grade 2
Communication			
Consolidate Mathematical Thinking	Consolidate thinking in independent activities.	Present mathematical thinking through Math Journal activities.	Present mathematical thinking through Math Journal activities.
Communicate with Peers, Teachers, and Others	Discuss mathematical ideas in paired and small group activities.	Discuss mathematical ideas in Let's Explore activities. Work together in pairs or groups in Let's Explore, Games, and other activities.	Discuss mathematical ideas in Let's Explore activities. Work together in pairs or groups in Let's Explore, Games, and other activities.
Share Mathematical Thinking	Share mathematical ideas in paired and small group activities.	Share mathematical ideas with others during Let's Explore and Hands-On activities.	Share mathematical ideas with others during Let's Explore and Hands-On activities.
Express Mathematics Ideas	Express ideas in paired and small group activities.	Express ideas in Math Journal activities, using lesson vocabulary. Use chapter and lesson vocabulary correctly.	Express ideas in Math Journal activities, using lesson vocabulary. Use chapter and lesson vocabulary correctly.
Connections			
Recognize Connections in Mathematical Ideas	Understand the connection between quantities and written numerals.	Understand the relationship between counting and addition and subtraction. Understand the relationships between the numbers in fact families. Connect addition and multiplication (repeated addition). Recognize and apply different strategies for adding and subtracting 1-and 2-digit numbers	Examine and apply the inverse relationship between addition and subtraction. Connect geometric concepts with halves, thirds, and fourths. Connect subtraction and division (repeated subtraction). Recognize and apply different strategies for multiplication and division facts.
Understand How Concepts Build on One Another	Explore relationships among counting, ordering, and ordinal numbers.	Learn how place-value concepts apply to regrouping in addition and subtraction.	Understand how patterns can be described using numbers, operations, and data displays. Recognize the relationship between bar models, number sentences, and number patterns.

	Kindergarten	Grade 1	Grade 2
Connections (continued)			
Solve Real-World Problems in Contexts Outside of Mathematics	Solve real-world problems involving *more* and *less*.	Solve real-world problems involving addition, subtraction, and measurement.	Solve real-world problems involving addition, subtraction, multiplication, division, and measurement and data analysis.
Representation			
Use Representations to Model, Organize, and Record	Use concrete models to create a set with a given number of objects (up to 20).	Use concrete and pictorial models to create a set with a given number of objects (up to 100).	Use concrete and pictorial models to create a set with a given number of objects (up to 1,000).
	Use numbers and numerals to represent quantities up to 20.	Represent numbers to 100 on a number line.	Represent numbers to 1,000 on a number line.
	Use picture cards to communicate understanding of comparisons (*bigger, taller, smaller*).		Use symbolic notation (<, >) to compare numbers.
	Understand the meaning of the +, −, and = sign in number sentences.	Use the +, −, and = symbols to represent addition and subtraction situations.	Use bar models to represent addition and subtraction situations.
	Model addition and subtraction stories with addition and subtraction number sentences.	Represent numerical data using picture graphs, tally charts and bar graphs.	Represent numerical data using picture graphs with scales, tally charts, and bar graphs.
	Represent addition and subtraction stories.	Represent sharing equally making equal groups.	Use the x, ÷, and = symbols to represent multiplication and division situations.
			Represent multiplication with skip counting, dot paper arrays, and bar models.
			Represent division as repeated subtraction.
	Describe and extend shape patterns.	Identify, describe and extend two- and three-dimensional shape patterns.	Describe, extend and create two-dimensional shape patterns.
	Describe a rule for sorting objects.	Identify a rule for sorting objects.	

	Kindergarten	Grade 1	Grade 2
Representation (continued)			
Use Representations to Model, Organize, and Record (continued)		Identify and extend growing and repeating patterns.	Identify rules for number and table patterns.
Select and Apply Representations to Model Problems	Represent quantities with objects, number cubes, and numerals.	Use number bonds to represent number combinations.	Use place-value models to create equivalent representations of numbers.
		Use a variety of concrete, pictorial, and symbolic models for addition and subtraction.	Use a variety of concrete, pictorial, and symbolic models for addition, subtraction, multiplication, and division.
Interpret Phenomena Through Representations	Show understanding of *big, middle-sized, small,* and *same size.*	Measure and compare lengths and weights using non-standard units.	Use metric and customary units to measure length, volume (capacity), weight and mass.
	Describe and compare objects by position.	Use positional words to describe location.	
	Name flat shapes that make up real-world objects.	Identify real-world two- and three-dimensional shapes.	
	Represent measurements and data in picture graphs and bar graphs.	Represent data in picture graphs.	Represent data in bar graphs and picture graphs.
	Order a number of objects according to length, height, or weight.	Solve problems about sharing equally and making equal groups.	Solve real-world problems about social phenomena.
	Use one-to-one correspondence.	Use a variety of models for adding and subtracting.	Use bar models to represent addition, subtraction, multiplication, and division situations.
		Use technology (virtual manipulatives and computers) to model and draw.	Use technology (virtual manipulatives and computers) to model and draw.

Table of Contents

■ Big Book ■ Student Book ■ Teacher's Edition Only

Chapter 2

Numbers to 9

1 Pairing Sets: All About 6 [2 DAY Lesson] 28

1 **Investigate:** Number 6

2 **Investigate:** Concept of 6

3 **Explore:** Pairs

4 **Apply:** Match One-to-One

5 **Apply:** Draw 1 to 6

2 Pairing More Sets: All About 7 [3 DAY Lesson] 33

1 **Investigate:** Number 7

2 **Investigate:** Concept of 7

3 **Apply:** Concept of 7

4 **Apply:** Match One-to-One

5 **Apply:** Draw 1 to 7

6 **Explore:** Make Matches Using Pictures

7 **Apply:** Write Numerals 1 to 7

8 **Apply:** Count Groups

9 **Apply:** Concepts of 1 to 7

10 **Apply:** Problem Solving Situations

3 All About 8 [2 DAY Lesson] 40

1 **Investigate:** Number 8

2 **Apply:** Concept of 8

3 **Apply:** Draw 1 to 8

4 **Apply:** Match One-to-One

5 **Apply:** Draw 1 to 8

6 **Apply:** Write Numerals 1 to 8

4 Numbers 0 to 9 [3 DAY Lesson] 45

1 **Investigate:** Number 9; Number Comparisons

2 **Apply:** Concept of 9 • Recall, Reinforce, and Review

3 **Apply:** Counting Skills

4 **Apply:** Number 0; Sequence and Pattern

5 **Apply:** Match One-to-One

6 **Apply:** Draw 1 to 9

7 **Apply:** Write Numerals 1 to 9

8 **Apply:** Solve Part-Part-Whole Problems

5 Number Games [2 DAY Lesson] 52

1 **Explore:** Count Spaces on a Game Board

2 **Explore:** Count Spaces on a Game Board

Chapter 3 — Order by Length or Weight

■ Big Book   ■ Student Book   ■ Teacher's Edition Only

Chapter 4 — Counting and Numbers 0 to 10

Chapter 5 — Size and Position

■ Big Book   ■ Student Book   ■ Teacher's Edition Only

Chapter 6 — Counting and Numbers to 20

■ Big Book   ■ Student Book   ■ Teacher's Edition Only

Table of Contents

Chapter 7 — Solid and Flat Shapes

Chapter 8

Counting by 2s and 5s

1 Making Pairs `1 DAY` Lesson **18**

1 Investigate: Pairs and Twos

2 Apply: Match Pairs

3 Explore: Count by Twos

2 Counting by 2s `1 DAY` Lesson **20**

1 Investigate: Count by Twos

2 Explore: Count People and Objects

• Recall, Reinforce, and Review

3 Apply: Count Objects in Pictures by Twos

3 Counting by 5s `2 DAY` Lesson **22**

1 Investigate: Fives and Tally

2 Explore: Count by Fives to 20

3 Apply: Complete a Tally Chart

4 Odd and Even Numbers `2 DAY` Lesson **24**

1 Investigate: Skip-count

2 Discover: Odd and Even Numbers

3 Apply: Odd and Even Sets

4 Apply: Odd and Even Clapping

5 Apply: Odd and Even Numbers in a Counting Sequence

5 Number Conservation `1 DAY` Lesson **28**

1 Explore: Match One-to-One; Number Conservation

2 Discover: Match One-to-One

3 Apply: Match Equal Sets

■ Big Book   ■ Student Book   ■ Teacher's Edition Only

Chapter 9 — Comparing Sets

Chapter 10 — Ordinal Numbers

Chapter 11 — Calendar Patterns

■ Big Book   ■ Student Book   ■ Teacher's Edition Only

Chapter 12   Counting On and Counting Back

Chapter 13 Patterns

1 Repeating Shape Patterns 2 DAY Lesson **80**

1 Investigate: Repeating Pattern

2 Explore: Create a Repeating Pattern

3 Apply: Identify the Next Shape

4 Apply: Identify a Missing Shape • Recall, Reinforce, and Review

2 Repeating Patterns 1 DAY Lesson **83**

1 Explore: Create a Repeating Pattern

3 Making Patterns with Things 1 DAY Lesson **84**

1 Explore: Continue Patterns

2 Explore: Replicate a Given Pattern • Recall, Reinforce, and Review

Chapter 14 Counting On to 15

1 Combining Two Sets to Make 10 1 DAY Lesson **88**

1 Investigate: Count On to 10

2 Apply: How Many More

2 Numbers 10 to 20 2 DAY Lesson **90**

1 Investigate: Relate Numbers to Numerals • Recall, Reinforce, and Review

2 Discover: Count On From 11 to 20

3 Apply: Identify Sets and Trace Numerals

4 Apply: Identify Sets and Write Numerals

3 Counting On 1 DAY Lesson **94**

1 Investigate: Number Comparisons to 20

2 Apply: Count On to 15; How Many More • Recall, Reinforce, and Review

3 Apply: Total Number of Objects; How Many More

■ Big Book ■ Student Book ■ Teacher's Edition Only

■ Big Book   ■ Student Book   ■ Teacher's Edition Only

Chapter 19 Measurement

Chapter 20 Money

1 Coin Values **[1 DAY Lesson]**

1 Investigate: Penny, Nickel, Dime, Quarter, and Cent **2 Apply:** Match Coins to Their Values

2 Counting Coins **[1 DAY Lesson]**

1 Explore: Add and Subtract Money; Change **2 Apply:** Buy Objects with Pennies

3 Different Coins, Same Value **[1 DAY Lesson]**

1 Explore: Coin Combinations **2 Apply:** Coins Needed to Make a Purchase
• Recall, Reinforce, and Review

Teacher Resources

■ Big Book   ■ Student Book   ■ Teacher's Edition Only

Math Background

Children's understanding of shapes begins at a very young age when they observe the world that surrounds them. When they start school, instruction focuses on expanding and enhancing prior knowledge. Children are taught more precise names for shapes and they learn to describe them. From there, children begin to compare and contrast shapes.

It is important to provide many concrete examples of flat and solid shapes to help children make real-world connections. They should be able to identify examples and non-examples of different shapes. For example, a window pane is a rectangle, but the bottom of a cylindrical wastebasket is not.

Vocabulary

corners	places where two sides or edges meet
edges	the outsides of a three-dimensional shape
sides	the outsides of a two-dimensional shape
pattern	a repeated sequence

○ circle   △ triangle   ☐ square   ▭ rectangle

Cross-Curricular Connections

Reading/ Language Arts Read aloud *Shapes, Shapes, Shapes* by Tana Hoban (HarperTrophy ©1996). The author asks the reader to look for all the shapes that can be found in the book's photographs. As you read the story, and the children name the shapes, ask them for other examples of shapes that they see in the classroom.

Art Tell children that many artists use shapes in their artwork. If possible, show examples. You may wish to find examples on the Internet and print them out ahead of time. Have children create their own shape artwork. Provide a variety of shapes that can be traced and colored. Another option is to give children shapes cut from construction paper that they glue onto paper. Invite children to use shape vocabulary to describe their work.

Skills Trace

| Grade K | Identify circles, triangles, squares, and rectangles. |
| Grade 1 | Use shapes to make patterns. (Chap. 5) |

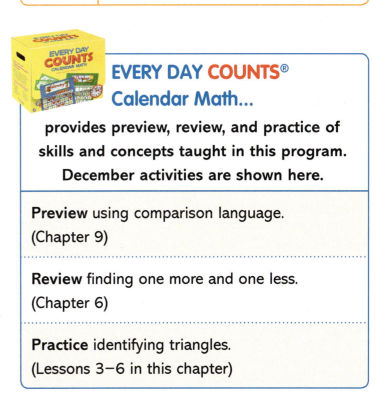

EVERY DAY COUNTS® Calendar Math...

provides preview, review, and practice of skills and concepts taught in this program. December activities are shown here.

Preview using comparison language. (Chapter 9)

Review finding one more and one less. (Chapter 6)

Practice identifying triangles. (Lessons 3–6 in this chapter)

Chapter Resources

Activity Cards

Also available on Teaching Resources CD.

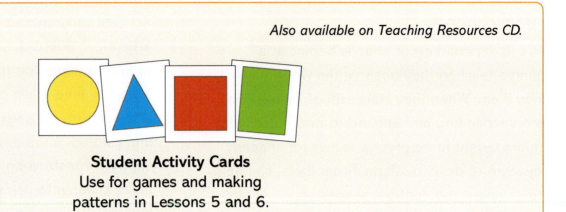

Student Activity Cards
Use for games and making
patterns in Lessons 5 and 6.

Manipulatives from the Manipulatives Kit

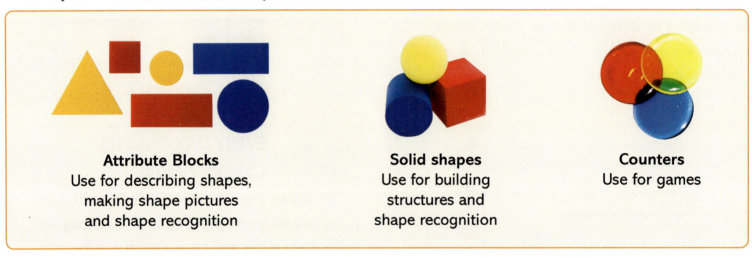

Attribute Blocks
Use for describing shapes,
making shape pictures
and shape recognition

Solid shapes
Use for building
structures and
shape recognition

Counters
Use for games

Technology Resources

- *Math in Focus*® eBooks
- *Math in Focus*® Teacher Resources CD
- Online Web Resources
- *Math in Focus*® Virtual Manipulatives
  for Lessons 1–6

Classroom/Household Items

- Crayons
- Paper
- Adhesive tape
- Classroom objects that resemble shapes, such as a box, a ball, a triangular cushion, and so on
- Colored pencils

Differentiation and Assessment

Differentiation for Special Populations (Resources in the Teacher's Edition)

	English Language Learners	Children Needing Reinforcement	Children Needing a Challenge
Lesson 1	Math Talk, Student Book B, Part 1, pp. 2–3		
Lesson 2	Math Talk, Teacher's Edition B, p. 6		
	Math Talk, Student Book B, Part 1, p. 4		
Lesson 3	Math Talk, Teacher's Edition B, p. 9		
Lesson 6		Teacher's Edition B, p. 15	Teacher's Edition B, p. 15

Lead children on a shape search in the playground to look for shapes: circles, triangles, squares, and rectangles. Ask: Which type of shape do you see most often?

Chapter 7 Assessments

On-Going Assessment	Formal Assessment
See the check questions in the Teacher's Edition on these pages	*Find Formal Assessment Blackline Masters in the Assessments book*
Teacher's Edition B	**Assessments Book**
Lesson 2, pp. 6, 7 Lesson 3, p. 10 Lesson 4, p. 12 Lesson 5, pp. 13, 14 Lesson 6, p. 16	Assessment 3 for Book B, Part 1 (Chapters 7–10), is on pages 14–18 of Assessments. Interview Assessment is on pages 19–20.

Chapter 7 Planning Guide

Lessons and Pacing	Activity	Component	Objectives and Math Focus
Lesson 1	**Solid Shapes,** pp. 2–4		• Recognize basic solid and flat shapes. • Understand that some shapes have corners and flat sides, and some do not.
DAY 1 Activities	1 Investigate	**Big Book B,** pp. 2–3	Build awareness of plane figures.
	2 Discover	**Teacher's Edition B,** p. 3	Discover plane shapes within the classroom.
DAY 2 Activities	3 Explore	**Teacher's Edition B,** p. 3	Introduce *corners, edges,* and *sides* of solid shapes.
	4 Apply	**Student Book B, Part 1,** pp. 2–3	Match a solid shape to the shape of one face.
Lesson 2	**Solid Shapes in Everyday Things,** pp. 5–7		• Describe basic solid and flat shapes. • Name basic flat shapes. • Recognize the relationship between solid shapes and flat shapes.
DAY 1 Activities	1 Investigate	**Big Book B,** pp. 2–3	Introduce *circle, triangle, square,* and *rectangle.*
	2 Discover	**Teacher's Edition B,** p. 6	Discover geometric shapes in classroom objects.
DAY 2 Activities	3 Explore	**Teacher's Edition B,** p. 6	Explore the outlines of solid shapes.
	4 Apply	**Student Book B, Part 1,** p. 4	Match a solid figure to the outline of one of its faces.
Lesson 3	**Flat Shapes,** pp. 8–10		• Draw flat shapes. • Understand *big* and *small.*
DAY 1 Activities	1 Investigate	**Big Book B,** pp. 2–3	Build awareness of flat shapes.
	2 Apply	**Teacher's Edition B,** p. 9	Draw a given flat shape.
	3 Apply	**Student Book B, Part 1,** pp. 5–6	Draw large and small plane figures.
Lesson 4	**Flat Shape Pictures,** pp. 11–12		• Identify basic shapes within a scene. • Make a picture using basic flat shapes.
DAY 1 Activities	1 Investigate	**Big Book B,** pp. 4–5	Identify and count flat shapes in a picture.
	2 Apply	**Student Book B, Part 1,** p. 7	Color flat shapes to match a key.
DAY 2 Activities	3 Explore	**Teacher's Edition B,** p. 12	Create and describe pictures, using attribute blocks.

Vocabulary	Manipulatives/Materials	Class Organization	NTCM Focal Points & Process Standards
		Whole class	Identify, name, and describe plane shapes; connect them to solid shapes.
	• Attribute blocks (minus the hexagons), 1 per child • Crayons, 1 per child • Paper, 1 sheet per child • Adhesive tape	Whole class	
corners, edges, sides	• Solid shapes, 6 per pair	Pairs	• Communication • Connections
		Independent	
circle, triangle, square, rectangle		Whole class	Identify, name, and describe plane shapes; connect them to solid shapes.
	• Classroom objects that resemble shapes, such as a box, a ball, a triangular cushion, and so on	Whole class	
	• Circle (TR17), Triangle (TR18), Square (TR19), and Rectangle (TR20), 1 copy of each per group • Solid shapes, 4 per group (1 cone or hemisphere, 1 pyramid or triangular prism, 1 rectangular prism, and 1 cube or cylinder)	Small groups	• Communication • Representation • Connections • Problem solving
		Independent	
		Whole class	Identify, name, and describe plane shapes.
	• Circle (TR17), Triangle (TR18), Square (TR19), and Rectangle (TR20), 1 copy of each per pair	Pairs	
		Independent	• Communication • Representation
		Whole class	Identify, name, and describe plane and shapes.
	• Colored pencils, 4 per pair (1 red, 1 green, 1 yellow, and 1 blue)	Independent	
	• Attribute blocks (minus the hexagons), 10 per pair	Pairs	• Communication • Connections • Problem solving

Chapter 7 Planning Guide

Lessons and Pacing	Activity	Component	Objectives and Math Focus
Lesson 5	**Name That Shape,** pp. 13–14		• Guess a shape from its description.
DAY 1 Activities	1 Investigate	**Big Book B,** pp. 4–5	Identify flat shapes by their properties.
	2 Explore	**Teacher's Edition B,** p. 14	Identify matching flat shapes quickly.
DAY 2 Activities	3 Explore	**Teacher's Edition B,** p. 14	Search for flat shapes in the classroom.
Lesson 6	**Shapes Patterns,** pp. 15–16		• Guess a shape from its description. • Describe a basic flat shape. • Identify and continue a shape pattern.
DAY 1 Activities	1 Explore	**Teacher's Edition B,** p. 15	Verbalize properties of flat shapes.
DAY 2 Activities	2 Explore	**Teacher's Edition B,** p. 16	Introduce patterns of shapes.
	3 Apply	**Student Book B, Part 1,** p. 8	Continue a pattern of shapes.

Vocabulary	Manipulatives/Materials	Class Organization	NTCM Focal Points & Process Standards
	• Counters, 20–30 • Student Activity Cards 7.5a–d, 2 sets per pair	Whole class Pairs	Identify, name, and describe plane shapes.
	• Circle (TR17), Triangle (TR18), Square (TR19), and Rectangle (TR20), 1 copy of each • Attribute blocks, 20 (5 circles, 5 triangles, 5 squares, and 5 rectangles)	Small groups	• Communication • Representation • Reasoning / Proof
		Small groups	Identify and extend simple patterns of shapes.
pattern	• Student Activity Cards 7.5a–d, 1 set per child	Small groups Independent	• Communication • Connections • Problem solving

Lesson 1
Solid Shapes

LESSON OBJECTIVES
• Recognize basic solid and flat shapes.
• Understand that some shapes have corners and flat sides, and some do not.

MATERIALS
• Attribute blocks
• Crayons
• Paper
• Adhesive tape
• Solid shapes

<table>
<tr><td>**Vocabulary**</td></tr>
<tr><td>corners</td></tr>
<tr><td>edges</td></tr>
<tr><td>sides</td></tr>
</table>

DAY 1

Teacher's Edition B, pp. 2–3
Big Book B, pp. 2–3

DAY 2

Teacher's Edition B, pp. 3–4
Student Book B, Part 1, pp. 2–3

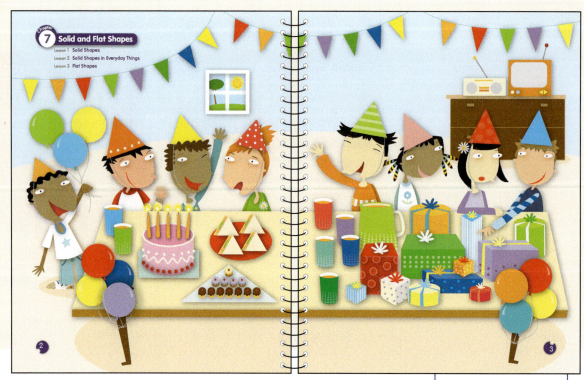

Big Book B, pp. 2–3

DAY 1

ACTIVITY 1
Investigate

Math Focus: Build awareness of plane figures.
Resource: Big Book B, pp. 2–3
Classroom Setup: Whole class, in front of the Big Book

1. *Ask* children to sit so that everyone can see the Big Book.

2. *Ask* children to describe the shapes they can see in the birthday party picture.

Best Practices There is no need to name the solid shapes. Accept any suitable shape descriptions including size descriptions. Focus on the four basic shapes: circle, triangle, square, and rectangle, including the faces on solid figures.

It is big, blue, and round.

ACTIVITY 2
Discover

Math Focus: Discover plane shapes within the classroom.
Materials: Attribute blocks (minus the hexagons), 1 per child
Crayons, 1 per child
Paper, 1 sheet per child
Adhesive tape
Classroom Setup: Whole class

1. *Encourage* children to return to their places.

2. *Show* children the attribute blocks one at a time and ask them to describe what they see.

3. *Ask* children to look for things around the classroom that are of a similar shape to the four basic shapes.

4. *Distribute* materials to the children.

5. Have them lay their attribute block on their sheet of paper, tape it down, and turn the paper over.

6. *Ask* them to lightly color over the area where the attribute block is. The shape of the block will appear on the paper.

7. *Model* steps 5 and 6 if necessary.

> **Best Practices** Hang children's work on the walls of your classroom to remind them of the shapes they are learning.

ACTIVITY 3
Explore

Math Focus: Introduce *corners*, *edges*, and *sides* of solid shapes.
Materials: Solid shapes, 6 per pair
Classroom Setup: Children work in pairs.

1. *Distribute* materials to the children.

2. Children are to build structures, such as animals, buildings or monsters with their solid shapes.

3. *Ask* children to explain why certain shapes fit together and why some do not fit easily together. (Some shapes have only one *corner* at their top, so they cannot balance other shapes. Some shapes have curved *edges* or are round, so they too cannot balance or support other shapes. Shapes with flat tops can balance on or support other shapes.)

4. *Direct* children's attention to the cube. *Say:* Each flat part of a solid shape is called a *side*. How many sides does this figure have? (6)

5. *Repeat* step 4 using the square pyramid.

> **Best Practices** There is no need to name the solid shapes at this time. When you want to talk about a particular solid, simply hold it up.

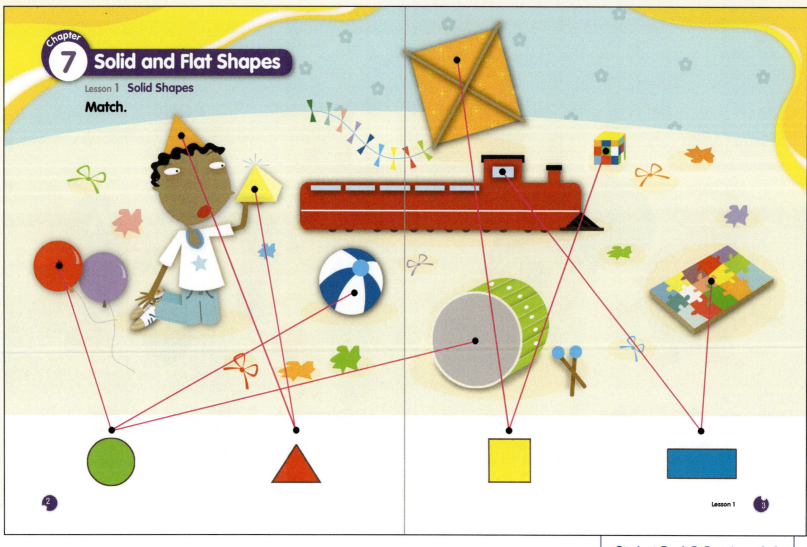

Student Book B, Part 1, pp. 2–3

ACTIVITY 4
Apply

Math Focus: Match a solid shape to the shape of one face.
Resource: Student Book B, Part 1, pp. 2–3
Classroom Setup: Children work independently.

1. Children draw a line between the picture of a solid shape and the corresponding flat shape.

2. *Ask* children to explain why they have matched the shapes in this manner.

3. **Math Talk** Encourage children to justify their choices in terms of what they notice about the differences between the shapes. Help them focus on the different shapes rather than the size of the shape.

Lesson 2
Solid Shapes in Everyday Things

LESSON OBJECTIVES
- Describe basic solid and flat shapes.
- Name basic flat shapes.
- Recognize the relationship between solid shapes and flat shapes.

MATERIALS
- Classroom objects that resemble shapes, such as a box, a ball, a triangular cushion, and so on
- Circle (TR17), Triangle (TR18), Square (TR19), and Rectangle (TR20)
- Solid shapes

Vocabulary
circle

triangle

square

rectangle

DAY 1

Teacher's Edition B, pp. 5–6
Big Book B, pp. 2–3

DAY 2

Teacher's Edition B, pp. 6–7
Student Book B, Part 1, p. 4

Big Book B, pp. 2–3

DAY 1

ACTIVITY 1
Investigate

Math Focus: Introduce *circle*, *triangle*, *square*, and *rectangle*.
Resource: Big Book B, pp. 2–3
Classroom Setup: Whole class, in front of the Big Book

1. *Ask* children to sit so that everyone can see the Big Book.

2. *Ask* children to describe the shapes they can see in the birthday party picture.

3. As the names of shapes are introduced, describe the differences in terms of length, number of sides, corners, and curved, round or straight edges.

4. Next, ask children to add any more description they can think of, such as size.

Best Practices With solid objects, the faces may be more than one flat shape. For example, a box may have two square faces and four rectangular ones, but there is no need to name the solid shape.

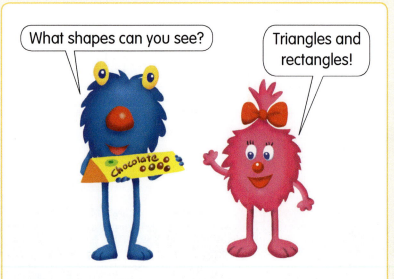

ACTIVITY 2
Discover

Math focus: Discover geometric shapes in classroom objects.

Materials: Classroom objects that resemble shapes, such as a box, a ball, a triangular cushion, and so on

Classroom Setup: Continue with whole class setup as in Activity 1.

1. *Hold* up an object and *ask:* What shapes can you see in this?

2. Next, explain the shapes. *Say:* This shape is called a triangle, and so on.

3. *Ask* children to use a finger to draw the shape in the air.

4. As the name of each shape is introduced, have children describe it in terms of lengths and number of sides, corners, and curved, round, or straight edges.

5. *Repeat* until you have included all four basic shapes.

6. *Compare* each shape to previous shapes as you go along.

ACTIVITY 3
Explore

Math Focus: Explore the outlines of solid shapes.

Materials: Circle (TR17), Triangle (TR18), Square (TR19), and Rectangle (TR20), 1 copy of each per group
Solid shapes, 4 per group (1 cone or hemisphere, 1 pyramid or triangular prism, 1 rectangular prism, and 1 cube or cylinder)

Classroom Setup: Children work in small groups.

1. *Distribute* materials to the children.

2. *Ask* children to trace around the bottom of a solid shape inside each corresponding shape outline.

Best Practices Have children pass around the solid shapes within their group until everyone has traced at least one of each shape.

3. *Point* out that when the solid shapes are traced onto paper, their outlines are flat shapes in the form of circles, triangles, squares or rectangles.

✔ 4. While children engage in the activity, ask check questions such as:
   • Why did you draw around this object here?
   • Could you have used a different object?
   • How do you know? Are you sure?

5. **Math Talk** Encourage descriptions of the shape in terms of the number of sides, number of corners, curved, round or straight edges, and the name of the shape drawn.

Best Practices There is no need to name the solid shapes at this time as this might confuse the children.

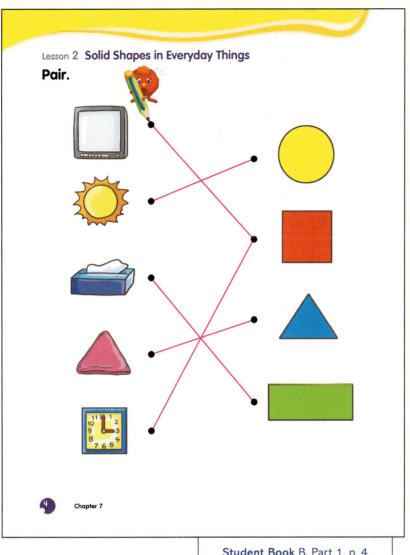

Lesson 2 **Solid Shapes in Everyday Things**

Pair.

Student Book B, Part 1, p. 4

ACTIVITY 4
Apply

Math Focus: Match a solid figure to the outline of one of its faces.
Resource: Student Book B, Part 1, p. 4
Classroom Setup: Children work independently.

1. Children draw a line between the picture of the solid shape and the corresponding flat shape outline.

✔ 2. While children engage in the activity, ask check questions such as:
   • Why have you drawn this line here?
   • Could you draw it to this shape instead?
   • Why not? Are you sure?

3. **Math Talk** Encourage descriptions of the shape in terms of the number of sides, number of corners, curved, round, or straight edges, and the name of the shape.

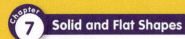

Chapter 7 — Solid and Flat Shapes

Lesson 3
Flat Shapes

LESSON OBJECTIVES
- Draw flat shapes.
- Understand *big* and *small*.

MATERIALS
- Circle (TR17), Triangle (TR18), Square (TR19), and Rectangle (TR20)

DAY 1

Teacher's Edition B, pp. 8–10
Big Book B, pp. 2–3
Student Book B, Part 1, pp. 5–6

Big Book B, pp. 2–3

DAY 1

ACTIVITY 1
Investigate

Math Focus: Build awareness of flat shapes.
Resource: Big Book B, pp. 2–3
Classroom Setup: Whole class, in front of the Big Book

1. *Ask* children to sit so that everyone can see the Big Book.

2. *Ask* children to describe the shapes they see in the birthday party picture.

3. *Remind* children about the number and length of sides, corners, and round, curved, or straight edges.

ACTIVITY 2
Apply

Math Focus: Draw a given flat shape.

Materials: Circle (TR17), Triangle (TR18), Square (TR19), and Rectangle (TR20), 1 copy of each per pair

Classroom Setup: Children work in pairs.

1. *Encourage* children to return to their places.

2. *Distribute* materials to the children.

3. *Ask* children to draw an object from memory. The object should have the same shape as shown on the paper, and be drawn inside the shape on the paper.

4. *Ask:* Why have you drawn this object here?

5. **Math Talk** Encourage descriptions of the shape in terms of the number and length of sides, corners, round, curved, or straight edges, and the name of the shape.

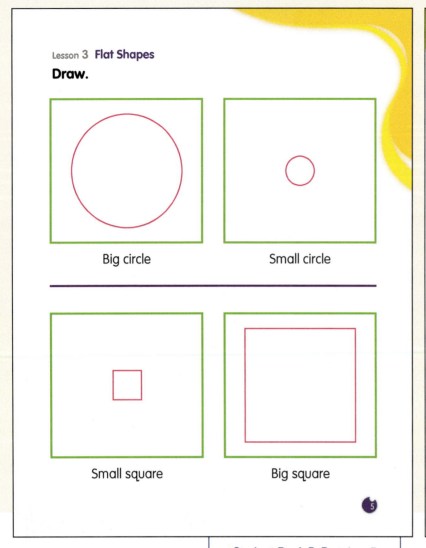

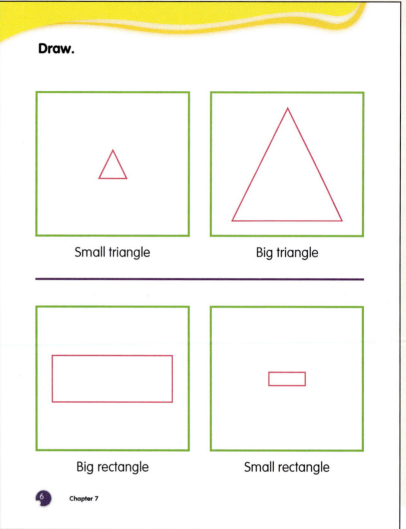

ACTIVITY 3
Apply

Math Focus: Draw large and small plane figures.
Resource: Student Book B, Part 1, pp. 5–6
Classroom Setup: Children work independently.

1. Children draw the stated shapes in each box.

2. *Remind* children about the number and length of sides, corners, round, curved, or straight edges, and the size (big or small).

✓ 3. While children engage in the activity, ask check questions such as:
   • Is this the correct shape? How do you know?
   • Is this a small triangle? Why do you think it is small?

Lesson 4
Flat Shape Pictures

LESSON OBJECTIVES
- Identify basic shapes within a scene.
- Make a picture using basic flat shapes.

MATERIALS
- Colored pencils
- Attribute blocks

DAY 1

Teacher's Edition B, pp. 11–12
Big Book B, pp. 4–5
Student Book B, Part 1, p. 7

DAY 2

Teacher's Edition B, p. 12

Lesson 4 Flat Shape Pictures
Lesson 5 Name That Shape

Big Book B, pp. 4–5

DAY 1

ACTIVITY 1
Investigate

Math Focus: Identify and count flat shapes in a picture.
Resource: Big Book B, pp. 4–5
Classroom Setup: Whole class, in front of the Big Book.

1. *Ask* children to sit so that everyone can see the Big Book.

2. *Ask* children to count silently the number of circles, triangles, squares, and rectangles they see in the picture. Then, check with the class as a whole. (10 circles, 6 triangles, 7 squares, 7 rectangles)

3. *Remind* children about the number and length of sides, corners, and round, curved, or straight edges each shape has irrespective of its size.

Lesson 4 **Flat Shape Pictures**

**Color the squares red. Color the rectangles green.
Color the circles yellow. Color the triangles blue.**

⑦

Student Book B, Part 1, p. 7

ACTIVITY 2
Apply 👤

Math Focus: Color flat shapes to match a key.
Resource: Student Book B, Part 1, p. 7
Materials: Colored pencils, 4 per pair (1 red, 1 green, 1 yellow, and 1 blue)
Classroom Setup: Children work independently.

1. *Encourage* children to return to their places and open their Student Books to page 7.

2. *Distribute* materials to the children.

3. Children color the squares red, the rectangles green, the circles yellow, and the triangles blue. Direct their attention to the furries at the top of the page who will help them choose the correct color for each shape.

4. *Help* children, especially those who need more time, to recall the properties of the four basic shapes.

ACTIVITY 3
Explore 👥

Math Focus: Create and describe pictures, using attribute blocks.
Materials: Attribute blocks (minus the hexagons), 10 per pair
Classroom Setup: Children work in pairs.

1. *Distribute* materials to the children.

2. *Ask* children to make a picture of their choice using all the attribute blocks.

✓3. While children engage in the activity, ask check questions such as:
  • Why have you put this shape here?
  • Will this one fit instead?
  Encourage answers that include size and shape properties.

Lesson 5
Name That Shape

LESSON OBJECTIVE
• Guess a shape from its description.

MATERIALS
• Counters
• Student Activity Cards 7.5a–d
• Circle (TR17), Triangle (TR18), Square (TR19), and Rectangle (TR20)
• Attribute blocks

DAY 1

Teacher's Edition B, pp. 13–14
Big Book B, pp. 4–5

DAY 2

Teacher's Edition B, p. 14

Lesson 4 Flat Shape Pictures
Lesson 5 Name That Shape

Big Book B, pp. 4–5

DAY 1

ACTIVITY 1
Investigate

Math Focus: Identify flat shapes by their properties.
Resource: Big Book B, pp. 4–5
Materials: Counters, 20–30
Classroom Setup: Whole class, in front of the Big Book

1. *Ask* children to sit so that everyone can see the Big Book.

2. *Tell* children that you will describe a shape to them and look for the first child to raise his or her hand. That child can then come up to the Big Book, point out the particular shape, and win a counter. The first child to get three counters is the winner.

3. *Say*, for example:
   • This shape is green and has a round edge. (green circle)
   • This shape is red and has three edges. (red triangle)
   • This shape is blue, has four sides, but two sides are longer than the other two sides. (blue rectangle)

 4. When the child comes up to the Big Book to point out the shape, ask check questions such as:
   • Are you sure this is a triangle?
   • Why? (Because it has three sides.)

ACTIVITY 2
Explore

Math Focus: Identify matching flat shapes quickly.
Materials: Student Activity Cards 7.5a–d, 2 sets per pair
Classroom Setup: Children work in pairs.

1. *Encourage* children to return to their places.

2. *Distribute* materials to the children.

3. One child of each pair mixes up the cards and places them face down.

4. The same child turns one card over. Then, his or her partner turns a card over.

5. If the cards have the same shape picture, they whisper 'Snap'.

6. The first player to whisper 'Snap' keeps the cards.

7. *Continue* until all the cards are used.

✓ 8. While children engage in the activity, ask check questions such as:
   • How do you know these cards are the same?
   • Why won't this card do instead?

ACTIVITY 3
Explore

Math Focus: Search for flat shapes in the classroom.
Materials: Circle (TR17), Triangle (TR18), Square (TR19), and Rectangle (TR20), 1 copy of each
   Attribute blocks, 20 (5 circles, 5 triangles, 5 squares, and 5 rectangles)
Classroom Setup: Children work in small groups.

1. *Hide* the attribute blocks in the classroom.

2. *Divide* children into four groups and assign each group a shape.

3. *Distribute* TR17, TR18, TR19, and TR20 to the respective groups to remind them of their assigned shape.

4. *Remind* children of the shape properties before the game begins.

5. Each group searches for its shape. The group that collects the most blocks, or finds all of them in the least time, wins.

Chapter 7 — Solid and Flat Shapes

Lesson 6
Shape Patterns

LESSON OBJECTIVES
- Guess a shape from its description.
- Describe a basic flat shape.
- Identify and continue a shape pattern.

MATERIALS
- Student Activity Cards 7.5a–d

Vocabulary
pattern

DAY 1
Teacher's Edition B, p. 15

DAY 2
Teacher's Edition B, p. 16
Student Book B, Part 1, p. 8

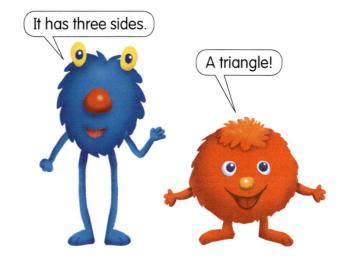

ACTIVITY 1
Explore

Math Focus: Verbalize properties of flat shapes.
Classroom Setup: Children work in small groups.

1. *Select* children to give shape clues to their group, who will guess the name of the shape, such as: It is big, has three corners and three flat sides.

2. *Ensure* that children across the ability range are invited to give clues. If their clues fail to give guidance, suggest that they check their set of basic shapes (found on the bottom of pages 2 and 3 of Student Book B, Part 1) and check that they have included all the features.

Differentiated Instruction for Activity 1

Reinforcement

Classroom Setup: *Teacher with a child or two*

Give suggestions about edges, sides, lengths of sides, and corners.

Challenge

Classroom Setup: *Teacher with a child or two*

Give a partial description that would fit more than one figure. Then, ask what clue could be added to make a unique answer.

DAY 2

ACTIVITY 2
Explore

Math Focus: Introduce patterns of shapes.
Materials: Student Activity Cards 7.5a–d, 1 set per child
Classroom Setup: Children work in small groups.

1. *Distribute* materials to the children.

2. *Ask:* Can you make this pattern – triangle, square, circle, rectangle?

3. *Ask:* Can you continue the pattern by repeating the figures – triangle, square, circle, rectangle, triangle, square, circle, rectangle?

4. *Ask:* Can you make this pattern – two squares followed by two triangles?

5. *Ask:* Can you continue the pattern by repeating the figures – two squares followed by two triangles, then two more squares followed by two more triangles?

6. *Devise* any suitable repeated pattern for children to follow.

Best Practices If children have difficulty following the pattern sequence verbally, draw the pattern on the board.

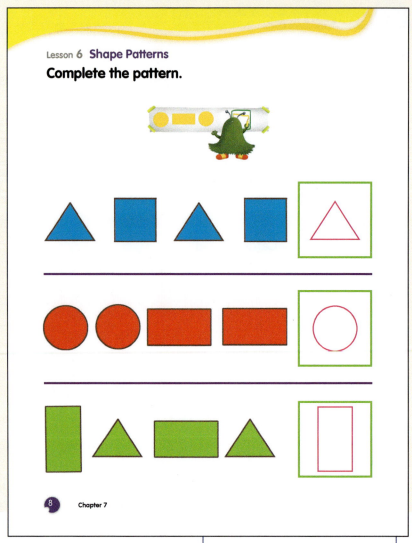

Lesson 6 Shape Patterns
Complete the pattern.

8 Chapter 7

Student Book B, Part 1, p. 8

ACTIVITY 3
Apply

Math Focus: Continue a pattern of shapes.
Resource: Student Book B, Part 1, p. 8
Classroom Setup: Children work independently.

1. Children draw the missing shape in each box to continue the pattern.

2. While children engage in the activity, ask check questions such as:
   • Is this the correct shape? How do you know?
   • Is your shape the right color? How do you know?
   • Is your shape the right size? How do you know?

Chapter Overview
Counting by 2s and 5s

Math Background

Skip-counting is a skill that can help children connect many mathematics topics. Children understand that counting connects numbers and number words with particular quantities and objects. Skip-counting is a shorter way to count objects since the objects are grouped in twos or fives. Teachers can relate skip-counting to the operation of addition. Each number is two or five more than the previous number. Eventually children will see the relationship between skip-counting and multiplication.

Skip-counting also relates to the algebraic concept of understanding and extending patterns. In order to extend a skip-counting pattern, children must understand the rule. For example, to find the next number in the pattern, add two or add five. This understanding provides a foundation for learning about functions.

Vocabulary

pairs	a set of two objects either used together or regarded as a unit
twos	a group of two people or objects
fives	a group of five people or objects
tally	a record of an amount that groups by fives
skip-counting	counting in twos or fives
odd	numbers which have a remainder of 1 when divided by 2, such as 1, 3, 5, and so on
even	numbers which are divisible by 2, such as 2, 4, 6, and so on

Cross-Curricular Connections

Reading/ Language Arts The vocabulary in this chapter includes several plurals: *twos, pairs, fives, tallies.* Review with children the meanings of these plurals, explaining that most words are made plural by adding –s or –es. Have students use counters and follow your instructions. *Say:* Show me a pair of counters. Show me three pairs. Show me two counters. Show me three twos, and so on.

Physical Education Play a game of *Simon Says* with children. Tell them that they must do the exercises you say and they must count by ones, twos, or fives as instructed. *Say*, for example: Simon says, do 10 jumping jacks while counting by twos. Simon says do 20 push-ups while counting by fives.

Continue with other simple exercises, such as hop on one foot, do arm circles, bring your knees to your chest, and so on.

Skills Trace

Grade K	Count by twos to 10.
	Keep a count with a tally.
Grade 1	Count by twos to 100. (Chaps. 7, 12, and 16)
	Use a tally chart to make a bar graph. (Chap. 11)

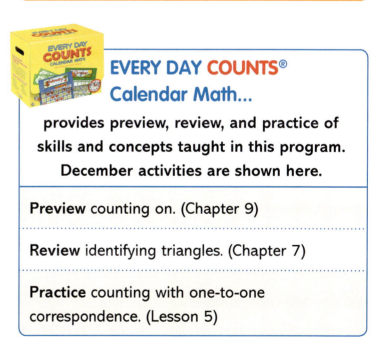

EVERY DAY COUNTS® Calendar Math...

provides preview, review, and practice of skills and concepts taught in this program. December activities are shown here.

Preview counting on. (Chapter 9)

Review identifying triangles. (Chapter 7)

Practice counting with one-to-one correspondence. (Lesson 5)

Chapter Resources

Manipulatives from the Manipulatives Kit

Connecting Cubes
Use for counting by 2s, counting by 5s, and matching activities

Counters
Use for matching activities

Technology Resources

- *Math in Focus®* eBooks
- *Math in Focus®* Teacher Resources CD
- Online Web Resources
- *Math in Focus®* Virtual Manipulatives for Lessons 1–5

Classroom/Household Items

- Socks (or mittens)
- Paper clips
- Colored pencils
- Pencils
- Erasers

Differentiation and Assessment

Differentiation for Special Populations (Resources in the Teacher's Edition)

	English Language Learners	Children Needing Reinforcement	Children Needing a Challenge
Lesson 1		Teacher's Edition B, p. 19	Teacher's Edition B, p. 19
Lesson 2		Student Book B, Part 1, p. 10	
Lesson 4		Big Book B, p. 9	
Lesson 5		Teacher's Edition B, p. 29	Teacher's Edition B, p. 29

To practice the process of pairing and counting by 2s, try this activity every day for the duration of this chapter. Have the class stand and 'pair up', then count by 2s to see how many children are present. Try this at different times of the day with different numbers of children.

Chapter 8 Assessments

On-Going Assessment	Formal Assessment
See the check questions in the Teacher's Edition on these pages	Find Formal Assessment Blackline Masters in the Assessments book
Teacher's Edition B	**Assessments Book**
Lesson 1, p. 19 Lesson 2, p. 21 Lesson 3, p. 23 Lesson 4, p. 26 Lesson 5, p. 29	Assessment 3 for Book B, Part 1 (Chapters 7–10), is on pages 14–18 of Assessments. Interview Assessment is on pages 19–20.

Chapter 8 Planning Guide

Lessons and Pacing	Activity	Component	Objectives and Math Focus
Lesson 1	**Making Pairs**, pp. 18–19		• Recognize and use pairs for counting. • Count by twos.
DAY 1 Activities	1 Investigate	**Teacher's Edition B**, p. 18	Introduce *counting by pairs* and *twos*.
	2 Apply	**Student Book B, Part 1**, p. 9	Match up pairs.
	3 Explore	**Teacher's Edition B**, p. 19	Count by twos to find how many.
Lesson 2	**Counting by 2s**, pp. 20–21		• Use the *counting by twos* sequence to count up to 10 objects.
DAY 1 Activities	1 Investigate	**Big Book B**, p. 6	Build awareness of the *counting by twos* sequence of numbers.
	2 Explore	**Teacher's Edition B**, p. 21	Count people and objects in the classroom by twos. **Recall, Reinforce, and Review** Count by 2s up to 10.
	3 Apply	**Student Book B, Part 1**, p. 10	Apply counting by twos to objects in a picture.
Lesson 3	**Counting by 5s**, pp. 22–23		• Count by fives up to 20. • Keep count of numbers using tallies.
DAY 1 Activities	1 Investigate	**Big Book B**, pp. 7–8	Introduce *fives* and *tally*.
DAY 2 Activities	2 Discover	**Teacher's Edition B**, p. 23	Discover how to count by fives to 20.
	3 Apply	**Student Book B, Part 1**, p. 11	Complete a tally chart.
Lesson 4	**Odd and Even Numbers**, pp. 24–27		• Skip-count. • Know and understand *odd* and *even* numbers.
DAY 1 Activities	1 Investigate	**Big Book B**, p. 9	Introduce *skip-counting*.
	2 Discover	**Teacher's Edition B**, p. 25	Introduce *odd* and *even* numbers.
	3 Apply	**Student Book B, Part 1**, pp. 12–13	Identify sets with odd or even number of objects.
DAY 2 Activities	4 Apply	**Teacher's Edition B**, p. 27	Identify odd and even numbers in a clapping sequence.
	5 Apply	**Student Book B, Part 1**, p. 14	Identify odd and even numbers in a counting sequence.
Lesson 5	**Number Conservation**, pp. 28–30		• Number conservation with or without counting (up to 7).
DAY 1 Activities	1 Explore	**Teacher's Edition B**, p. 28	Match two sets one-to-one; number conservation.
	2 Discover	**Teacher's Edition B**, p. 29	Match up two sets mentally one-to-one.
	3 Apply	**Student Book B, Part 1**, p. 15	Match equivalent sets.

Vocabulary	Manipulatives/Materials	Class Organization	NTCM Focal Points & Process Standards
pairs, twos	• Several pairs of cleans socks (or mittens)	Whole class	Count sets of a given size.
		Independent	
	• Paper clips (or connecting cubes), 6 per pair	Pairs	• Communication • Connections
		Whole class	Count sets of a given size.
		Whole class	• Communication • Representation • Connections
		Independent	
fives, tally		Whole class	Count groups of a given size.
	• Connecting cubes, 20	Whole class	• Communication • Representation
		Independent	
skip-counting odd, even		Whole class	Count groups of a given size.
		Whole class	
		Independent	• Communication • Representation • Connections • Problem solving
		Whole class	
	• Colored pencils, 2 per child (1 red and 1 green)	Independent	
	• Connecting cubes, 10 per pair	Pairs	Compare sets using models.
	• Connecting cubes, 3 • Counters, 2 • Pencils, 3 • Erasers, 2	Whole class	• Communication • Problem solving
		Independent	

Lesson 1
Making Pairs

LESSON OBJECTIVES
- Recognize and use pairs for counting.
- Count by twos.

MATERIALS
- Socks (or mittens)
- Paper clips (or connecting cubes)

Vocabulary

pairs

twos

DAY 1

Teacher's Edition B, pp. 18–19
Student Book B, Part 1, p. 9

DAY 1

ACTIVITY 1
Investigate

Math Focus: Introduce *counting by pairs* and *twos*.
Materials: Several pairs of clean socks (or mittens)
Classroom Setup: Whole class

1. *Put* the socks (or mittens) in a stack.

2. *Ask* children what they think would be the best way to count the pairs of socks. Discuss ways of arranging the socks.

3. Next, together with children, count the socks in pairs. Help them notice that each pair has the same color or pattern.

4. *Guide* children to understand that counting in pairs is the same as counting in twos. Help them to see that counting by twos makes it easier to find how many pairs and how many socks there are in all.

Chapter 8 Counting by 2s and 5s

Lesson 1 **Making Pairs**

Pair.

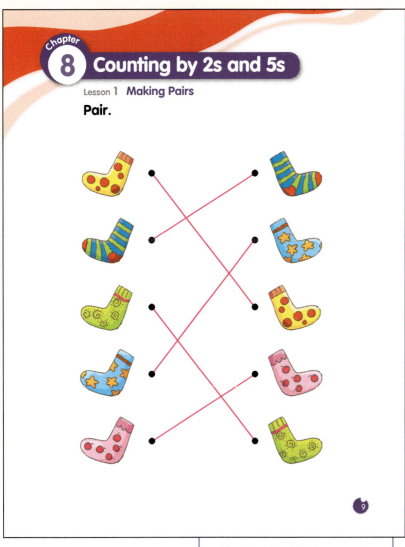

Student Book B, Part 1, p. 9

2, 4!

ACTIVITY 2
Apply

Math Focus: Match up pairs.
Resource: Student Book B, Part 1, p. 9
Classroom Setup: Children work independently.

1. Children draw a line between any two socks that make a pair.

2. *Ask* children to explain why they think two particular socks make a pair.

✓ 3. While children engage in the activity, ask check questions such as:
   • Why do these two socks make a pair?
   • Could you pair this sock with that sock instead?
   • Why? or Why not?
   • Are you sure?

4. *Encourage* children to count the socks in twos.

5. *Ask* how many socks cannot be counted in twos. (1, 3, 5, and so on.)

ACTIVITY 3
Explore

Math Focus: Count by twos to find how many.
Materials: Paper clips (or connecting cubes), 6 per pair
Classroom Setup: Children work in pairs.

1. *Distribute* materials to the children.

2. *Ask* children to put the paper clips (or connecting cubes) in sets of two.

3. *Ask:* Who can count in twos and tell me how many paper clips (or connecting cubes) they have in all?

Differentiated Instruction for Activity 3

Reinforcement

Materials: *Paper clips (or connecting cubes)*
Classroom Setup: *Teacher with a child or two*

Give fewer items for children to count in twos.

Challenge

Materials: *Paper clips (or connecting cubes)*
Classroom Setup: *Teacher with a child or two*

Give more items for children to count in twos.

Lesson 2
Counting by 2s

LESSON OBJECTIVE
• Use the *counting by twos* sequence to count up to 10 objects.

DAY 1

Teacher's Edition B, pp. 20–21
Big Book B, p. 6
Student Book B, Part 1, p. 10

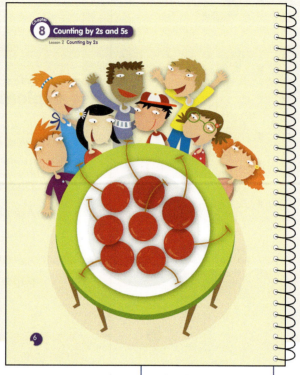

Big Book B, p. 6

DAY 1

ACTIVITY 1
Investigate

Math Focus: Build awareness of the *counting by twos* sequence of numbers.
Resource: Big Book B, p. 6
Classroom Setup: Whole class, in front of the Big Book

1. *Ask* children to sit so that everyone can see the Big Book.

2. *Talk* about the easiest way to count the cherries on the plate. Elicit that counting in pairs, or twos, helps count objects more quickly.

3. *Count* the number of children in the picture by twos.

4. *Ask:* What else can be counted by twos? (table legs, eyes, noses, mouths, and cherry stems)

5. Then, count each of the above-mentioned objects by twos.

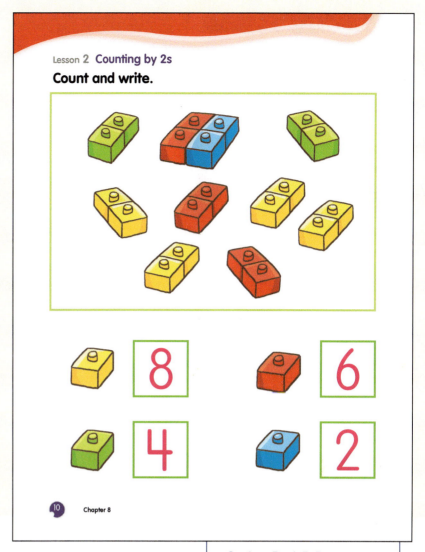

ACTIVITY 2
Explore

Math Focus: Count people and objects in the classroom by twos.

Classroom Setup: Whole class

1. *Encourage* children to return to their places.

2. *Ask* ten children (by name) to stand in front of the classroom without revealing the number of children to the others.

3. *Ask* the remaining children to tell the quickest way of counting the number of standing children. (counting by twos)

4. Next, ask children to look around the room and count by twos any interesting objects they see. They do not need to be in pairs.

5. *Remind* children that counting in pairs, or by twos, helps them count objects more quickly.

Recall, Reinforce, and Review

Ask children to count by 2s up to 10. Show each number with fingers as they count.

ACTIVITY 3
Apply

Math Focus: Apply counting by twos to objects in a picture.
Resource: Student Book B, Part 1, p. 10
Classroom Setup: Children work independently.

1. Children count the connecting cubes of each color by twos.

2. Then, they write the number of connecting cubes of each color in the corresponding boxes.

3. *Check* that children are pointing to each *pair* of cubes as they count.

Differentiated Instruction for Activity 3

Reinforcement

Classroom Setup: *Teacher with a child or two*

Review the 'counting by twos' sequence of numbers with children who are counting individual cubes by pointing to each one.

Lesson 3
Counting by 5s

LESSON OBJECTIVES
- Count by fives up to 20.
- Keep count of numbers using tallies.

MATERIALS
- Connecting cubes

Vocabulary
fives

tally

DAY 1

Teacher's Edition B, p. 22
Big Book B, pp. 7–8

DAY 2

Teacher's Edition B, pp. 23
Student Book B, Part 1, p. 11

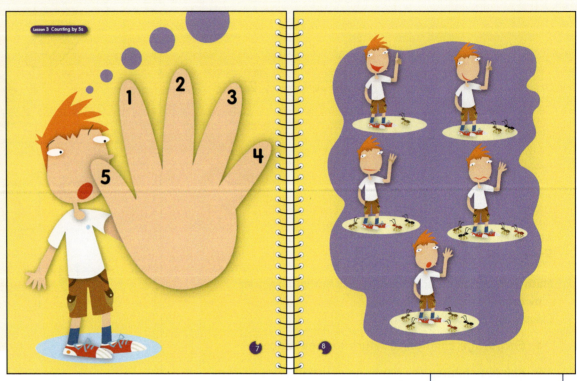

Big Book B, pp. 7–8

DAY 1

ACTIVITY 1
Investigate

Math Focus: Introduce *fives* and *tally*.
Resource: Big Book B, pp. 7–8
Classroom Setup: Whole class, in front of the Big Book

1. *Ask* children to sit so that everyone can see the Big Book.

2. *Talk* about the number of fingers the boy is holding up in the picture on page 7.

3. *Ask* children to raise one hand and to count the total number of fingers on one of their own hands as you point to the boy's fingers in the picture. Ensure that the thumb is counted as '5'.

4. *Repeat* the process while keeping a tally of the number of times the children count to 5.

5. *Help* children see the connection between counting words, fingers, and tally marks.

6. *Help* children see the connection between the boy's fingers and the number of ants in the pictures on page 8.

7. *Ask:*
   - What do you notice about the boy's facial expression? (He is getting more nervous.)
   - Why? (Because more ants are coming towards him.)

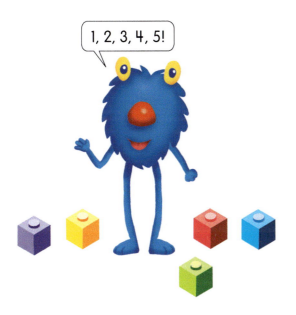

ACTIVITY 2
Discover

Math Focus: Discover how to count by fives to 20.
Materials: Connecting cubes, 20
Classroom Setup: Whole class

1. *Invite* children to gather around a table.

2. *Lay* the connecting cubes out on the table for children to see.

3. *Ask* children to count the number of cubes.

4. *Explain* that they will use a different way to count the cubes – counting by fives.

5. *Begin* by counting 10 cubes. Encourage children to pair each cube counted with one finger as they count, and at the first set of 5, to cross their thumb over their palm.

6. Next, show children how to write the tally marks (4 marks side by side, with the fifth mark crossing the 4 like this: 卌).

7. *Count* out another 5 and repeat the process. Afterward, count the number of sets of 5. (2)

8. *Repeat* until all 20 cubes are counted.

9. *Help* children see the connection between counting words, fingers, and tally marks.

Circle the groups of 5 ants.

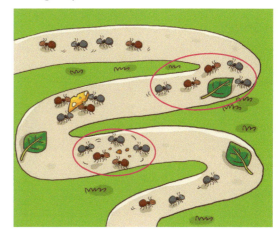

Make the tally.

Student Book B, Part 1, p. 11

ACTIVITY 3
Apply

Math Focus: Complete a tally chart.
Resource: Student Book B, Part 1, p. 11
Classroom Setup: Children work independently.

1. Children circle the groups of 5 ants.

2. Then, they write a tally mark for each ant in the box at the bottom of the page.

3. *Remind* children to make one tally mark for each ant counted, up to 4, and on the fifth ant, to make a mark crossing the other 4.

4. *Ask* children to count how many sets of 5 tally marks they have made.

5. While children engage in the activity, ask check questions such as:
   • Does each of your groups have 5 ants in it? Are you sure?
   • Does the number of ants match the number of tallies? Are you sure? How do you know?

Best Practices Note that there are 21 ants, so there will be a single stand-alone tally mark.

Lesson 4
Odd and Even Numbers

LESSON OBJECTIVES
- Skip-count.
- Know and understand *odd* and *even* numbers.

MATERIALS
- Colored pencils

Vocabulary
skip-counting

odd

even

DAY 1

Teacher's Edition B, pp. 24–26
Big Book B, p. 9
Student Book B, Part 1,
pp. 12–13

DAY 2

Teacher's Edition B, p. 27
Student Book B, Part 1, p. 14

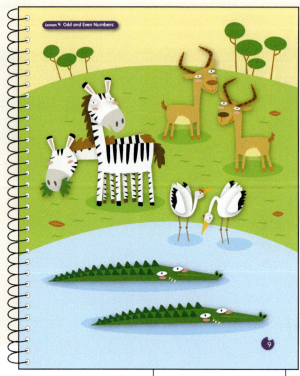

Big Book B, p. 9

DAY 1

ACTIVITY 1
Investigate

Math Focus: Introduce *skip-counting*.
Resource: Big Book B, p. 9
Classroom Setup: Whole class, in front of the Big Book

1. *Ask* children to sit so that everyone can see the Big Book.

2. *Ask* each child to count the total number of animals.

3. *Ask:* Which will be the easiest way to count all the animals?

4. *Explain* that counting by twos can be called skip-counting. It is a quick way of counting objects.

Differentiated Instruction for Activity 1

Reinforcement

Classroom Setup: *Teacher with a child or two*

Ask children to count fewer animals in the picture, such as the animals in the water.

ACTIVITY 2
Discover

Math Focus: Introduce *odd* and *even* numbers.

Classroom Setup: Continue with whole class setup as in Activity 1.

1. *Invite* children to sit on the floor with their legs stretched out in front of them.

2. *Ask:*
   • Which is the quickest way to count all our legs?
   • What about our arms?

3. *Explain* that when you count objects by twos, or pairs, then you are counting objects with partners, just like when you count your legs and arms. Every leg has a partner and so does every arm.

   Best Practices Be alert to children in class with physical limitations or sensitivities. Choose other body parts to pair up if arms or legs would make some children uncomfortable.

4. *Ask:* Which other objects have partners? Let's check our fingers. If every finger has a partner, the number is *even*. If a finger lacks a partner, it is an *odd* number.

5. *Ask:*
   • How many fingers are on one hand? (5)
   • Is the number 5 an odd or even number? (odd)

6. *Emphasize* that when you can count sets of objects in pairs, then you have an even number of objects. If there is an object without a partner, then you have an odd number of objects.

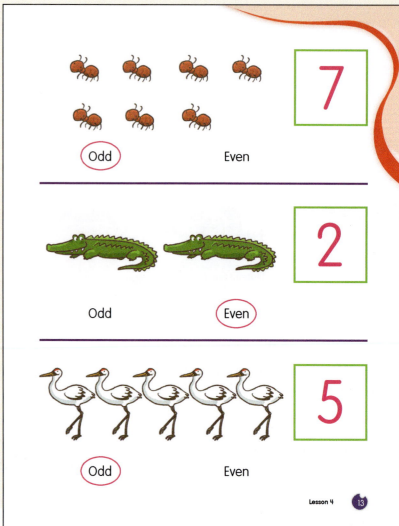

Student Book B, Part 1, p. 12

Student Book B, Part 1, p. 13

ACTIVITY 3
Apply

Math Focus: Identify sets with odd or even number of objects.
Resource: Student Book B, Part 1, pp. 12–13
Classroom Setup: Children work independently.

1. *Encourage* children to return to their places and open their Student Books to page 12.

2. Children count the number of animals in each exercise.

3. Then, they write the number in the empty box, decide if the number is odd or even, and circle the appropriate word.

4. *Emphasize* that when you can count sets of objects in pairs, you have an *even* number of objects. If there is an object without a partner, you have an *odd* number of objects.

✓ 5. *Check* that children are identifying odd and even numbers appropriately. If not, you may want to have them draw a box around each pair of animals before deciding if the number of animals is odd or even.

DAY 2

ACTIVITY 4
Apply

Math Focus: Identify odd and even numbers in a clapping sequence.
Classroom Setup: Whole class

1. **Ask** children to count to 10. As they count, ask them to clap on odd numbers and not to clap on even numbers.

2. **Ask:**
   - When we clap on odd numbers, do we clap the first number? (Yes)
   - Do we clap the next number? (No)

3. **Repeat** the activity for even numbers.

4. **Remind** children that if they are uncertain whether the number is odd or even, they can count a set of objects that total that particular number to see if any object is without a partner.

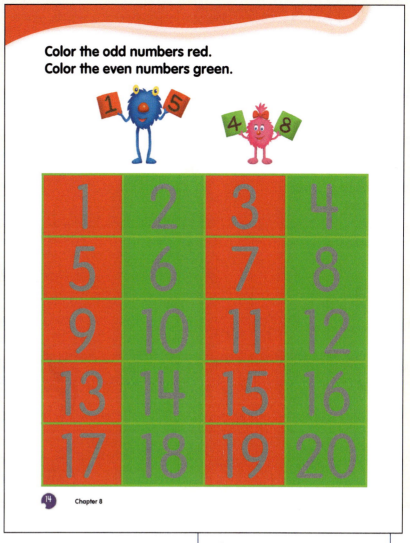

Color the odd numbers red.
Color the even numbers green.

1	2	3	4
5	6	7	8
9	10	11	12
13	14	15	16
17	18	19	20

14   Chapter 8

Student Book B, Part 1, p. 14

ACTIVITY 5
Apply

Math Focus: Identify odd and even numbers in a counting sequence.
Resource: Student Book B, Part 1, p. 14
Materials: Colored pencils, 2 per child (1 red and 1 green)
Classroom Setup: Children work independently.

1. **Distribute** materials to the children.

2. Children color the odd numbers red and the even numbers green.

3. **Remind** children that if they are uncertain whether a number is odd or even, they can make a set with that number of objects. Then, they can check to see if any object is without a partner.

Lesson 5
Number Conservation

LESSON OBJECTIVE
- Number conservation with or without counting (up to 7).

MATERIALS
- Connecting cubes
- Counters
- Pencils
- Erasers

DAY 1

Teacher's Edition B, pp. 28–30
Student Book B, Part 1, p. 15

DAY 1

ACTIVITY 1
Explore

....

Math Focus: Match two sets one-to-one; number conservation.

Materials: Connecting cubes, 10 per pair

Classroom Setup: Children work in pairs.

1. **Distribute** materials to the children.

2. **Ask** children to place five connecting cubes in a row. Be sure that the cubes are touching each other.

3. Next, ask children to arrange the remaining five cubes also in a row, but now with more space between the cubes.

4. **Ask** if there is the same number of cubes in both rows or if one row has more or less.

5. **Ask** how they can find out. (Without counting, they can match the cubes in one-to-one correspondence.)

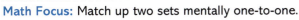

ACTIVITY 2
Discover

Math Focus: Match up two sets mentally one-to-one.
Materials: Connecting cubes, 3
   Counters, 2
   Pencils, 3
   Erasers, 2
Classroom Setup: Whole class

1. *Choose* any seven of the materials and arrange them in two rows.

2. *Invite* children to look at the objects. Then, ask them to close their eyes.

3. *Rearrange* the order and layout of the objects, but keep them in two rows.

4. *Ask* children to open their eyes and look to see if the arrangement is still the same or if they think it is different.

5. *Ask:*
   • How do you know?
   • What is the same and what is different?

6. *Note* which children need to count and which children realize the number is the same just by looking. Watch to see whether children can check the number mentally by one-to-one correspondence.

Differentiated Instruction for Activity 2

Reinforcement

Materials: *Connecting cubes, counters, pencils, erasers*
Classroom Setup: *Teacher with a child or two*

Use fewer objects for children to compare in one-to-one correspondence.

Challenge

Materials: *Connecting cubes, counters, pencils, erasers*
Classroom Setup: *Teacher with a child or two*

Use more objects for children to compare in one-to-one correspondence.

Lesson 5 **Number Conservation**
Pair.

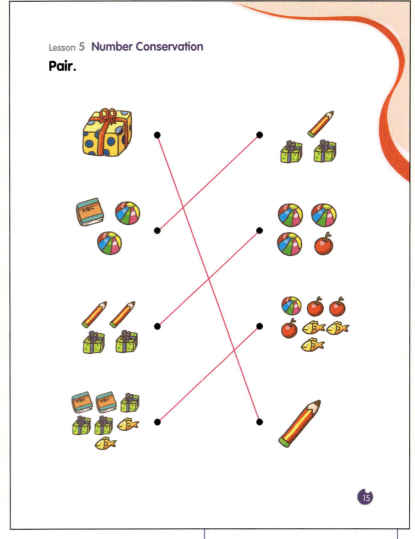

Student Book B, Part 1, p. 15

ACTIVITY 3
Apply

Math Focus: Match equivalent sets.
Resource: Student Book B, Part 1, p. 15
Classroom Setup: Children work independently.

1. *Encourage* children to return to their places and open their Student Books to page 15.

2. Children pair up the equivalent sets by drawing a line between the sets that have the same number.

Best Practices Refrain from telling children they are to pair up the sets with the same number of objects. Instead, ask: How will you match up these sets? What rule do you think you will use?

3. While children engage in the activity, ask check questions such as:
   • Why have you joined these sets?
   • Could you join it to this set instead?
   • Why? or Why not?

4. *Encourage* children not to count, but to note equivalence by one-to-one correspondence.

5. *Note* which children can join the sets without counting.

Notes

Math Background

As children continue to develop skills in counting, their number sense becomes stronger. They are soon able to compare quantities. At first, children match sets in a one-to-one correspondence to determine which set has more objects and which has fewer objects. This leads to the discovery that one number is greater or less than another. Through one-to-one correspondence activities, children also learn how much more or less one number is than another. These concepts pave the way to an understanding of addition and subtraction.

The number line, introduced in Lesson 1, is a powerful mathematical model that children will see every year in their mathematics classes. The number line used in Kindergarten (and called a counting tape in Grade 1) shows only a limited amount of numbers. Each year, children will add to it, extending it to thousands, millions, fractions, decimals, integers, and finally irrational numbers. The model will grow with them as they become aware of new numbers around them.

Vocabulary

fewer	a smaller number of people or objects
few	a small number of people or objects
most	greatest number of people or objects
fewest	least number of people or objects
in between	in the space separating two objects

Cross-Curricular Connections

Reading/Language Arts In this chapter children will use the terms *more/most* and *fewer/fewest* to compare quantities. Introduce the use of *−er* and *−est* endings. First, check that children know the meaning of *few* (not many). Point out that *−er* is added to *few* to compare two things and *−est* is added to few to compare three or more things. Ask children to name other words they know that have these endings.

Social Studies Tell children that a number line shows numbers in order. Make the connection between a number line and a time line. Explain that time lines show events in order. Discuss some different transportation methods such as airplanes, cars, trains, and horse-drawn carriages. Make a time line with children to show the order in which the methods were invented (horse-drawn carriages, trains, cars, airplanes).

Skills Trace

Grade K	Compare two sets one-to-one to find the difference in the number of objects.
Grade 1	Use subtraction to find the difference between two two-digit numbers. (Chaps. 8 and 13)

EVERY DAY COUNTS® Calendar Math...

provides preview, review, and practice of skills and concepts taught in this program. January activities are shown here.

Preview position words. (Chapter 10)

Review solid figures. (Chapter 7)

Practice one-to-one correspondence. (Lesson 1 in this chapter)

Chapter Resources

Activity Cards

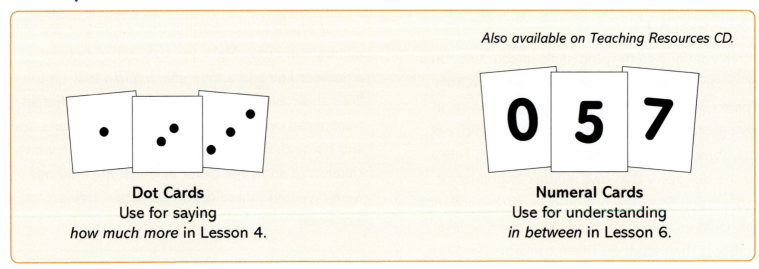

Also available on Teaching Resources CD.

Dot Cards
Use for saying
how much more in Lesson 4.

Numeral Cards
Use for understanding
in between in Lesson 6.

Manipulatives from the Manipulatives Kit

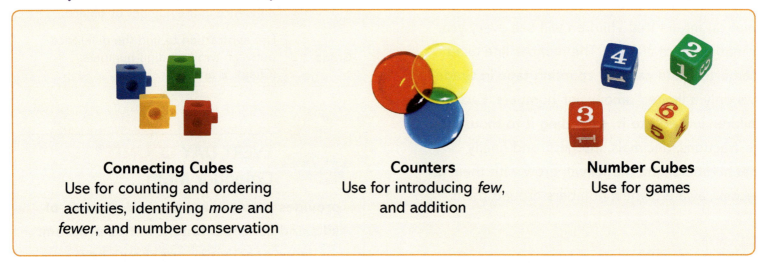

Connecting Cubes
Use for counting and ordering
activities, identifying *more* and
fewer, and number conservation

Counters
Use for introducing *few*,
and addition

Number Cubes
Use for games

Technology Resources

- *Math in Focus*® eBooks
- *Math in Focus*® Teacher Resources CD
- Online Web Resources
- *Math in Focus*® Virtual Manipulatives
  for Lessons 1–3, 5–6

Classroom/Household Items
- Salt (or sand)
- Colored pencils
- Paper clips

Differentiation and Assessment

Differentiation for Special Populations (Resources in the Teacher's Edition)

	English Language Learners	Children Needing Reinforcement	Children Needing a Challenge
Lesson 2			Teacher's Edition B, pp. 34–35
Lesson 3	Math Talk, Teacher's Edition B, p. 38		
Lesson 4		Student Book B, Part 1, p. 20	Big Book B, p. 11
Lesson 5		Teacher's Edition B, p. 42	Teacher's Edition B, p. 42
Lesson 6		Teacher's Edition B, p. 45	Teacher's Edition B, p. 45
Lesson 7		Teacher's Edition B, p. 47	Teacher's Edition B, p. 47

Have two children choose to place 4, 5, 6, or 7 counters on the overhead. *Ask:* Who has more? Who has fewer?

Match the counters up one-to-one and ask again. Repeat this numerous times over many days. Then, advance to having three children place counters on the overhead and compare.

Chapter 9 Assessments

On-Going Assessment	Formal Assessment
See the check questions in the Teacher's Edition on these pages	*Find Formal Assessment Blackline Masters in the Assessments book*
Teacher's Edition B	**Assessments Book**
Lesson 1, p. 33 Lesson 2, p. 36 Lesson 3, p. 39 Lesson 5, p. 43	Assessment 3 for Book B, Part 1 (Chapters 7–10), is on pages 14–18 of Assessments. Interview Assessment is on pages 19–20.

Chapter 9 Planning Guide

Lessons and Pacing	Activity	Component	Objectives and Math Focus
Lesson 1	**Comparing Sets One-to-One**, pp. 32–33		• Compare sets in one-to-one correspondence. • Recognize and understand number lines.
DAY 1 Activities	1 Investigate	**Big Book B**, p. 10	Introduce the number line.
DAY 2 Activities	2 Explore	**Teacher's Edition B**, p. 33	Represent numbers with concrete materials.
	3 Apply	**Student Book B, Part 1**, p. 16	Count on to 9 objects by skip-counting by twos.
Lesson 2	**Number Lines**, pp. 34–36		• Compare sets in one-to-one correspondence. • Recognize and understand number lines. • Recognize number words. • Review *one more*. • Order numbers. • Add using a number line.
DAY 1 Activities	1 Discover	**Teacher's Edition B**, p. 34	Clap to a counting rhyme.
DAY 2 Activities	2 Explore	**Teacher's Edition B**, p. 35	Build number towers for numbers 1 to 9.
	3 Apply	**Student Book B, Part 1**, pp. 17–18	Count on two more on a number line.
Lesson 3	**Fewer and More**, pp. 37–39		• Compare sets in one-to-one correspondence. • Understand *few* and *fewer*. • Understand *more*.
DAY 1 Activities	1 Investigate	**Big Book A**, p. 24	Introduce *fewer*.
	2 Discover	**Teacher's Edition B**, p. 38	Introduce *few*.
DAY 2 Activities	3 Explore	**Teacher's Edition B**, p. 38	Compare two number trains.
	4 Apply	**Student Book B, Part 1**, p. 19	Compare two numbers by comparing two sets.

Vocabulary	Manipulatives/Materials	Class Organization	NTCM Focal Points & Process Standards
	• Connecting cubes, 10 • Number Line 1–10 (TR21)	Whole class	Compare sets and numerals.
	• Number Line 1–10 (TR21), 1 per group • Connecting cubes, 60 per group	Small groups Independent	• Communication • Representation • Connections
	• *Counting Claps* rhyme (TR22) • Number Line 0–10 (TR23)	Whole class	Identify and repeat simple number patterns.
	• Connecting cubes, 60 per group • Number Line 0–10 (TR23), 1 per group and 1 for the teacher	Small groups Independent	• Communication • Representation • Problem solving
fewer few	• Counters, 15 • Salt (or sand)	Whole class Whole class	Compare sets and numerals. • Communication • Representation
	• Number cubes, 2 (one with '5' and '6' covered) • Connecting cubes, 20 per pair • Red colored pencils, 1 per child	Pairs Independent	

Chapter 9 Planning Guide

Lessons and Pacing	Activity	Component	Objectives and Math Focus
Lesson 4	**Comparing Sets to Find the Difference, pp. 40–41**		• Understand *most* and *fewest*. • Count the difference through comparing sets in one-to-one correspondence.
DAY 1 Activities	1 Investigate	**Big Book B,** p. 11	Introduce *most* and *fewest*.
DAY 2 Activities	2 Explore	**Teacher's Edition B,** p. 41	Tell how many more quickly.
	3 Apply	**Student Book B, Part 1,** p. 20	Create and compare two sets.
Lesson 5	**How Many in All?, pp. 42–43**		• Count on. • Add using number lines.
DAY 1 Activities	1 Discover	**Teacher's Edition B,** p. 42	Discover how to count on.
	2 Apply	**Student Book B, Part 1,** pp. 21–22	Count on using a number line.
Lesson 6	**What's the Difference?, pp. 44–45**		• Add using number lines. • Understand the concept of how many numbers are *in between* two numbers.
DAY 1 Activities	1 Explore	**Teacher's Edition B,** p. 44	Count on using connecting cubes and a number line.
DAY 2 Activities	2 Discover	**Teacher's Edition B,** p. 45	Introduce *in between*.
	3 Apply	**Teacher's Edition B,** p. 45	Compare two numbers using concrete objects and a number line. **Recall, Reinforce, and Review** Count how many more fingers to make 5 and 10.
Lesson 7	**Counting On Using Fingers, pp. 46–48**		• Count on using fingers.
DAY 1 Activities	1 Investigate	**Big Book B,** p. 12	Build awareness of combining two sets into one.
DAY 2 Activities	2 Discover	**Teacher's Edition B,** p. 47	Find how many more are needed.
	3 Apply	**Student Book B, Part 1,** pp. 23–24	Find how many in all.

Vocabulary	Manipulatives/Materials	Class Organization	NTCM Focal Points & Process Standards
most, fewest		Whole class	Compare sets and numerals.
	• Dot Cards 1–9, 1 set per pair • Colored pencils	Pairs Independent	• Communication • Representation • Problem solving
	• Counters, 10	Whole class Independent	Extend simple number patterns. • Communication • Representation • Problem solving
	• Connecting cubes, 10 • Number Line 0–10 (TR23)	Whole class	Acquire simple strategies for joining two sets.
in between	• Teacher Numeral Cards 0–10 • Number Line 0–10 (TR23) • Connecting cubes (or paper clips), 20 per pair • Number Line 0–10 (TR23), 1 copy per pair	Whole class Pairs	• Communication • Representation • Problem solving
		Whole class	Separate a set into two sets using models.
		Whole class Independent	• Communication • Representation • Connections • Problem solving

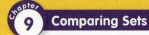

Lesson 1
Comparing Sets One-to-One

LESSON OBJECTIVES
- Compare sets in one-to-one correspondence.
- Recognize and understand number lines.

MATERIALS
- Connecting cubes
- Number Line 1–10 (TR21)

DAY 1

Teacher's Edition B, p. 32
Big Book B, p. 10

DAY 2

Teacher's Edition B, p. 33
Student Book B, Part 1, p. 16

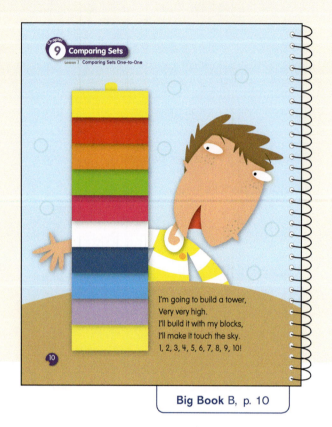

I'm going to build a tower,
Very very high.
I'll build it with my blocks,
I'll make it touch the sky.
1, 2, 3, 4, 5, 6, 7, 8, 9, 10!

Big Book B, p. 10

DAY 1

ACTIVITY 1
Investigate

Math Focus: Introduce the number line.
Resource: Big Book B, p. 10
Materials: Connecting cubes, 10
   Number Line 1–10 (TR21)
Classroom Setup: Whole class, in front of the Big Book

1. *Ask* children to sit so that everyone can see the Big Book.

2. As children recite the rhyme, build a tower with connecting cubes.

3. *Remind* children to say the counting word as each cube is added to the tower.

4. *Show* children TR21. Have children note some of the properties of a number line:
   - The spaces are all the same size.
   - The numbers are in order, starting at 1.
   - It can be longer when we learn new numbers.

5. As children repeat the rhyme, point to the numbers on the number line.

ACTIVITY 2
Explore

Math Focus: Represent numbers with concrete materials.
Materials: Number Line, 1–10 (TR21) 1 per group
Connecting cubes, 60 per group
Classroom Setup: Children work in small groups.

1. **Distribute** materials to the children. Be sure that each child gets at least 1 set of 10 connecting cubes.

2. **Ask** children to build towers with the cubes to show each number on the number line.

3. **Suggest** to children that a tower of 10 cubes can be used to make two towers – a tall one and a shorter one.

4. **Remind** children to check that the number of cubes in each tower corresponds to the number on the number line.

5. When children finish the activity, be sure that they put the cubes together in stacks of 10 by color. This reinforces their counting skills and gets the cubes ready for the next time.

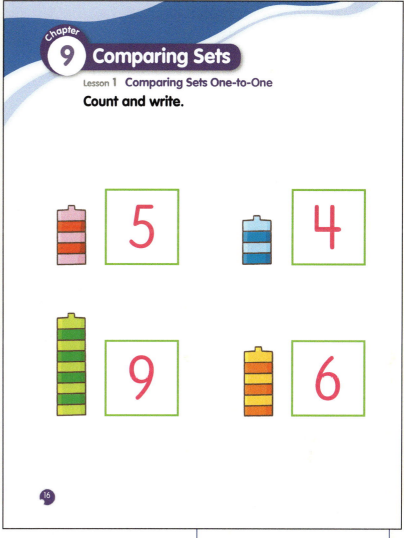

Student Book B, Part 1, p. 16

ACTIVITY 3
Apply

Math Focus: Count on to 9 objects by skip-counting by twos.
Resource: Student Book B, Part 1, p. 16
Classroom Setup: Children work independently.

1. Children write the number of cubes each tower represents in the corresponding box.

2. **Notice** which children count in ones and which children count by twos. Remind children it is easier to count large numbers by twos and add on the ones left over.

3. **Check** that children are counting the cubes correctly, especially those who are counting by twos. If children who are counting by twos are off by 1 cube, help them use the color pattern to correct their mistakes.

Lesson 2
Number Lines

LESSON OBJECTIVES
- Compare sets in one-to-one correspondence.
- Recognize and understand number lines.
- Recognize number words.
- Review *one more.*
- Order numbers.
- Add using a number line.

MATERIALS
- *Counting Claps* rhyme (TR22)
- Number Line 0–10 (TR23)
- Connecting cubes

DAY 1

Teacher's Edition B, pp. 34–35

DAY 2

Teacher's Edition B, pp. 35–36
Student Book B, Part 1,
pp. 17–18

DAY 1

One, one,
All clap one.

Two, two,
All clap two.

ACTIVITY 1
Discover

Math Focus: Clap to a counting rhyme.
Materials: *Counting Claps* rhyme (TR22)
   Number Line 0–10 (TR23)
Classroom Setup: Whole class

1. *Recite* the *Counting Claps* rhyme to the children.

2. *Recite* the rhyme again, this time encouraging children to clap according to the number mentioned in the rhyme.

   Best Practices The rhyme does not need to be recited in the number sequence.

3. Once children are familiar with the rhyme, point to the numbers on the number line to cue their rhyme. Encourage children to clap the number you are pointing at. Remember to include 0, which means they do not clap.

4. *Write* the number words *zero* to *ten* on the board.

5. *Point* to the number words as the rhyme is repeated, with children clapping according to the number word.

6. *Direct* children's attention back to the number line. Point at a number and *say:* Clap one more than this number.
   Vary the numbers.

7. *Repeat* step 6, this time pointing at a number word on the board.

8. *See* Differentiated Instruction idea on page 35.

ACTIVITY 2
Explore

Math Focus: Build number towers for numbers 1 to 9.
Materials: Connecting cubes, 60 per group
Number Line 0–10 (TR23) 1 per group and 1 for the teacher
Classroom Setup: Children work in small groups.

1. ***Distribute*** materials to the children.

   Best Practices Be sure that each child gets at least 10 connecting cubes. Some may get more.

2. ***Point*** to numbers on the number line at random.

3. For each number selected, children are to join that many cubes into a number tower until nearly all the cubes are used.

4. Next, ask children to place their number towers beside the numbers on their number lines from the least to the greatest number.

   Best Practices Suggest that children take turns making towers for the big numbers. Then, see if they have any leftovers that could be used for a smaller number.

5. ***Remind*** children that when the number is small, the number of cubes used will be small. Similarly, greater numbers will use a bigger number of cubes.

6. Have children sort and put away the cubes in towers of 10 cubes of the same color.

Differentiated Instruction for Activity 1

Challenge

Materials: *Number Line 0–10 (TR23)*
Classroom Setup: *Teacher with a child or two*

Ask children to clap one less than a number on the number line, or a number word on the board.

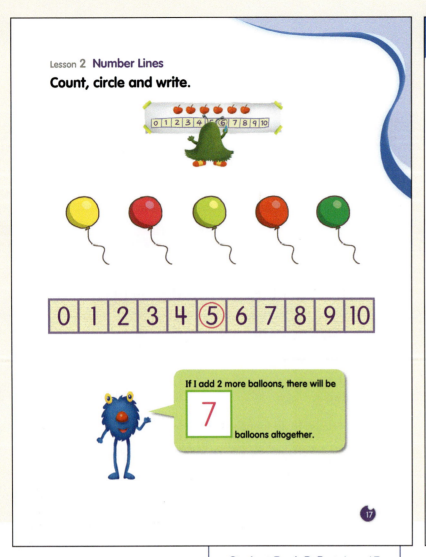

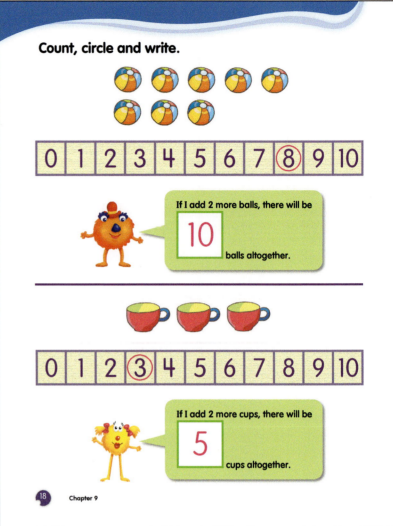

Student Book B, Part 1, p. 17

Student Book B, Part 1, p. 18

ACTIVITY 3
Apply

Math Focus: Count on two more on a number line.
Resource: Student Book B, Part 1, pp. 17–18
Classroom Setup: Children work independently.

1. Children count the objects in each exercise and find the total number on the number line.

2. Then, they circle this number.

3. Next, they use the number line and add two more objects to find the total number of objects altogether. Then, they write the number in the box.

> **Best Practices** Model the activity first. Emphasize that it is important to count each object carefully, point to that number on the number line and then count up two more.

4. While children engage in the activity, ask check questions such as:
   - How many objects did you count?
   - Is the number you wrote two more than this?
   - How do you know?

Lesson 3
Fewer and More

LESSON OBJECTIVES
- Compare sets in one-to-one correspondence.
- Understand *few* and *fewer*.
- Understand *more*.

MATERIALS
- Counters
- Salt (or sand)
- Number cubes
- Connecting cubes
- Red colored pencils

Vocabulary

fewer

few

DAY 1

Teacher's Edition B, pp. 37–38
Big Book A, p. 24

DAY 2

Teacher's Edition B, pp. 38–39
Student Book B, Part 1, p. 19

Lesson 2 Ordering Numbers from 0 to 10

I went to the shelves and what did I see?
One pumpkin,
Two potatoes,
Three onions,
Four cabbage,
Five beans,
Six peppers,
Seven lettuce,

Eight mushrooms,
Nine tomatoes,
Ten carrots,
And up on the shelf,
A nice round bagel for me!

Big Book A, p. 24

DAY 1

ACTIVITY 1
Investigate

Math Focus: Introduce *fewer*.
Resource: Big Book A, p. 24
Classroom Setup: Whole class, in front of the Big Book

1. *Note* that this activity relies on a page from Big Book A.

2. *Ask* children to sit so that everyone can see the Big Book.

3. *Talk* about number sizes to 10.

4. *Refer* to the picture of the vegetables. Count the number of each type of vegetable with the children.

5. *Remind* children that when a number is small, there are fewer objects than when the number is big.

There are fewer balls here.

There is less sand here.

ACTIVITY 2
Discover

Math Focus: Introduce *few*.
Materials: Counters, 15
  Salt (or sand)
Classroom Setup: Whole class

> **Best Practices** *Few* is a better word to use than *less* when talking about objects that can be counted. We say *few(er)* objects rather than *less* objects. Use *less* to refer to objects that you cannot count, for example, less sugar, less rice, and so on.

1. **Invite** children to stand around a table.

2. **Place** two mounds of salt on the table, one smaller than the other.

3. **Point** to the smaller mound and **say:** There is less salt here.

4. **Place** 3 counters on the table.

5. **Say:** There are a *few* counters here.

6. **Place** a group of 5 counters on the table.

7. **Point** to the group of 3 counters and **say:** 3 counters are fewer than 5 counters.

8. **Vary** the number of counters within each group. Then, ask children which group has fewer counters.

9. **Math Talk** Encourage children to state the comparison when responding. For example: That group, because 1 counter is fewer than 5 counters.

10. **Remind** children that when a number is small, there are fewer objects than when the number is big.

ACTIVITY 3
Explore

Math Focus: Compare two number trains.
Materials: Number cubes, 2 (one with '5' and '6' covered)
  Connecting cubes, 20 per pair
Classroom Setup: Children work in pairs.

1. **Distribute** connecting cubes to the children.

2. **Toss** the uncovered number cube.

3. **Ask** children to link that number of cubes into a tower.

4. **Repeat** several times starting a new tower each time.

5. Next, toss both number cubes, first one and then the other.

6. After the first number cube has been tossed, children form a tower of cubes according to the number on the number cube.

7. After the second number cube has been tossed, children form another tower of cubes according to the total number on both number cubes.

8. **Talk** about which tower has more cubes and which tower has fewer cubes. (The second tower has more cubes because it is the total of the numbers shown on both number cubes. The first tower has fewer cubes because it is only the number shown on the first number cube.)

9. **Encourage** comparisons rather than counting.

10. **Remind** children that when a number is small, there are fewer objects than when the number is big.

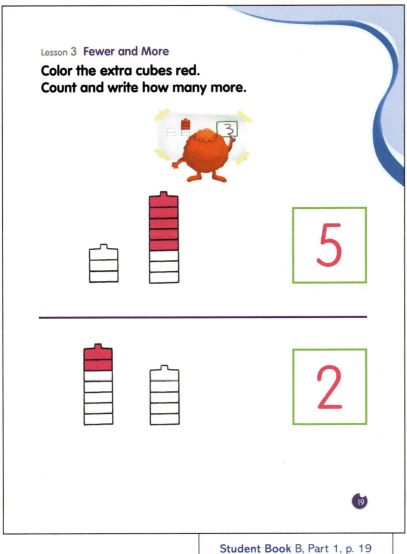

Lesson 3 **Fewer and More**

Color the extra cubes red.
Count and write how many more.

5

2

19

Student Book B, Part 1, p. 19

ACTIVITY 4
Apply

Math Focus: Compare two numbers by comparing two sets.
Resource: Student Book B, Part 1, p. 19
Materials: Red colored pencils, 1 per child
Classroom Setup: Children work independently.

1. Children compare the cubes in each tower and decide which tower has more cubes.

2. Then, they color these extra cubes red and write the number of extra cubes in the box.

3. *Encourage* children to compare the towers in one-to-one correspondence (side by side), rather than count the number of cubes in each tower.

✔ 4. *Check* that children color the excess cubes at the top of the tower, and not at the bottom. Use the work being done by the furry as a model.

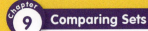

Lesson 4
Comparing Sets to Find the Difference

LESSON OBJECTIVES
• Understand *most* and *fewest*.
• Count the difference through comparing sets in one-to-one correspondence.

MATERIALS
• Dot Cards 1–9
• Colored pencils

Vocabulary
most

fewest

DAY 1

Teacher's Edition B, pp. 40–41
Big Book B, p. 11

DAY 2

Teacher's Edition B, p. 41
Student Book B, Part 1, p. 20

Big Book B, p. 11

DAY 1

ACTIVITY 1
Investigate

Math Focus: Introduce *most* and *fewest*.
Resource: Big Book B, p. 11
Classroom Setup: Whole class, in front of the Big Book

1. **Ask** children to sit so that everyone can see the Big Book.

2. **Talk** about the picture of the four teddy bears wearing coats with buttons. One coat has 3 buttons, another has 5 buttons, another has 7 buttons, and another has 9 buttons.

3. **Point** to Amy. **Ask:**
   • Which bear has more buttons on his or her coat than Amy? (Bob)
   • Which bears have fewer buttons on their coats than Amy? (Cory and Dina)

4. **Ask:** Which bear has the most buttons? (Bob) Which bear has the fewest buttons? (Dina)

5. **Remind** children to compare rather than count the buttons.

Best Practices If children have difficulty comparing the buttons in the picture, draw the buttons in columns on the board for each bear. This will make one-to-one comparisons more apparent to the children.

6. **See** Differentiated Instruction idea on page 41.

My card has 2 more dots than your card!

Lesson 4 Comparing Sets to Find the Difference
Draw, count and write.

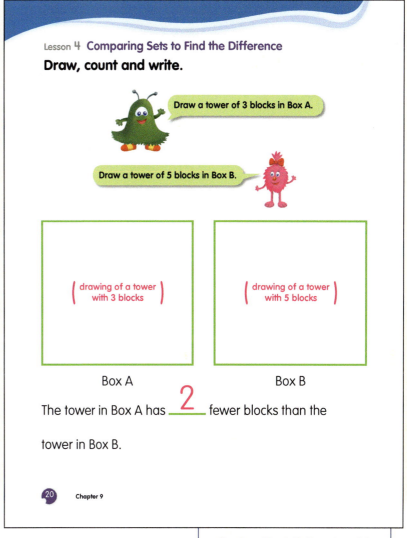

Draw a tower of 3 blocks in Box A.

Draw a tower of 5 blocks in Box B.

(drawing of a tower with 3 blocks) (drawing of a tower with 5 blocks)

Box A   Box B

The tower in Box A has __2__ fewer blocks than the

tower in Box B.

20   Chapter 9

Student Book B, Part 1, p. 20

ACTIVITY 2
Explore

Math Focus: Tell how many more quickly.
Materials: Dot Cards 1–9, 1 set per pair
Classroom Setup: Children work in pairs.

1. *Distribute* materials to the children.

2. *Ask* children to place their cards in a stack facing down. They take turns with their partner to turn over their top cards.

3. The first player who touches the card with more dots can keep the two cards if he or she can tell how many more dots this card has than the other card. If this child is not correct, his or her partner can tell how many more and keep the two cards.

4. Have children play for a certain time limit or until one child runs out of cards.

5. The player with more cards is the winner.

Best Practices Model the activity first. Ask children to compare the dots. Have them note the extra dots and count these rather than counting all the dots on each card.

ACTIVITY 3
Apply

Math Focus: Create and compare two sets.
Resource: Student Book B, Part 1, p. 20
Classroom Setup: Children work independently.

1. Children draw a tower of 3 blocks in Box A and a tower of 5 blocks in Box B.

2. Then, they compare and note which tower has fewer cubes and write this number in the answer blank.

Differentiated Instruction for Activity 1 (p. 40)

Challenge

Classroom Setup: *Teacher with a child or two*

Ask children to figure out which bear's coat has the most button holes, even though some of them are hidden behind name tags. Ask children to explain how they know. (Because every button has a button hole, Bob has the most button holes.)

Differentiated Instruction for Activity 3

Reinforcement

Materials: *Colored pencils*
Classroom Setup: *Teacher with a child or two*

Ask children to color the extra cubes before counting them and writing the answer in the answer blank.

Lesson 5
How Many in All?

LESSON OBJECTIVES
• Count on.
• Add using number lines.

MATERIALS
• Counters

DAY 1

Teacher's Edition B, pp. 42–43
Student Book B, Part 1,
pp. 21–22

DAY 1

ACTIVITY 1
Discover

Math Focus: Discover how to count on.
Materials: Counters, 10
Classroom Setup: Whole class

1. *Show* children 4 counters and ask them to show that number with their fingers.

2. *Add* 2 more counters and again ask children to show the number with their fingers.

3. *Ask* them how they know how many counters there are in all.

4. *Encourage* them to put the first number in their heads and to count on. *Say:* Four and one is five, and another one is six. Six in all.

5. *Demonstrate* with your fingers. Show four, raise one more, and *say:* Five.

6. *Raise* another finger and *say:* Six.

7. *Repeat* with children joining in.

8. *Repeat* the activity with a different number of counters, adding on two each time.

9. *Help* children see that when they put a number in their head, they do not need to count from one but instead start from that number.

Differentiated Instruction for Activity 1

Reinforcement

Materials: *Counters*
Classroom Setup: *Teacher with a child or two*
Add smaller numbers.

Challenge

Materials: *Counters*
Classroom Setup: *Teacher with a child or two*
Add bigger numbers.

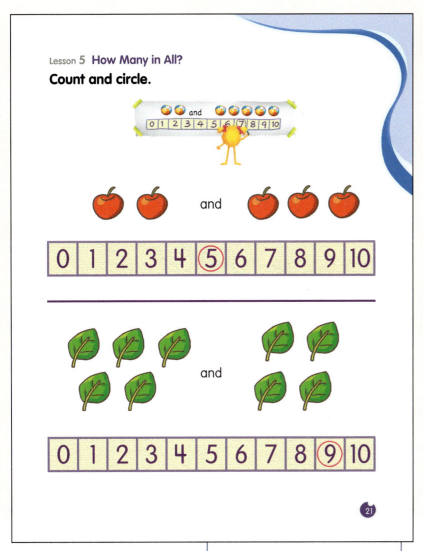

Student Book B, Part 1, p. 21

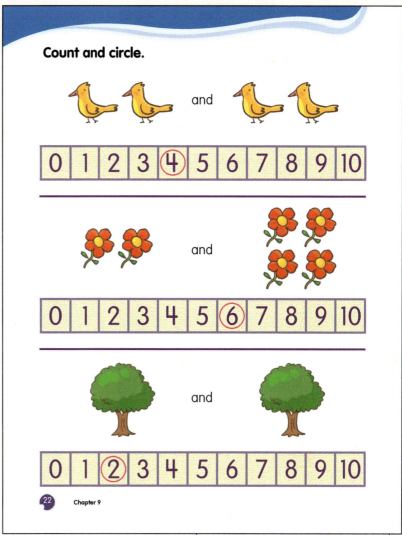

Student Book B, Part 1, p. 22

ACTIVITY 2
Apply

Math Focus: Count on using a number line.
Resource: Student Book B, Part 1, pp. 21–22
Classroom Setup: Children work independently.

1. For each exercise, children count the first set of objects and find that number on the number line.

2. Next, they count the second set of objects and count on the number line from the first number.

3. Children circle the total of the two sets on the number line.

✓ 4. *Check* that children are starting at the correct number, and that when they count on, they do not include the number that the first count ended on.

Lesson 6
What's the Difference?

LESSON OBJECTIVES
- Add using number lines.
- Understand the concept of how many numbers are *in between* two numbers.

MATERIALS
- Connecting cubes
- Number Line 0–10 (TR23)
- Teacher Numeral Cards 0–10
- Paper clips

Vocabulary

in between

DAY 1

Teacher's Edition B, p. 44

DAY 2

Teacher's Edition B, p. 45

DAY 1

ACTIVITY 1
Explore

Math Focus: Count on using connecting cubes and a number line.
Materials: Connecting cubes, 10
Number Line 0–10 (TR23)
Classroom Setup: Whole class

1. ***Invite*** four children to the front of the classroom. Give three of them three connecting cubes each, and the last child one cube.

2. ***Arrange*** the children in a row, with the child holding the single cube standing furthest from you.

3. ***Begin*** the counting with the first child by placing one hand on your head. ***Say:*** Zero and count on three. 0, 1, 2, 3.
Touch each of the first child's cubes as you count.

4. ***Continue*** around the group with each child adding on the number of cubes he or she is holding.

5. ***Repeat*** the activity, beginning at another child in the group. This time, instead of touching the cubes as they are counted, point at the numbers on the number line as the cubes are counted one by one.

6. ***Ask:***
   - What do you think the next number will be?
   - Can you find it on the number line?

7. ***Emphasize*** that there is no need to start counting from the beginning again, but to count on from the number stated.

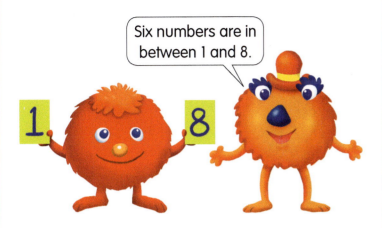

Six numbers are in between 1 and 8.

ACTIVITY 2
Discover

Math Focus: Introduce *in between*.
Materials: Teacher Numeral Cards 0–10
Number Line 0–10 (TR23)
Classroom Setup: Whole class

1. *Hold* up numeral cards '2' and '7'. *Ask:*
   - Can you read these numbers? What are they?
   - Can you point to them on the number line?
   - Can you say how many numbers are there in between these 2 numbers? (four – 3, 4, 5, and 6)
   Repeat with different numeral cards.

Differentiated Instruction for Activity 2

Reinforcement

Materials: *Number Line 0–10 (TR23)*
Classroom Setup: *Teacher with a child or two*

Choose two numbers that are near each other on the number line.

Challenge

Materials: *Number Line 0–10 (TR23)*
Classroom Setup: *Teacher with a child or two*

Choose two numbers that are far apart on the number line.

My tower has 3 more cubes than yours.

My tower has 3 fewer cubes than yours.

ACTIVITY 3
Apply

Math Focus: Compare two numbers using concrete objects and a number line.
Materials: Connecting cubes (or paper clips), 20 per pair
Number Line 0–10 (TR23), 1 copy per pair
Classroom Setup: Children work in pairs.

1. *Distribute* materials to the children.

2. *Ask* children to make two different towers (or two different paper clip snakes) and to compare them. Let them say which has more and which has fewer, and by how many.

3. Next, ask children to check their answers on the number line.

4. *Ask* children to identify the smaller number. Then, ask them to count on until they point to the bigger number.

Recall, Reinforce, and Review

Ask children to show a number up to 5 with their fingers. Then, have them count the number of fingers left to get to 5. Increase to 10 fingers once children can make up to 5.

Lesson 7
Counting On Using Fingers

LESSON OBJECTIVE
• Count on using fingers.

DAY 1

Teacher's Edition B, p. 46
Big Book B, p. 12

DAY 2

Teacher's Edition B, pp. 47–48
Student Book B, Part 1,
pp. 23–24

Big Book B, p. 12

DAY 1

ACTIVITY 1
Investigate

Math Focus: Build awareness of combining two sets into one.
Resource: Big Book B, p. 12
Classroom Setup: Whole class, in front of the Big Book

1. *Ask* children to sit so that everyone can see the Big Book.

2. *Ask* children to look at the leaves in the picture.

3. *Say:* 9 leaves are falling. 1 leaf has already fallen to the ground. How many leaves are there in all? (10)

4. *Ask* children to hold up 9 fingers to represent the 9 falling leaves. Raise 1 more finger to represent the fallen leaf. Guide them to see that counting on 1 from 9 gives 10 in all.

5. *Repeat* the activity by counting the apples (5 on the tree and 5 on the ground), the birds (7 in the tree and 3 flying away, or 8 yellow birds and 2 blue birds), and the flowers (4 red flowers and 6 blue flowers, or 4 flowers on the left of the tree and 6 flowers on the right of the tree).

ACTIVITY 2
Discover

Math Focus: Find how many more are needed.
Classroom Setup: Whole class

1. *Draw* a tree on the board.

2. *Invite* children to think of a number of apples (such as 8). Tell them you will put some of these apples (perhaps 5) on the tree.

3. *Draw* them (5 apples) on the tree.

4. *Ask:* How many apples should I draw on the ground if there were (8) apples in all to begin with? (3)

5. *Ask* children to raise 8 fingers and pretend these fingers are apples. Since there are 5 apples on the tree, they put down 5 fingers and count the remaining fingers to check how many are left.

6. *Demonstrate* with other number combinations.

Differentiated Instruction for Activity 2

Reinforcement

Classroom Setup: *Teacher with a child or two*

Use a smaller number of total apples.

Challenge

Classroom Setup: *Teacher with a child or two*

Use a greater number of total apples.

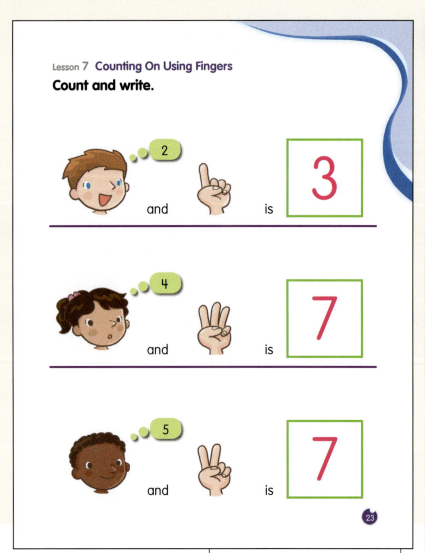

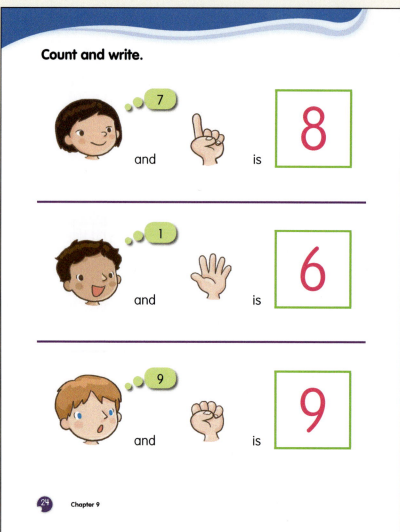

ACTIVITY 3
Apply 👤

Math Focus: Find how many in all.
Resource: Student Book B, Part 1, pp. 23–24
Classroom Setup: Children work independently.

1. Children look at the number the child in each exercise is thinking about and then count on the number of fingers shown.

2. Then, they write the total number in the corresponding box.

Chapter Overview
Ordinal Numbers

Math Background

Sequence and order are important concepts in all school subjects and in daily life. In science, children perform experiments that follow a specific sequence. In history, they learn that events happen in chronological order. In language there are rules that dictate appropriate word order in sentences. When children count, they learn that numbers follow sequential order.

One of the big ideas in elementary mathematics is that numbers can be used for different purposes and they can also be represented in different ways. The relationship between cardinal and ordinal numbers is one example that illustrates this big idea.

Vocabulary

first	coming before all others in time or space
next	coming immediately after the present one in time or space
last	coming after all others in time or space
second	constituting number two in a sequence; coming after the first in time or space
third	constituting number three in a sequence
before	in front of
after	behind

Cross-Curricular Connections

Reading/Language Arts Read a short story from a reading book or from a classroom book. Select a story that can be summarized in drawings. As you read, encourage children to think about what happens *first*, *next*, *last*, and so on. Ask children to summarize the story with drawings and words if they are able to. Suggest that they include three or four main events in the story. Have children label each drawing with an appropriate sequence word.

Drama Put children in groups of four, and give each group a different scenario to dramatize. Each scenario should present some type of sequence, for example, the finish of a race, a line at the cafeteria, or sitting in seats on a bus. Ask groups to present a short skit for their assigned scenario. Have audience members use sequence words to talk about the skit. (Mario finished the race last. Jen sat in the third seat on the bus.)

Skills Trace

Grade K	Order small sets using *first*, *second*, *third*, and *last*.
Grade 1	Order sets using ordinal numbers *first* through *tenth*. (Chap. 6)

EVERY DAY COUNTS®
Calendar Math...

provides preview, review, and practice of skills and concepts taught in this program. January activities are shown here.

Preview days of the week and months of the year. (Chapter 11)

Review counting on. (Chapter 9)

Practice position words.
(Lessons 1–3 in this chapter)

Chapter Resources

Activity Cards

Also available on Teaching Resources CD.

Student Activity Cards
Use for sequencing activities
in Lesson 2.

Technology Resources

- *Math in Focus*® eBooks
- *Math in Focus*® Teacher Resources CD
- Online Web Resources

Classroom/Household Items

- Colored pencils
- Classroom objects, such as pencils, rulers, and erasers
- Adhesive tape
- Poster paper (optional)

Differentiation and Assessment

Differentiation for Special Populations (Resources in the Teacher's Edition)

	English Language Learners	Children Needing Reinforcement	Children Needing a Challenge
Lesson 1	Math Talk, Teacher's Edition B, p. 51		
Lesson 2	Math Talk, Teacher's Edition B, pp. 53, 54		

When reading storybooks, discuss which events come first, second, and third in the story. Or, when children relate stories from home, you might inquire about the order of those real-life events using the terms *first*, *second*, and *third*. When children are lining up, discuss who is first, second, and third.

Chapter 10 Assessments

On-Going Assessment	Formal Assessment
See the check questions in the Teacher's Edition on these pages	*Find Formal Assessment Blackline Masters in the Assessments book*
Teacher's Edition B	**Assessments Book**
Lesson 1, p. 51 Lesson 2, p. 54	Assessment 3 for Book B, Part 1 (Chapters 7–10), is on pages 14–18 of Assessments. Interview Assessment is on pages 19–20.

Chapter 10 Planning Guide

Lessons and Pacing	Activity	Component	Objectives and Math Focus
Lesson 1	**'First', 'Next', and 'Last',** pp. 50–52		• Sequence events. • Understand *first*, *next*, and *last* to sequence events.
DAY 1 Activities	1 Investigate	**Big Book B**, p. 13	Introduce *first*, *next*, and *last*.
	2 Apply	**Student Book B, Part 1**, p. 25	Match a sequence of events with *first*, *next*, and *last*.
DAY 2 Activities	3 Explore	**Teacher's Edition B**, p. 51	Use *first*, *next*, and *last* to order everyday events.
	4 Apply	**Student Book B, Part 1**, p. 26	Identify first, next, and last events.
Lesson 2	**'First', 'Second', 'Third', and 'Last',** pp. 53–54		• Understand *first*, *second*, *third*, and *last* to sequence events.
DAY 1 Activities	1 Investigate	**Teacher's Edition B**, p. 53	Introduce *second* and *third*.
	2 Apply	**Student Book B, Part 1**, p. 27	Identify the order of four events.
DAY 2 Activities	3 Explore	**Teacher's Edition B**, p. 54	Order a sequence of events shown in pictures.
Lesson 3	**Physical Position,** pp. 55–56		• Understand *first*, *second*, and *third* in terms of physical position. • Understand *before* and *after*.
DAY 1 Activities	1 Investigate	**Big Book B**, p. 14	Identify positions in a line.
	2 Explore	**Teacher's Edition B**, p. 56	Introduce *before* and *after*.
	3 Apply	**Student Book B, Part 1**, p. 28	Identify who comes *before* and *after* in a picture.
Lesson 4	**Winning Order,** p. 57		• Understand *first*, *second*, and *third* in terms of winning position.
DAY 1 Activities	1 Investigate	**Teacher's Edition B**, p. 57	Identify first, second, and third children in an activity.
Lesson 5	**Showing Your Preferences,** pp. 58–60		• Rank preferences using *first*, *second*, and *third*.
DAY 1 Activities	1 Investigate	**Big Book A**, p. 20	Rank preferences *first*, *second*, and *third*.
	2 Apply	**Student Book B, Part 1**, p. 29	Record first, second, and third preferences.
DAY 2 Activities	3 Explore	**Teacher's Edition B**, p. 60 **Student Book B, Part 1**, p. 29	Make and interpret a picture graph.

Vocabulary	Manipulatives/Materials	Class Organization	NTCM Focal Points & Process Standards
first, next, last		Whole class Independent	Order events using ordinal numbers.
	• Colored pencils, 3 per child (1 red, 1 yellow, and 1 blue)	Whole class Independent	• Communication • Connections • Problem solving
second, third	• Colored pencils, 1 per child	Whole class Independent	Order events using ordinal numbers.
	• Student Activity Cards 10.2a–p, 1 set per group	Small groups	• Communication • Representation • Connections • Problem solving
before, after	• Colored pencils, 1 box per pair	Whole class Whole class Independent	Order sets using ordinal numbers. • Communication • Representation • Connections
	• Classroom objects, such as pencils, rulers, and erasers, 1 set per child	Whole class	Order sets using ordinal numbers. • Communication • Connections
		Whole class Independent	Collect data to answer questions.
	• Lion Faces (TR24), Elephant Faces (TR25), and Bear Faces (TR26) • Adhesive tape, 1 short strip per child • Poster paper (optional)	Whole class	• Communication • Representation • Connections

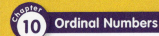

Lesson 1
'First', 'Next', and 'Last'

LESSON OBJECTIVES
• Sequence events.
• Understand *first*, *next*, and *last* to sequence events.

MATERIALS
• Colored pencils

Vocabulary
first
next
last

DAY 1

Teacher's Edition B, pp. 50–51
Big Book B, p. 13
Student Book B, Part 1, p. 25

DAY 2

Teacher's Edition B, pp. 51–52
Student Book B, Part 1, p. 26

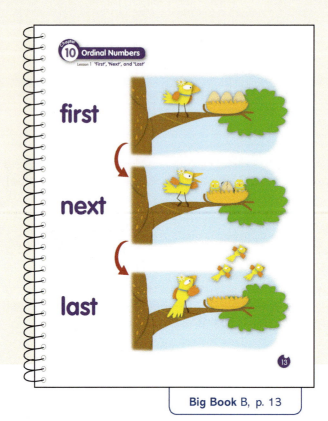

Big Book B, p. 13

DAY 1

ACTIVITY 1
Investigate

Math Focus: Introduce *first*, *next*, and *last*.
Resource: Big Book B, p. 13
Classroom Setup: Whole class, in front of the Big Book

1. *Ask* children to sit so that everyone can see the Big Book.

2. *Ask:*
   • What is happening in the first picture? (Mother Bird is looking at her eggs that have not hatched yet.)
   • What is happening in the next picture? (The eggs are starting to hatch.)
   • What is happening in the last picture? (The chicks are grown and are flying away.)

   Best Practices Point to the correct picture as the questions are asked.

3. *Provide* other examples that happened in order during the day. You might say, for example: First, we read a story. Next, we drew a picture about it. Last, we put our things away.

Lesson 1 'First', 'Next' and 'Last'

Pair.

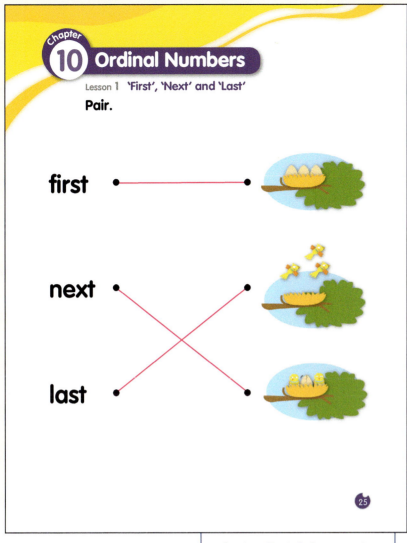

first

next

last

Student Book B, Part 1, p. 25

ACTIVITY 2
Apply

Math Focus: Match a sequence of events with *first*, *next*, and *last*.
Resource: Student Book B, Part 1, p. 25
Classroom Setup: Children work independently.

1. *Encourage* children to return to their places and open their Student Books to page 25.

2. Children draw lines between events in the pictures in the order they occur with the labels *first*, *next*, and *last*.

3. While children engage in the activity, ask check questions such as:
   • Why is this picture first?
   • Could it be last instead?
   • Why not?

DAY **2**

First, I comb my hair. Next, I tie up my hair. Last, I put my comb away.

ACTIVITY 3
Explore

Math Focus: Use *first*, *next*, and *last* to order everyday events.
Classroom Setup: Whole class

1. *Talk* about the sequential activities in everyday life. For example:
   • First, you put on your socks. Next, you put on your shoes. Last, you tie your shoelaces.
   • First, you take out your toys. Next, you play with your toys. Last, you put your toys away.
   • First, you squeeze toothpaste onto your toothbrush. Next, you brush your teeth. Last, you rinse your mouth.

2. **Math Talk** Ask children to describe similar events or classroom activities and elicit the use of the words *first*, *next*, and *last*.

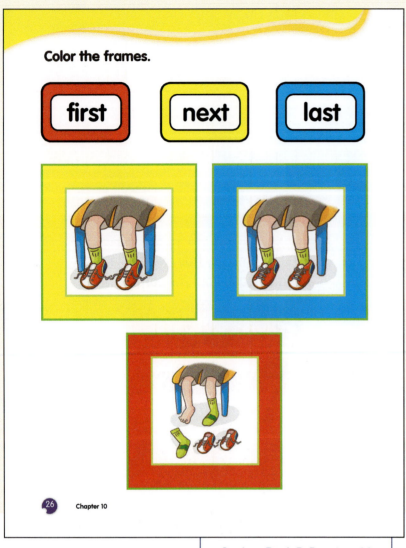

Color the frames.

first next last

Student Book B, Part 1, p. 26

ACTIVITY 4
Apply

Math Focus: Identify first, next, and last events.
Resource: Student Book B, Part 1, p. 26
Materials: Colored pencils, 3 per child (1 red, 1 yellow, and 1 blue)
Classroom Setup: Children work independently.

1. *Distribute* materials to the children.

2. Children color the frames according to what they think the sequence of the events is. Ask children to color the first event red, the next event yellow, and the last event blue.

3. *Remind* children to think about the order of events before they begin the activity.

Best Practices Some children may interpret the sequence of events as removing one's shoes and socks, instead of putting them on. Accept this answer, too, if children can explain their choices.

Lesson 2
'First', 'Second', 'Third', and 'Last'

LESSON OBJECTIVE
• Understand *first*, *second*, *third*, and *last* to sequence events.

MATERIALS
• Colored pencils
• Student Activity Cards 10.2a–p

Vocabulary
| second |
| third |

DAY 1
Teacher's Edition B, pp. 53–54
Student Book B, Part 1, p. 27

DAY 2
Teacher's Edition B, p. 54

DAY 1

First, I get a bowl and a spoon. Second, I pour some cereal into the bowl. Third, I pour in some milk. Last, I eat my cereal!

ACTIVITY 1
Investigate

Math Focus: Introduce *second* and *third*.
Classroom Setup: Whole class

1. *Talk* about the sequential activities in everyday life that come in four parts. For example:
   • First, take a banana from a bunch.
   • Second, peel the banana.
   • Third, eat the banana.
   • Last, throw away the banana peel.

2. *Write* the words *second* and *third* on the board. Also, write *first* and *last* for review.

3. *Encourage* children to offer their own four-part sequences. Prompt them if they are unable to think of their own examples. For example, *say:* To make a birthday card, first you fold the paper into a card.

4. **Math Talk** Elicit sample responses using three prompts: Second, you (draw a picture on the front). Third, you (write a message and sign your name). Last, you (put it in an envelope).

5. *Repeat* the activity with other examples, such as eating a bowl of cereal, getting ready for bed, and so on.

Lesson 2 'First', 'Second', 'Third' and 'Last'

Color.

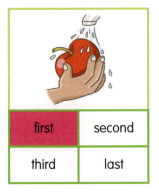

first	second
third	last

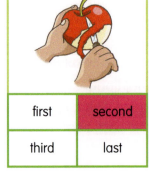

first	second
third	last

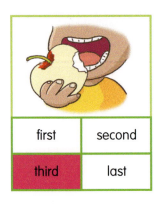

first	second
third	last

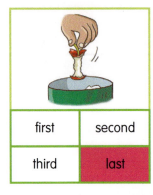

first	second
third	last

27

Student Book B, Part 1, p. 27

ACTIVITY 2
Apply

Math Focus: Identify the order of four events.
Resource: Student Book B, Part 1, p. 27
Materials: Colored pencils, 1 per child
Classroom Setup: Children work independently.

1. Children look at the four parts of the sequence of washing, peeling, eating, and discarding the apple core.

2. Then, they decide the order of events by coloring the corresponding *first*, *second*, *third*, or *last* boxes.

Best Practices Remind children that they should always ask an adult to help peel their apples.

ACTIVITY 3
Explore

Math Focus: Order a sequence of events shown in pictures.
Resource: Student Activity Cards 10.2a–p, 1 set per group
Classroom Setup: Children work in small groups.

1. **Distribute** materials to the children.

2. **Ask** children to place all four sets of cards in the correct sequence. If there are variations in the sequences, ask the groups to explain their sequences.

3. **Math Talk** Encourage the use of the words *first*, *second*, *third*, and *last* as the children describe the events.

4. While children engage in the activity, ask check questions such as:
   • How do you know this is the first event? Second event, and so on.
   • Why is this not the first event?

Lesson 3
Physical Position

LESSON OBJECTIVES
• Understand *first*, *second*, and *third* in terms of physical position.
• Understand *before* and *after*.

MATERIALS
• Colored pencils

Vocabulary
before
after

DAY 1

Teacher's Edition B, pp. 55–56
Big Book B, p. 14
Student Book B, Part 1, p. 28

Big Book B, p. 14

DAY 1

ACTIVITY 1
Investigate

Math Focus: Identify positions in a line.
Resource: Big Book B, p. 14
Classroom Setup: Whole class, in front of the Big Book

1. *Ask* children to sit so that everyone can see the Big Book.

2. *Talk* about the line of children waiting at the bus stop. *Ask:*
    • Who will board the bus first? (the boy wearing the blue jeans)
    • Who will board the bus second? (the girl)
    • Who will board the bus third? (the boy wearing the blue shirt)

3. *Elicit* the positions of the children by asking: Which position in the line is (this boy)?

4. *Repeat* the activity for the ants and the birds.

Best Practices You may want to discuss with children how they can tell who is at the front of the line. (By looking at which way they are facing.)

ACTIVITY 2
Explore

Math Focus: Introduce *before* and *after*.

Classroom Setup: Continue with whole class setup as in Activity 1.

1. *Write* 1st, 2nd, and 3rd on the board before beginning the activity. Then, write *first* under 1st, *second* under 2nd, and *third* under 3rd. This is to show children the mathematical representation of the ordinal words.

2. *Role-play* the situation of lining up for a bus.

3. *Ask* three children to stand back to front in a line. Ask the other children:
   • Who is 1st in line?
   • Who is 3rd in line?
   • Who is 2nd in line?

4. *Explain* to children that when you are standing in line, the person *before* you is the person in front of you, and that the person *after* you is the person behind you.

5. Then, *ask:*
   • Who comes before (name of 3rd child)?
   • Who comes after (name of 1st child)?
   • Who comes before (name of 2nd child)?
   • Who comes after (name of 2nd child)?

Lesson 3 Physical Position

Color the child that comes before Baby Bear.
Circle the child that comes after Baby Bear.

(Color this child.)

28

Student Book B, Part 1, p. 28

ACTIVITY 3
Apply

Math Focus: Identify who comes *before* and *after* in a picture.
Resource: Student Book B, Part 1, p. 28
Materials: Colored pencils, 1 box per pair
Classroom Setup: Children work independently.

1. *Encourage* children to return to their places and open their Student Books to page 28.

2. *Distribute* materials to the children.

3. *Ask* children to look carefully at the picture of the line of children and Baby Bear.

4. Children color the child that comes before Baby Bear, and circle the child that comes after Baby Bear.

5. You may want to extend this activity by asking children to circle the bug that comes after the ladybug or the orange butterfly. They can also put an X on the bug that comes before the ladybug and the orange butterfly.

Lesson 4
Winning Order

LESSON OBJECTIVE
• Understand *first*, *second*, and *third* in terms of winning position.

MATERIALS
• Classroom objects, such as pencils, rulers, and erasers

DAY 1

Teacher's Edition B, p. 57

DAY 1

ACTIVITY 1
Investigate

Math Focus: Identify first, second, and third children in an activity.
Materials: Classroom objects, such as pencils, rulers, and erasers, 1 set per child
Classroom Setup: Whole class

1. *Ask* children to place the materials so they are accessible.

2. *Explain* to children that they are going to play the game *Scavenger Hunt*.

3. *Draw* the following charts on the board to give a visual representation of the children's positions in the game.

	1st	2nd	3rd
Pencil			

	1st	2nd	3rd
Ruler			

	1st	2nd	3rd
Eraser			

4. *Ask:* Who can show me a pencil?
   The first child to raise a hand with a pencil has his or her name recorded on the chart, as do the second and third children to hold up a pencil.

   Best Practices If several children raise their hands at once, call on three children one by one.

5. *Explain* that (Child A) was first to show you a pencil, (Child B) was the second, and (Child C) was the third.

6. *Repeat* the activity for the ruler and eraser.

7. *Extend* the activity by making a chart about colors. For example, *say:*
   • Who can show me something that is blue?
   • Who can show me something that is yellow?

Lesson 5
Showing Your Preferences

LESSON OBJECTIVE
• Rank preferences using *first, second,* and *third.*

MATERIALS
• Lion Faces (TR24), Elephant Faces (TR25), and Bear Faces (TR26)
• Adhesive tape
• Poster paper (optional)

DAY 1

Teacher's Edition B, pp. 58–59
Big Book A, p. 20
Student Book B, Part 1, p. 29

DAY 2

Teacher's Edition B, p. 60
Student Book B, Part 1, p. 29

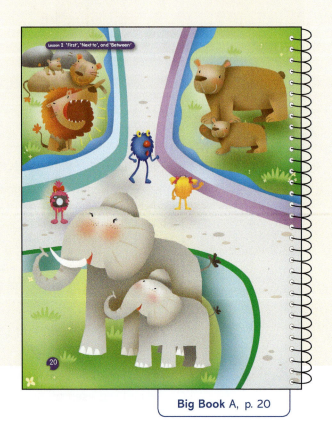

Big Book A, p. 20

DAY 1

ACTIVITY 1
Investigate

Math Focus: Rank preferences *first, second,* and *third.*
Resource: Big Book A, p. 20
Classroom Setup: Whole class, in front of the Big Book.

1. *Note* that this activity relies on a page from Big Book A.

2. *Ask* children to sit so that everyone can see the Big Book.

3. *Point* out the three animals in the Big Book – lion, elephant, and bear, and talk about the animal (among these three) that is your favorite.

4. *Ask* children to decide which one is their favorite animal and explain that this will be their first choice of animal.

5. Next, explain that their next favorite animal will be their second choice, and that their favorite animal after that will be their third choice.

6. *Ask* children to remember the way they have ranked the animals in terms of preference.

Lesson 5 **Showing Your Preferences**

Pair.

(Varies from child to child.)

1st choice •   •

2nd choice •   •

3rd choice •   •

29

Student Book B, Part 1, p. 29

ACTIVITY 2
Apply

Math Focus: Record first, second, and third preferences.
Resource: Student Book B, Part 1, p. 29
Classroom Setup: Children work independently.

1. *Encourage* children to return to their places and open their Student Books to page 29.

2. Children draw lines between the ordinal numbers and their favorite animals.

3. *Emphasize* that the most favorite is the 1st choice, the next favorite is the 2nd choice, and the least favorite is the 3rd choice.

ACTIVITY 3
Explore

Math Focus: Make and interpret a picture graph.
Resource: Student Book B, Part 1, p. 29
Materials: Lion Faces (TR24), Elephant Faces (TR25), and
Bear Faces (TR26)
Adhesive tape, 1 short strip per child
Poster paper (optional)
Classroom Setup: Whole class

1. Before the lesson, cut out the animal faces from TR24, TR25, and TR26.

   Best Practices Make more copies of the animal faces if necessary.

2. **Draw** this chart on the board (or poster paper):

```
|
|
|
|
|
|
|
|_____
   Lion    Elephant    Bear
```

3. **Ask** children to look at page 29 of their Student Book and remember the animal that they have chosen as their favorite animal (the animal matched to 1st choice).

4. **Ask** each child: Which animal did you choose as your favorite animal?

5. With each response, have the child come to the board (or poster paper) and give him or her a short strip of adhesive tape and a cut-out of his or her favorite animal head. Then, have the child place this animal head in the appropriate column as shown:

Lion   Elephant   Bear

Best Practices Encourage children to keep the space left between two animal heads within a column constant throughout the chart. This will allow them to make a visual one-to-one comparison rather than to count the animal heads when asked the questions that follow.

6. **Ask:**
   • Which is the tallest column?
   • Why is this?
   • What does this mean? (It is the most popular first choice.)

7. **Ask:**
   • Which is the shortest column?
   • Why is this?
   • What does this mean? (It is the least popular first choice.)

8. If two columns are of the same height, **ask:**
   • Which columns have the same number of animal heads?
   • Why is this?
   • What does this mean? (The same number of children prefer these animals as their first choice.)

   Best Practices If no two columns have the same number of animal heads, add on or remove some animal heads to create two equal columns.

Math Background

In Chapter 10, children learned the importance of order and sequence in the many facets of school and daily life. This chapter presents another application of sequence – the days of the week and the months of the year. Children should understand that the seven days of the week and the twelve months of the year always follow the same order and repeat continuously.

Everything that children do, from attending school, to playing sports, to watching television, is related to the concept of time. (On Tuesdays and Thursdays, we have music. My favorite show is on Wednesday nights, and so on.) Children should recognize the names of the days of the week and the months of the year and understand their relationship. Question children about time concepts often during the school day.

Vocabulary

day	a period of 24 hours
week	a period of 7 days
Sunday, Monday, Tuesday, Wednesday, Thursday, Friday, Saturday	the days of the week
month	each of the 12 named periods into which a year is divided
year	a period of 365 days (or 366 days in leap years)
January, February, March, April, May, June, July, August, September, October, November, December	the months of the year
warmer	of a higher temperature
cooler	of a lower temperature

Cross-Curricular Connections

Reading/Language Arts On the board, make a calendar for the current month, or focus children's attention on the classroom calendar if there is one. Ask them to look for capital letters on the calendar and to describe what they find. Guide children to see that the days of the week and the months of the year begin with capital letters.

Science Talk about the weather forecast feature on news programs. Explain that scientists (meteorologists) study patterns and predict what the weather will be like ahead of time. Bring in a newspaper that has a five or seven-day forecast. Discuss the forecast with children. Have them make a one-week calendar on which they will draw pictures and write temperatures to show the weather forecast.

Skills Trace

Grade K	Recognize the names of the days of the week and months of the year.
	Recognize the pattern in the days and months.
Grade 1	Learn the sequence of days and months, and the number of days in each month. (Chap. 15)

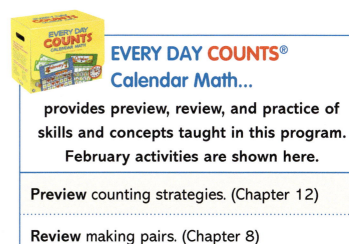

EVERY DAY COUNTS®
Calendar Math...

provides preview, review, and practice of skills and concepts taught in this program. February activities are shown here.

Preview counting strategies. (Chapter 12)

Review making pairs. (Chapter 8)

Practice calendar concepts.
(Lessons 1 and 2 in this chapter)

Chapter Resources

Activity Cards

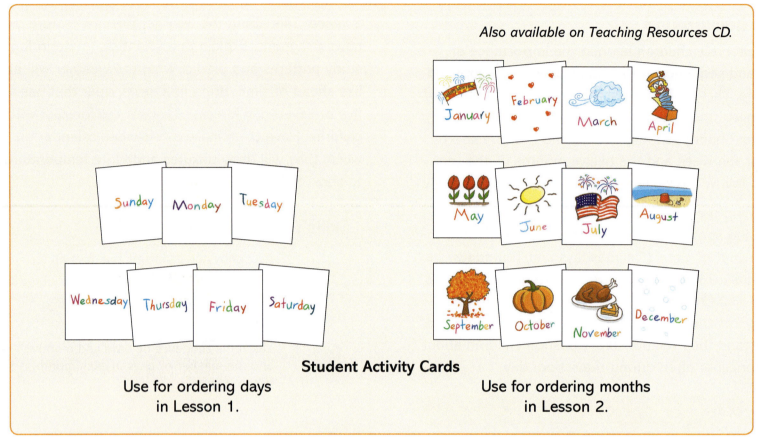

Also available on Teaching Resources CD.

Student Activity Cards

Use for ordering days
in Lesson 1.

Use for ordering months
in Lesson 2.

Technology Resources

- *Math in Focus®* eBooks
- *Math in Focus®* Teacher Resources CD
- Online Web Resources
- *Math in Focus®* Virtual Manipulatives
  for Lessons 1 and 2

Classroom/Household Items

- A calendar
- Adhesive tape
- Colored pencils

Differentiation and Assessment

Differentiation for Special Populations (Resources in the Teacher's Edition)

	English Language Learners	Children Needing Reinforcement	Children Needing a Challenge
Lesson 1	Math Talk, Teacher's Edition B, p. 63		
Lesson 2	Math Talk, Teacher's Edition B, p. 64		
Lesson 3		Teacher's Edition B, pp. 66–67	Teacher's Edition B, pp. 66–67

During this chapter and subsequent chapters, ask children for the name of the day and the date of the month. Alternate questions about what day is today, what day was yesterday, and what day will tomorrow be. Which month came before this month and which month will come after this month?

Chapter 11 Assessments

On-Going Assessment	Formal Assessment
See the check questions in the Teacher's Edition on these pages	*Find Formal Assessment Blackline Masters in the Assessments book*
Teacher's Edition B	**Assessments Book**
Lesson 1, p. 63 Lesson 2, p. 65	Assessment 4 for Book B, Part 1 (Chapters 11–14), is on pages 21–26 of Assessments. Interview Assessment is on page 27.

Chapter 11 Planning Guide

Lessons and Pacing	Activity	Component	Objectives and Math Focus
Lesson 1	**Days of the Week,** pp. 62–63		• Know the days of the week and how many there are. • Understand how to read a weekly calendar. • Review *before*, *after*, and *between*. • Order the days of the week.
DAY 1 Activities	1 Investigate	**Big Book B,** p. 15	Introduce the days of the week.
DAY 2 Activities	2 Discover	**Teacher's Edition B,** p. 63	Discover relationships among days of the week.
	3 Apply	**Teacher's Edition B,** p. 63	Order the days of the week.
Lesson 2	**Months of the Year,** pp. 64–65		• Know the months of the year and how many there are. • Order the months of the year. • Review *before*, *after*, and *between*.
DAY 1 Activities	1 Investigate	**Teacher's Edition B,** p. 64	Introduce the months of the year.
DAY 2 Activities	2 Apply	**Teacher's Edition B,** p. 65	Order the months of the year.
	3 Apply	**Student Book B, Part** 1, p. 30	Apply the order of the months to solving problems.
Lesson 3	**Pictographs,** pp. 66–68		• Review the months of the year. • Make and interpret picture graphs.
DAY 1 Activities	1 Explore	**Teacher's Edition B,** pp. 66–67	Make and interpret a pictograph of birth months.
DAY 2 Activities	2 Explore	**Teacher's Edition B,** p. 67	Make and interpret pictographs of class favorites.

Vocabulary	Manipulatives/Materials	Class Organization	NTCM Focal Points & Process Standards
day, week, Sunday, Monday, Tuesday, Wednesday, Thursday, Friday, Saturday	• Calendar Page a–g (TR27a–g) • A calendar of the current year for reference	Whole class	The Focal Points do not address time relationships.
	• Calendar Page a–g (TR27a–g) • Student Activity Cards 11.1a–g, 1 set per group	Whole class Small groups	• Communication • Representation • Connections
month, year, January, February, March, April, May, June, July, August, September, October, November, December	• Calendar Page a–g (TR27a–g) • A calendar of the current year for reference • Adhesive tape	Whole class	The Focal Points do not address time relationships.
	• Student Activity Cards 11.2a–l, 1 set per group • Colored pencils, 1 per child	Small groups Independent	• Communication • Connections • Problem solving
	• Stick Figures (TR28) • Adhesive tape	Whole class	Collect data to answer questions.
	• Stick Figures (TR28) • Adhesive tape	Whole class	• Communication • Representation • Connections

Lesson 1
Days of the Week

LESSON OBJECTIVES

• Know the days of the week and how many there are.
• Understand how to read a weekly calendar.
• Review *before*, *after*, and *between*.
• Order the days of the week.

MATERIALS

• Calendar Page a–g (TR27a–g)
• A calendar
• Student Activity Cards 11.1a–g

Vocabulary
day
week
Sunday
Monday
Tuesday
Wednesday
Thursday
Friday
Saturday

DAY 1

Teacher's Edition B, p. 62
Big Book B, p. 15

DAY 2

Teacher's Edition B, p. 63

Big Book B, p. 15

DAY 1

ACTIVITY 1
Investigate

Math Focus: Introduce the days of the week.
Resource: Big Book B, p. 15
Materials: Calendar Page a–g (TR27a–g) to match the current month
   A calendar of the current year for reference
Classroom Setup: Whole class, in front of the Big Book

1. *Select* the appropriate calendar page and fill in the name of the current month and a date for the 31ˢᵗ, if needed.
2. *Ask* children to sit so that everyone can see the Big Book.
3. *Recite* the rhyme with children. *Ask:*
   • Which *day* of the *week* is it today? How do you know?
4. *Write* the days of the week on the board. *Ask:*
   • How many days are there in a week? (7) How do you know?
5. *Ask* children if they know which day of the week they were born.
6. Next, ask them to select their favorite day based on the rhyme.
7. *Introduce* children to the calendar of the current month (the selected TR27). Point to the days of the week on the calendar after introducing the days in the rhyme. Then, ask a child to point to today's date on the calendar.

Best Practices Be sure that children understand that the days on a calendar are read from left to right, starting with the top row. You may want to read aloud, and then together, the dates on the calendar, especially those past the twentieth of the month.

Which is the day before Thursday?

Wednesday!

Sunday	Monday	Tuesday	Wednesday	Thursday	Friday	Saturday
1	2	3	4	5	6	7
8	9	10	11	12	13	14
15	16	17	18	19	20	21
22	23	24	25	26	27	28
29	30	31				

ACTIVITY 2
Discover

Math Focus: Discover relationships among days of the week.
Materials: Calendar Page a–g (TR27a–g)
Classroom Setup: Whole class

Best Practices Use the calendar page from Activity 1.

1. **Point** out the special days of the week on the calendar. For example:
   • Saturday and Sunday make up the weekend.
   • Monday is the first day of school.
   • Ms. Moon comes to our class for music on Thursdays, and so on.

2. **Math Talk** Review the words *before*, *after*, and *between*. **Ask:**
   • Which is the day before Saturday? (Friday)
   • Which is the day after Monday? (Tuesday)
   • Which days are between Friday of one week and Tuesday of the next week? (Saturday, Sunday, and Monday)
   • What day comes before Sunday? (Saturday)

Best Practices Point to the days on the calendar page as each question is asked.

ACTIVITY 3
Apply

Math Focus: Order the days of the week.
Materials: Student Activity Cards 11.1a–g, 1 set per group
Classroom Setup: Children work in small groups.

1. **Distribute** materials to the children.

2. Children are to order the cards according to the days of the week. They may order them either on a tabletop, or by standing in a line.

3. While children engage in the activity, ask check questions such as:
   • Which day comes before (Tuesday)?
   • Which day comes after (Wednesday)?
   • Which day comes between (Thursday) and (Saturday)?
   • Which days come between (Monday) and (Friday)?

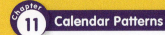

Lesson 2
Months of the Year

LESSON OBJECTIVES
- Know the months of the year and how many there are.
- Order the months of the year.
- Review *before*, *after*, and *between*.

MATERIALS
- Calendar Page a–g (TR27a–g)
- A calendar
- Adhesive tape
- Student Activity Cards 11.2a–l
- Colored pencils

Vocabulary
month
year
January
February
March
April
May
June
July
August
September
October
November
December
warmer
cooler

DAY 1

Teacher's Edition B, p. 64

DAY 2

Teacher's Edition B, p. 65
Student Book B, Part 1, p. 30

DAY 1

How many months are there between April and September?

May, June, July, and August. Four?

ACTIVITY 1
Investigate

Math Focus: Introduce the months of the year.
Materials: Calendar Page a–g (TR27a–g)
   A calendar of the current year for reference
   Adhesive tape
Classroom Setup: Whole class

1. ***Check*** to see how many months of the current year begin on each day of the week and make an appropriate number of copies of each Teacher's Resource Page (TR27a–g).

2. ***Write*** the name of the month on each calendar page, and add the 31st to the months that need it. White out 29 and 30 on your February page.

3. ***Tape*** the months of the year on the wall in order.

4. ***Ask:***
   - How many months are in a year? (12)
   - How can we find out? Let's count.

5. **Math Talk** Review the words *before*, *after*, and *between*. ***Ask:***
   - Which month comes before (July)?
   - Which month comes after (February)?
   - How many months are there between (March) and (October)? Let's count.

Best Practices Talk about the weather, seasons, and local events that happen during certain months. Ask if the weather is *warmer* (or *cooler*) in September (or August) when they start school, or in January.

Calendar Patterns

Lesson 2 **Months of the Year**

Make an X on the month before August. Circle the month after February. Color the month between October and December.

1 January	2 February	3 March
4 April	5 May	6 June
7 July	8 August	9 September
10 October	11 November	12 December

 30

Student Book B, Part 1, p. 30

DAY 2

ACTIVITY 2
Apply

Math Focus: Order the months of the year.
Materials: Student Activity Cards 11.2a–l, 1 set per group
Classroom Setup: Children work in small groups.

1. **Distribute** materials to the children.

2. **Ask** children what the picture on each card tells them about the month.

3. Children are to order the cards according to the months of the year.

✓ 4. While children engage in the activity, ask check questions such as:
   • Which month comes before (March)?
   • Which month comes after (June)?
   • Which months come between (July) and (October)?

ACTIVITY 3
Apply

Math Focus: Apply the order of the months to solving problems.
Resource: Student Book B, Part 1, p. 30
Materials: Colored pencils, 1 per child
Classroom Setup: Children work independently.

1. **Distribute** materials to the children.

2. **Help** children read the calendar months in their Student Book page.

3. **Explain** that the numbers show the order in which the months fall.

4. Ask children to make an X on the month before August, circle the month after February, and color the month between October and December.

Lesson 3
Pictographs

LESSON OBJECTIVES
• Review the months of the year.
• Make and interpret picture graphs.

MATERIALS
• Stick Figures (TR28)
• Adhesive tape

DAY 1

Teacher's Edition B, pp. 66–67

DAY 2

Teacher's Edition B, pp. 67–68

DAY 1

ACTIVITY 1
Explore

Math Focus: Make and interpret a pictograph of birth months.

Materials: Stick Figures (TR28)
Adhesive tape

Classroom Setup: Whole class

1. Before the lesson, cut out the stick figures from TR28, and have adhesive tape handy. Be sure you have enough figures so that each child will get one.

Jan Feb Mar Apr May Jun Jul Aug Sep Oct Nov Dec
Months of the Year

2. *Draw* the outline of a chart like the one shown above. It need only show the axes and the names of the months. You may want to draw vertical lines between the months so that the columns 'grow' straighter. Note that the graph will seldom have more than 4 stick figures in any column.

3. *Ask:* How many of you know what month your birthday is in?
If some children do not know their birthday month, be prepared to coach them. (See Differentiated Instruction idea on page 67.)

4. Have each child place his or her stick figure in the appropriate column.

(continued on page 67)

5. *Complete* the graph by adding a title, such as *Our Birthday Months*.

> **Best Practices** Try to make the vertical space between two figures in a column constant throughout the chart. This helps children make an easy visual one-to-one comparison rather than having to count the stick figures when asked to interpret the graph with the following questions.

6. *Ask:* How can you tell how many children have the same birthday month?
Elicit that they can look at the pictograph to see how many figures are shown for each month.

7. *Ask:* How many children were born in (month name)?

8. *Ask:*
   • Which month has the most birthdays?
   • Which month has the fewest birthdays?
   • Which months have the same number of birthdays?

9. *Encourage* the use of one-to-one correspondence for comparison of the months rather than counting.

Differentiated Instruction for Activity 1

Reinforcement

Classroom Setup: *Teacher with a child or two*

Pull together information on children's birthdays before starting this activity. If a child cannot recall his or her birthday month, write it on the bottom of his or her stick figure.

Challenge

Classroom Setup: *Teacher with a child or two*

Ask how many more birthdays there are in (June) than in (March).

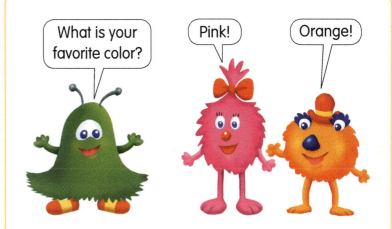

ACTIVITY 2
Explore

Math Focus: Make and interpret pictographs of class favorites.

Materials: Stick Figures (TR28)
Adhesive tape

Classroom Setup: Whole class

1. Before the lesson, cut out the stick figures from TR28, and have adhesive tape handy. Be sure you have enough figures so that every child will get one figure.

2. *Expand* the pictograph activity in Lesson 3, Activity 1, by showing favorite seasons of the year, favorite sports, favorite colors, and so on.

> **Best Practices** For each pictograph that you make, remember to ask children to suggest a label for the horizontal axis and a title for the graph.

3. *Encourage* children to use one-to-one correspondence, rather than counting, when making comparisons.

Notes

Chapter Overview

12 Chapter

Counting On and Counting Back

Math Background

Teachers in the early grades should encourage and foster a variety of problem-solving strategies, including those that are developed by the children themselves, as a way to lead to more general methods. In this chapter, children learn the counting on and counting back strategies. Within the context of these activities, children build an understanding of, and familiarity with, number pairs that make tens. The work in this chapter initiates an awareness of addition and subtraction, which will be taught using these and many other strategies throughout the elementary years.

Cross-Curricular Connections

Reading/Language Arts Display *Anno's Counting Book Big Book* by Mitsumasa Anno. Invite children to tell stories about the pictures. Have them count up and count back to compare the number of different objects that appear on the pages. Ask children to draw their own pictures for a counting book. Invite them to share their drawings and show how they can be used for counting on or counting back.

Physical Education Use masking tape to make a number line on the floor. Have children take turns hopping forward and backward as they count on and count back. For example, tell the child to start on five and hop and count on to ten. Encourage children to describe their movements. (I started on five, hopped up five hops, and ended on ten.)

Skills Trace

Grade K	Count on to 10; count back from 10.
Grade 1	Add and subtract numbers to 100. (Chaps. 3, 4, 8, 13, and 17)

EVERY DAY COUNTS® Calendar Math...

provides preview, review, and practice of skills and concepts taught in this program. February activities are shown here.

Preview making tens. (Chapter 14)

Review counting by 5s. (Chapter 8)

Practice counting strategies. (Lessons 1–4 in this chapter)

Chapter Resources

Activity Cards

Also available on Teaching Resources CD.

Teacher Activity Cards
Use for counting activities in Lesson 1.

Manipulatives from the Manipulatives Kit

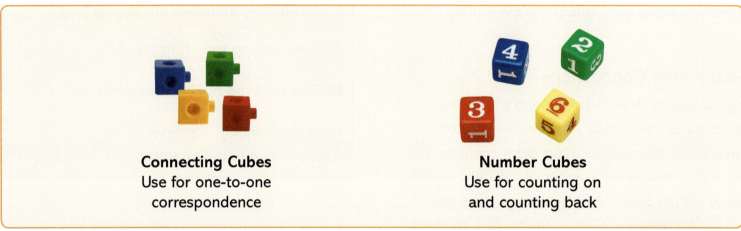

Connecting Cubes
Use for one-to-one
correspondence

Number Cubes
Use for counting on
and counting back

Technology Resources

- *Math in Focus*® eBooks
- *Math in Focus*® Teacher Resources CD
- Online Web Resources
- *Math in Focus*® Virtual Manipulatives
  for Lessons 1, 3, and 4

Classroom/Household Items

- String
- Adhesive tape
- Sticky notes
- Marking pen

Differentiation and Assessment

Differentiation for Special Populations (Resources in the Teacher's Edition)

	English Language Learners	Children Needing Reinforcement	Children Needing a Challenge
Lesson 1		Student Book B, Part 1, pp. 31–32	Student Book B, Part 1, pp. 31–32
Lesson 4		Big Book B, pp. 22–23	Big Book B, pp. 22–23

Encourage children to use their fingers to instantly show a number. Call out a number and have children represent it with their fingers. Can they show all numbers to 4 without counting? Do they know to use 5 on one hand to show a quantity over 5? Practice often, as this will help with automaticity in number and set recognition.

Chapter 12 Assessments

On-Going Assessment	Formal Assessment
See the check questions in the Teacher's Edition on these pages	*Find Formal Assessment Blackline Masters in the Assessments book*
Teacher's Edition B	**Assessments Book**
Lesson 1, p. 71 Lesson 3, p. 75	Assessment 4 for Book B, Part 1 (Chapters 11–14), is on pages 21–26 of Assessments. Interview Assessment is on page 27.

Lessons and Pacing	Activity	Component	Objectives and Math Focus
Lesson 1	**Counting On Using Fingers,** pp. 70–72		• Review associating fingers with numbers. • Review ordering numbers to 10. • Compare by using one-to-one correspondence. • Count on by using fingers to find the difference.
DAY 1 Activities	1 Investigate	**Big Book B,** pp. 16–17	Count by using fingers.
	2 Explore	**Teacher's Edition B,** p. 71	Review counting to 10.
DAY 2 Activities	3 Discover	**Teacher's Edition B,** p. 71	Discover how to use fingers to find how many more.
	4 Apply	**Student Book B, Part 1,** pp. 31–32	Solve problems by making 10.
Lesson 2	**Counting On Up to 10,** pp. 73–74		• Discover number conservation with or without counting (up to 10). • Count on using fingers to find a difference.
DAY 1 Activities	1 Investigate	**Big Book B,** pp. 18–19	Count on to make 10.
	2 Explore	**Teacher's Edition B,** p. 74	Count on using fingers.
Lesson 3	**Counting Back Using Fingers,** pp. 75–76		• Count back using fingers. • Count back to find the difference.
DAY 1 Activities	1 Investigate	**Big Book B,** pp. 20–21	Count back to find the difference.
	2 Explore	**Teacher's Edition B,** p. 76	Count back using fingers.
Lesson 4	**Finding Differences Using Fingers,** pp. 77–78		• Review *more* and *fewer*. • Count up and back to find the difference between two sets. • Investigate number conservation.
DAY 1 Activities	1 Investigate	**Big Book B,** pp. 22–23	Find how many more.

Vocabulary	Manipulatives/Materials	Class Organization	NTCM Focal Points & Process Standards
	• Teacher Activity Cards 12.1a–j	Whole class Whole class	Use numbers to solve quantitative problems.
	• Connecting cubes, 10 per child	Whole class Independent	• Communication • Representation • Problem solving
	• Number cubes, 1 per pair	Whole class Pairs	Use numbers to solve quantitative problems. • Communication • Representation
	• Number cubes, 1 per pair	Whole class Pair	Use numbers to solve quantitative problems. • Communication • Representation • Problem solving
	• String • Adhesive tape • Sticky notes, 6 • Marking pen	Whole class	Use numbers to solve quantitative problems. • Communication • Representation • Problem solving

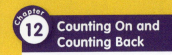
Lesson 1
Counting On Using Fingers

LESSON OBJECTIVES
- Review associating fingers with numbers.
- Review ordering numbers to 10.
- Compare by using one-to-one correspondence.
- Count on by using fingers to find the difference.

MATERIALS
- Teacher Activity Cards 12.1a–j
- Connecting cubes

DAY 1

Teacher's Edition B, pp. 70–71
Big Book B, pp. 16–17

DAY 2

Teacher's Edition B, pp. 71–72
Student Book B, Part 1,
pp. 31–32

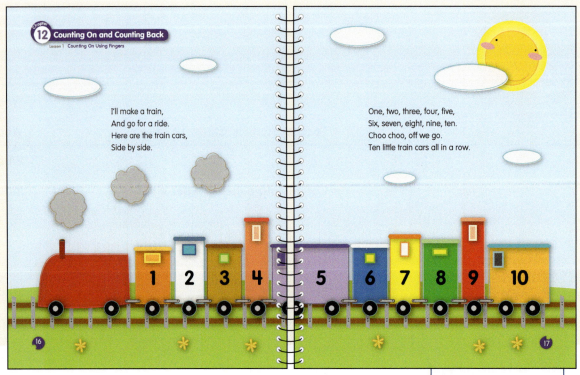

Big Book B, pp. 16–17

DAY 1

ACTIVITY 1
Investigate

Math Focus: Count by using fingers.
Resource: Big Book B, pp. 16–17
Classroom Setup: Whole class, in front of the Big Book

1. *Ask* children to sit so that everyone can see the Big Book.

2. *Model* counting the cars on the train by using fingers. Ask each child to raise and wiggle a finger or thumb in order to count the train cars as the rhyme is recited.

3. *Ask:*
   - Which number comes after 6? (7)
   - Which number comes before 3? (2)
   Vary values up to 10. These questions remind children of the number values and order to 10.

How many?

ACTIVITY 2
Explore

Math Focus: Review counting to 10.
Materials: Teacher Activity Cards 12.1a–j
Classroom Setup: Continue with whole class setup as in Activity 1.

1. **Show** the pictures of the trains to children, one by one, in random order.

2. **Ask** children how many train cars they can see. Remind them that the red engine is not one of the cars.

3. Then, have children raise their hands and show the correct number of fingers for each picture.

4. **Ask** a child to come up to the picture and count the cars to check, as needed.

4 more fingers to make 10.

ACTIVITY 3
Discover

Math Focus: Discover how to use fingers to find how many more.
Classroom Setup: Whole class

1. **Ask** children to raise 8 fingers.

2. **Ask:** How many more need to be raised to make 10 fingers?

3. While children engage in the activity, ask check questions such as:
   • How do you know?
   • Are you sure?

4. **Repeat** with different numbers (including 0). Guide children in working out the number of fingers needed to make 10 each time.

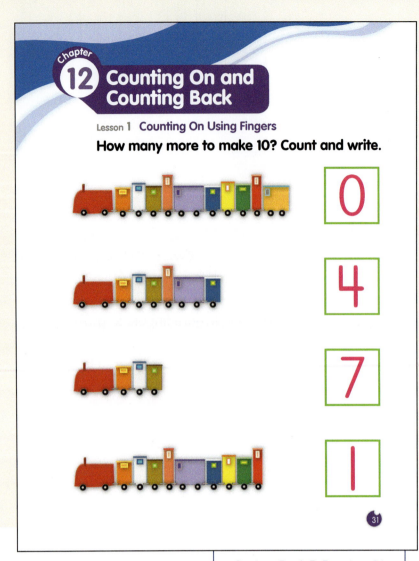

Chapter 12 — Counting On and Counting Back

Lesson 1 Counting On Using Fingers

How many more to make 10? Count and write.

0

4

7

1

31

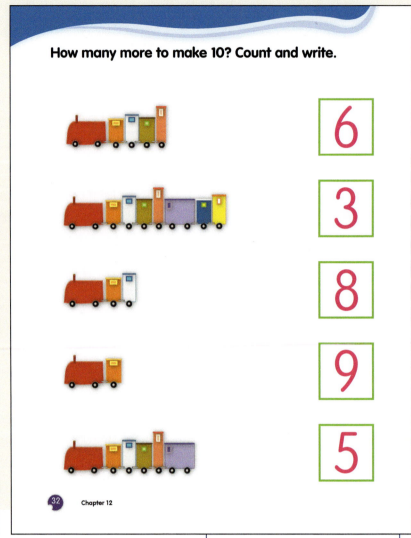

How many more to make 10? Count and write.

6

3

8

9

5

32   Chapter 12

Student Book B, Part 1, p. 31

Student Book B, Part 1, p. 32

ACTIVITY 4
Apply

Math Focus: Solve problems by making 10.

Resource: Student Book B, Part 1, pp. 31–32

Classroom Setup: Children work independently.

1. Children count the train cars in each exercise and use fingers to find how many more train cars would be needed to make 10 in all.

2. Then, they write this number in the adjacent box.

Best Practices Remind children that the train engine (the 1st red section of each train picture) is not a train car and should not be included when they count.

Differentiated Instruction for Activity 4

Reinforcement

Materials: *Connecting cubes, 10 per child*

Classroom Setup: *Teacher with a child or two*

Ask children to pair a connecting cube with each train car. Then, find how many more cubes are needed to make 10.

Challenge

Classroom Setup: *Teacher with a child or two*

Ask children to keep the number of train cars shown in their heads, and then count on to 10.

Chapter 12
Counting On and Counting Back

Lesson 2
Counting On Up to 10

LESSON OBJECTIVES
- Discover number conservation with or without counting (up to 10).
- Count on using fingers to find a difference.

MATERIALS
- Number cubes

DAY 1

Teacher's Edition B, pp. 73–74
Big Book B, pp. 18–19

Big Book B, pp. 18–19

DAY 1

ACTIVITY 1
Investigate

Math Focus: Count on to make 10.
Resource: Big Book B, pp. 18–19
Classroom Setup: Whole class, in front of the Big Book

1. *Ask* children to sit so that everyone can see the Big Book.
2. Have children count the number of T-shirts on the clothesline.
3. *Ask:* How many T-shirts are there in all? (10)
4. *Ask* children if the number of T-shirts will be the same if they start counting from the other end. *Ask:* Why? or Why not?

Best Practices If some children are unsure, demonstrate by asking another child to count the T-shirts, starting from the opposite end.

5. *Cover* 3 T-shirts and ask children to count how many T-shirts are uncovered. (7)
6. Next, ask children if they know how many T-shirts are covered, if there are 10 items in all.
7. *Model* the answer by saying: I see 7 T-shirts. So 1, 2, 3, T-shirts are covered by my hand. So for 7, I count up 3 to make 10 T-shirts in all.
8. *Repeat* steps 5 and 6 with different numbers of T-shirts covered.
9. *Repeat* steps 5 and 6 using 10 fingers.

CHAPTER 12: LESSON 2   **73**

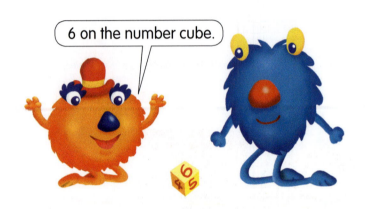

6 on the number cube.

ACTIVITY 2
Explore

Math Focus: Count on using fingers.
Materials: Number cubes, 1 per pair
Classroom Setup: Children work in pairs with teacher direction.

1. *Encourage* children to return to their places.

2. *Distribute* materials to the children.

3. Children take turns tossing the number cube.

4. Using fingers, children count on from the number shown on the number cube up to 10. For example, if the number cube shows 6, the pair counts up 7, 8, 9, 10.

5. *Model* how to arrive at the answer by saying: 6 is on the number cube. Put 6 in your head and put up fingers to count up: 7, 8, 9, 10. We need 4 fingers to make 10, so the answer is 4.

Lesson 3
Counting Back Using Fingers

LESSON OBJECTIVES
• Count back using fingers.
• Count back to find the difference.

MATERIALS
• Number cubes

DAY 1

Teacher's Edition B, pp. 75–76
Big Book B, pp. 20–21

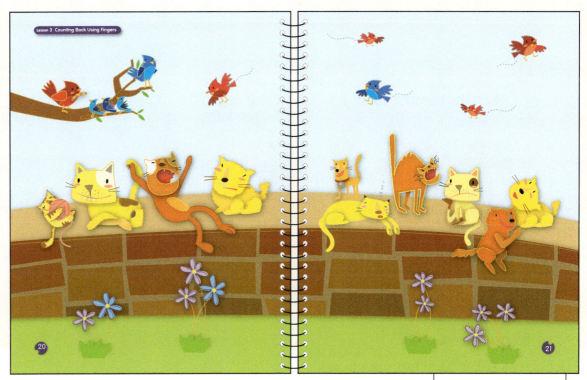

Big Book B, pp. 20–21

DAY 1

ACTIVITY 1
Investigate

Math Focus: Count back to find the difference.
Resource: Big Book B, pp. 20–21
Classroom Setup: Whole class, in front of the Big Book

1. *Ask* children to sit so that everyone can see the Big Book.
2. *Point* to the cats as you count them. *Ask:* How many cats are there in all? (10)
3. Next, point to the big cats and count them. *Ask:* How many big cats are there in all? (8)
4. *Ask* children to raise 10 fingers. Ask them to put down 8 fingers, one at a time, as they count back 8: 10, 9, 8, 7, 6, 5, 4, 3.
5. *Ask:* How many fingers are left when you count back 8? (2)
   The number of fingers still raised is the number of small cats.
6. *Repeat* by counting:
   • the 6 yellow and 4 orange cats,
   • the 5 large and 5 small birds,
   • the 5 blue and 5 red birds, and
   • the 2 blue and 8 purple flowers.
7. While children engage in the activity, ask check questions such as:
   • How did you find your answer?
   • Are you sure it is correct?
   • Could the answer be (6) instead?
   • Why? or Why not?

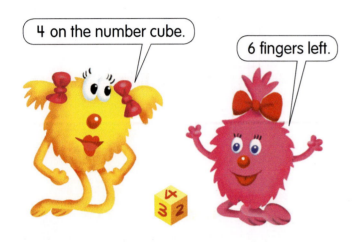

4 on the number cube.

6 fingers left.

ACTIVITY 2
Explore

Math Focus: Count back using fingers.

Materials: Number cubes, 1 per pair

Classroom Setup: Children work in pairs with teacher direction.

1. *Encourage* children to return to their places.

2. *Distribute* materials to the children.

3. Children take turns tossing the number cube.

4. *Ask* children to count back from 10 the number shown on the cube. For example, if the number cube shows 4, the pair raises 10 fingers and counts back 4: 10, 9, 8, 7.

5. *Model* how to find the answer by saying: I see 4 on the number cube. Show 10 fingers and count back 4 fingers. Now only 6 fingers are raised, so the answer is 6.

Chapter 12
Counting On and Counting Back

Lesson 4
Finding Differences Using Fingers

LESSON OBJECTIVES
- Review *more* and *fewer*.
- Count up and back to find the difference between two sets.
- Investigate number conservation.

MATERIALS
- String
- Adhesive tape
- Sticky notes
- Marking pen

DAY 1

Teacher's Edition B, pp. 77–78
Big Book B, pp. 22–23

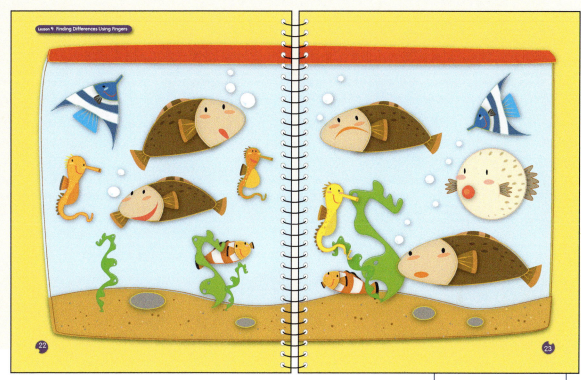

Big Book B, pp. 22–23

DAY 1

ACTIVITY 1
Investigate

Math Focus: Find how many more.
Resource: Big Book B, pp. 22–23
Materials: String
  Adhesive tape
  Sticky notes, 6
Classroom Setup: Whole class, in front of the Big Book

1. *Ask* children to sit so that everyone can see the Big Book.

2. *Ask* children to count the number of fish in the aquarium. (9)

3. Next, *ask* them to count the number of seahorses. (3)

4. Then, *ask:*
   - Are there more fish or more seahorses? (more fish)
   - How do you know?
   - Are there fewer fish or fewer seahorses? (fewer seahorses)
   - How do you know?

(continued on page 78)

5. *Ask:*
   - How many more (fewer)? (There are 6 more fish. There are 6 fewer seahorses.)
   - How do you know?

6. *Elicit* from children that they could match each seahorse to a fish and then count how many more there are.

Best Practices You may want to demonstrate how to form the seahorse-fish pairs in one or more of the following ways:
- Cover each seahorse-fish pair with a pair of hands.
- Match each seahorse to a fish using a piece of string. Once a seahorse-fish pair has been found, tape down the string.
- Use sticky notes to cover each seahorse-fish pair.

7. *Ask* if the number will be the same if they start to count from a different animal each time.

Differentiated Instruction for Activity 1

Reinforcement

Materials: *Marking pen*
Classroom Setup: *Teacher with a child or two*

Some children may be distracted by the seaweed that may seem to resemble the seahorses. For these children, trace around the animals and use the tracings to repeat the activity.

Challenge

Classroom Setup: *Teacher with a child or two*

Encourage children to use their fingers to count back 3 from 9.

Math Background

Patterns are as much a part of human behavior as speech. Even the ancients found the patterns of stars in the night sky (*constellations*), and the planets that wandered in and out of these star patterns. Kindergarten children already recognize simple patterns and find them appealing because of their need for organization and structure. They should be encouraged to look for them in their environment, such as tile patterns or the patterns in routine events.

The simple repeating patterns children create and use in Kindergarten provide a basis for increasingly complex patterns. In Grade 1, children will study number patterns that grow instead of simply repeat. These simple number patterns in turn 'grow up' to be number sequences and functions when children get to pre-algebra and algebra.

Vocabulary

| repeating pattern | a design that recurs uniformly |

Cross-Curricular Connections

Reading/Language Arts Present some patterns similar to the ones in this chapter, for example *square*, *triangle*, *heart*. Ask children to identify the beginning letter in each word and write these letters on the board (*s*, *t*, *h*). Have children create a word pattern by taking turns saying words they know that begin with *s*, *t*, *h*, *s*, *t*, *h*, and so on. Continue with other shape, letter, and word patterns.

Art Tell children that many artists use shapes and patterns to create their works. Have them create their own works of art using shapes and patterns. You may wish to provide shapes cut out from different color construction paper. Another option is to give children pattern blocks that they can trace and then color. You might also show children what a tessellation is and have them create that type of pattern.

Skills Trace

Grade K	Create and extend patterns of shapes.
Grade 1	Create and extend number patterns. (Chaps. 7, 12, and 16)

EVERY DAY COUNTS®
Calendar Math...

provides preview, review, and practice of skills and concepts taught in this program. March activities are shown here.

Preview making tens. (Chapter 14)

Review using position words. (Chapter 10)

Practice using patterns.
(Lessons 1–3 in this chapter)

Chapter Resources

Activity Cards

Also available on Teaching Resources CD.

Student Activity Cards
Use for creating repeating
patterns in Lesson 2.

Manipulatives from the Manipulatives Kit

Attribute Blocks
Use for creating repeating patterns

Connecting Cubes
Use for creating repeating patterns

Technology Resources

- *Math in Focus®* eBooks
- *Math in Focus®* Teacher Resources CD
- Online Web Resources
- *Math in Focus®* Virtual Manipulatives
  for Lessons 1–3

Classroom/Household Items

- Colored pencils (optional)
- Adhesive tape

Differentiation and Assessment

Differentiation for Special Populations (Resources in the Teacher's Edition)

	English Language Learners	Children Needing Reinforcement	Children Needing a Challenge
Lesson 1		Student Book B, Part 1, pp. 34–35	
Lesson 2			Teacher's Edition B, p. 83

Encourage children to clap their hands, tap their feet, or cluck their tongues to create ABAB or ABBABB patterns. For example, *clap clap tap* or *tap tap cluck* could model AAB. Practice the same patterns with connecting cubes and counters.

Chapter 13 Assessments

On-Going Assessment	Formal Assessment
See the check questions in the Teacher's Edition on these pages	*Find Formal Assessment Blackline Masters in the Assessments book*
Teacher's Edition B	**Assessments Book**
Lesson 1, p. 81 Lesson 2, p. 83	Assessment 4 for Book B, Part 1 (Chapters 11–14), is on pages 21–26 of Assessments. Interview Assessment is on page 27.

Chapter 13 Planning Guide

Lessons and Pacing	Activity	Component	Objectives and Math Focus
Lesson 1		**Repeating Shape Patterns, pp. 80–82**	• Recognize, continue, and create a repeating shape pattern. • Identify a missing portion of a repeating pattern.
DAY 1 Activities	1 Investigate	**Big Book B,** pp. 24–25	Introduce *repeating pattern*.
DAY 2 Activities	2 Explore	**Teacher's Edition B,** p. 81	Create a repeating pattern.
	3 Apply	**Student Book B, Part 1,** p. 33	Identify the next shape in a pattern.
	4 Apply	**Student Book B, Part 1,** pp. 34–35	Identify a missing shape in a repeating pattern. **Recall, Reinforce, and Review** Make a linear color pattern using connecting cubes and ask questions about it.
Lesson 2		**Repeating Patterns, p. 83**	• Create an ABABAB repeating pattern using cards.
DAY 1 Activities	1 Explore	**Teacher's Edition B,** p. 83	Select an attribute and create a repeating pattern.
Lesson 3		**Making Patterns with Things, pp. 84–86**	• Create ABABAB, AABAAB, and ABBABB repeating patterns using shapes.
DAY 1 Activities	1 Explore	**Teacher's Edition B,** p. 84	Continue ABAB, AABAAB, and ABBABB patterns.
	2 Explore	**Teacher's Edition B,** p. 85	Replicate a given pattern with other shapes. **Recall, Reinforce, and Review** Model a pattern using claps and taps, and ask what will come next.

Vocabulary	Manipulatives/Materials	Class Organization	NTCM Focal Points & Process Standards
repeating pattern		Whole class	Identify, create, and continue repeating patterns.
	• Attribute blocks, 12 per group (2 shapes, all of the same size)	Small groups	• Communication
		Independent	• Representation
	• Colored pencils, 1 box per pair (optional)	Independent	• Problem solving
	• Attribute blocks (1 circle, 1 triangle, 1 square, and 1 rectangle)		
	• Adhesive tape		
	• Connecting cubes (of 3 colors)		
	• Student Activity Cards 13.2a–h, 1 set per pair	Pairs	Identify, create, and continue repeating patterns.
			• Communication
			• Representation
			• Problem solving
	• Circle attribute blocks, 6 per group	Whole class	Identify, create, and complete repeating patterns.
	• Square attribute blocks, 6 per group	Small groups	
			• Communication
			• Representation
			• Problem solving

Lesson 1
Repeating Shape Patterns

LESSON OBJECTIVES
- Recognize, continue, and create a repeating shape pattern.
- Identify a missing portion of a repeating pattern.

MATERIALS
- Attribute blocks
- Colored pencils (optional)
- Adhesive tape
- Connecting cubes

Vocabulary

repeating pattern

DAY 1

Teacher's Edition B, p. 80
Big Book B, pp. 24–25

DAY 2

Teacher's Edition B, pp. 81–82
Student Book B, Part 1,
pp. 33–35

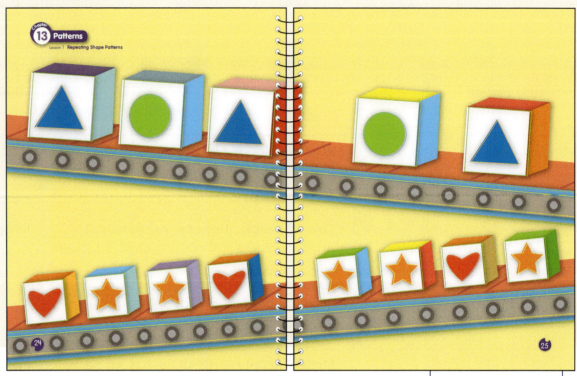

Big Book B, pp. 24–25

DAY 1

ACTIVITY 1
Investigate

Math Focus: Introduce *repeating pattern*.
Resource: Big Book B, pp. 24–25
Classroom Setup: Whole class, in front of the Big Book

1. **Ask** children to sit so that everyone can see the Big Book.

2. **Ask:**
   - Can you see a repeating pattern? Can you describe it to me? (yes; triangle, circle, triangle, circle)
   - How do you know this is a repeating pattern?

3. **Ask:**
   - Can you see another repeating pattern? How can you describe it? (yes; heart, star, star, heart, star, star)
   - Does this look like the other pattern? (no)
   - Why (not)? (Because this is an ABBABB pattern. The first one is an ABAB pattern.)

4. **Remind** children about repeating patterns: Items are usually repeated in a regular order, such as, ABABAB and ABBABBABB. Patterns can be made up of recognizable and abstract designs.

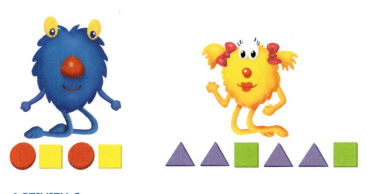

ACTIVITY 2
Explore

Math Focus: Create a repeating pattern.
Materials: Attribute blocks, 12 per group (2 shapes, all of the same size)
Classroom Setup: Children work in small groups.

1. **Distribute** materials to the children.

2. **Ask** children to make repeating patterns with their attribute blocks.

3. **Remind** children to decide first on the type of pattern they will make, such as an ABAB, ABBABB, or AABBAABB type.

> **Best Practices** Children should show at least three repetitions to adequately establish the pattern.

4. Have another group try to figure out the pattern and add one more shape to it.

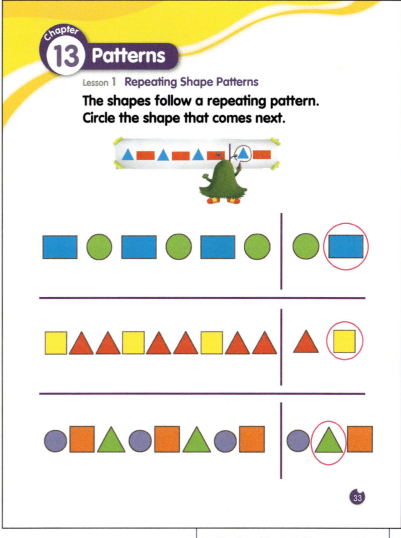

Chapter 13 Patterns

Lesson 1 Repeating Shape Patterns

The shapes follow a repeating pattern. Circle the shape that comes next.

Student Book B, Part 1, p. 33

ACTIVITY 3
Apply

Math Focus: Identify the next shape in a pattern.
Resource: Student Book B, Part 1, p. 33
Classroom Setup: Children work independently.

1. **Direct** children's attention to the green furry at the top of the page. Have them look at the repeating pattern on the furry's paper.

2. **Ask:** Which shape do you think should come next?

3. **Explain** that the green furry thinks that the blue triangle should come next and so, it is circling the blue triangle.

4. Children look at the repeating patterns in each exercise and circle the shape that comes next.

5. **Encourage** children to check how many of each shape are present in each pattern, and how often each shape is repeated.

✔ 6. While children engage in the activity, ask check questions such as:
  • Why did you choose this shape and not the other?
  • What type of pattern is this?
  • Is this the same type of pattern as the other one?
  • How do you know?

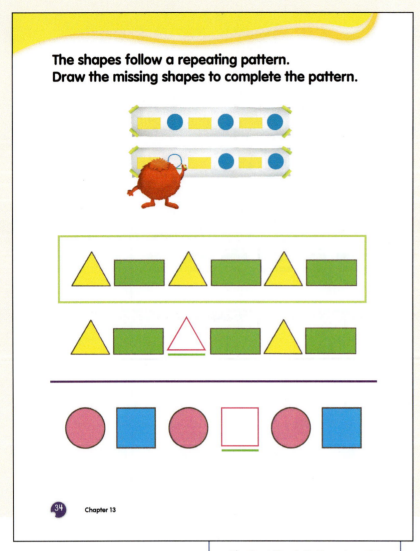

The shapes follow a repeating pattern.
Draw the missing shapes to complete the pattern.

Student Book B, Part 1, p. 34

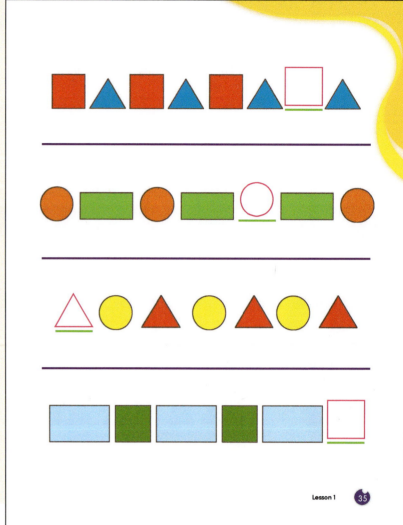

Student Book B, Part 1, p. 35

ACTIVITY 4
Apply

Math Focus: Identify a missing shape in a repeating pattern.
Resource: Student Book B, Part 1, pp. 34–35
Materials: Colored pencils, 1 box per pair (optional)
Classroom Setup: Children work independently.

1. *Direct* children's attention to the red furry at the top of the page. Explain that the furry is drawing the missing shape to complete the pattern.

2. *Explain* to children that they will have a guide only for the first exercise.

3. For the other exercises, children draw the missing shapes to complete the pattern. You may also want them to color the shape to match the pattern.

4. *Remind* children to check the shapes and type of pattern so that they can predict which shape is missing.

Differentiated Instruction for Activity 4

Reinforcement

Materials: Attribute blocks (1 circle, 1 triangle, 1 square, and 1 rectangle)
Adhesive tape
Classroom Setup: *Teacher with a child or two*

Have children select the two attribute blocks that make up each pattern. Place the blocks above the first two figures in each pattern and join them with a strip of tape. Then, slide this 'unit pattern' along so that it matches each unit of the pattern.

Recall, Reinforce, and Review

Using three colors of connecting cubes, make a linear pattern, such as: blue, yellow, red, blue, yellow, red, blue, yellow.
Ask: Which color will come next on this end of the pattern? On the other end of the pattern?

Lesson 2
Repeating Patterns

LESSON OBJECTIVE
• Create an ABABAB repeating pattern using cards.

MATERIALS
• Student Activity Cards 13.2a–h

DAY 1

Teacher's Edition B, p. 83

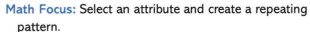

ACTIVITY 1
Explore

Math Focus: Select an attribute and create a repeating pattern.

Materials: Student Activity Cards 13.2a–h, 1 set per pair

Classroom Setup: Children work in pairs with teacher direction.

1. **Distribute** materials to the children.

2. **Remind** children of the ABAB pattern before they begin.

3. **Ask** children to make a repeating pattern using the cards.

✓ 4. While children engage in the activity, ask check questions such as:
   • How do you know this is a repeating pattern?
   • Is there any other way you can make a repeating pattern with the cards?
   • Why? or Why not?

> **Best Practices** The repeating pattern could either be of smiley faces and sad faces, or of hats and bows. Because children will need to select an attribute to alternate before they begin, it will take some children considerably longer to make this decision. They might also feel uncomfortable disregarding the other attribute.

Differentiated Instruction for Activity 1

Challenge

Materials: Student Activity Cards 13.2a–h

Classroom Setup: Teacher with a child or two

Ask children to create an AABAAB or ABBABB repeating pattern.

Lesson 3
Making Patterns with Things

LESSON OBJECTIVE
- Create ABABAB, AABAAB, and ABBABB repeating patterns using shapes.

MATERIALS
- Circle attribute blocks
- Square attribute blocks

DAY 1

Teacher's Edition B, pp. 84–86

DAY 1

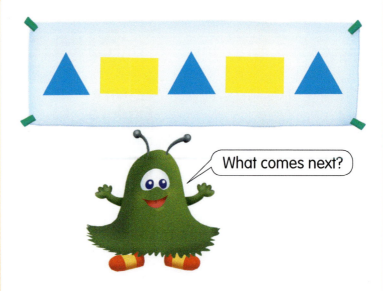

ACTIVITY 1
Explore

Math Focus: Continue ABAB, AABAAB, and ABBABB patterns.
Classroom Setup: Whole class

1. *Draw* an ABAB pattern on the board using two of the basic shapes: circle, triangle, square, and rectangle.

2. *Ask:*
   - What comes next?
   - How can you describe this pattern?

3. *Repeat* using other patterns such as AABAAB or ABBABB. Draw the following patterns on the board:

   - for AABAAB, and
   - ☐ △ △ ☐ △ △ for ABBABB.

   Best Practices Do not erase the patterns you have drawn on the board, because you will be using them in the next activity.

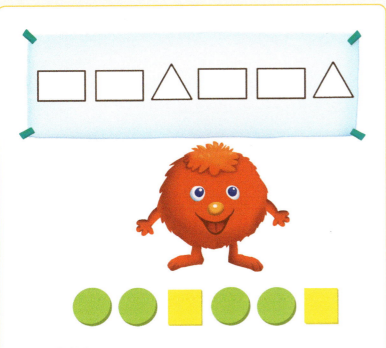

ACTIVITY 2
Explore

Math Focus: Replicate a given pattern with other shapes.

Materials: Circle attribute blocks, 6 per group
  Square attribute blocks, 6 per group
  Repeating patterns drawn on board in Activity 1

Classroom Setup: Children work in small groups with teacher direction.

1. *Distribute* attribute blocks to the children. Be sure that each group has all large or all small shapes, so that the size of the blocks is not a distraction when forming the pattern.

2. *Ask* children to look at the board and use the two shapes they have to make a pattern similar to the first pattern shown on the board.

   Best Practices Emphasize that children should focus on the blocks they have, and not the different shapes that are drawn on the board. Also, tell children to disregard the color of the blocks when making these patterns.

3. *Ask* children to describe their patterns once all groups have finished. Note that there are two patterns possible: square, square, circle, or circle, circle, square.

4. *Ask* children to match the second pattern on the board in the same way.

Recall, Reinforce, and Review

Model a pattern using claps and taps with your hands and feet. For example: tap, clap, tap, clap. Ask children what will come next. Repeat with other patterns, such as tap, tap, clap, clap. Continue making combinations and asking children to complete the pattern.

Notes

Chapter Overview
Counting On to 15

Math Background

In this chapter, children extend their counting abilities through the number 20. They count and combine groups of objects and they count back to find differences. These are all important readiness skills for addition and subtraction.

In Lesson 1, children count groups of objects and then find how many more are needed to make 10. This activity not only provides a foundation for addition and subtraction, but it can lead to the understanding that 10 is the basis for our numeration system. Counting and grouping tens is a basic place-value concept.

Cross-Curricular Connections

Reading/Language Arts Besides using the Big Book pages for the counting activities, you might also ask questions to elicit oral language practice. On pages 26 and 27, have children tell a story about the scene. Ask what the children in the picture are doing and what kind of event this is. On pages 28 and 29, ask the children to name the different bugs on the page and describe what they look like and what they are doing.

Science Use the Big Book pages in Lesson 3 (pages 28 and 29) to discuss insects. Point out that all insects have three pairs of legs. Their bodies have three parts. Insects have skeletons on the outside of their bodies. Many insects have wings and antennae. Ask children to look at the bugs in the picture or on the activity cards. Have them describe how the bugs are similar and different. Then, have them classify the bugs as insects or non-insects. (The bee, ant, and lady bug are insects; the slug and caterpillar are not.)

Skills Trace

Grade K	Count numbers to 20 and write the numerals.
	Count on to find how many more are needed.
Grade 1	Count and compare numbers to 100. (Chaps. 1, 7, 11, and 16)
	Add and subtract numbers to 100. (Chaps. 4, 5, 8, and 17)

EVERY DAY COUNTS® Calendar Math...

provides preview, review, and practice of skills and concepts taught in this program. March activities are shown here.

Preview language of size comparison. (Chapter 15)

Review comparing to find differences. (Chapter 12)

Practice counting small sets of objects. (Lesson 1 in this chapter)

Chapter Resources

Activity Cards

Also available on Teaching Resources CD.

Numeral Cards
Use for ordering and counting
on activities in Lessons 2 and 3.

Teacher Activity Cards
Use for counting on
activities in Lesson 3.

Manipulatives from the Manipulatives Kit

Connecting Cubes
Use for counting on activities

Technology Resources

- *Math in Focus*® eBooks
- *Math in Focus*® Teacher Resources CD
- Online Web Resources
- *Math in Focus*® Virtual Manipulatives
  for Lessons 1–3

Classroom/Household Items

- Scissors
- Adhesive tape

Differentiation and Assessment

Differentiation for Special Populations (Resources in the Teacher's Edition)

	English Language Learners	Children Needing Reinforcement	Children Needing a Challenge
Lesson 1		Student Book B, Part 1, pp. 36–37	Student Book B, Part 1, pp. 36–37

Invite two children to stand next to each other and count their 20 fingers aloud. Have one child raise one finger at a time until he or she is showing 10 fingers. Have the second child then also raise one finger at a time, counting out the numbers 11–20. Give different pairs of children a chance to demonstrate over the course of the chapter.

Chapter 14 Assessments

On-Going Assessment	Formal Assessment
See the check questions in the Teacher's Edition on these pages	*Find Formal Assessment Blackline Masters in the Assessments book*
Teacher's Edition B	**Assessments Book**
Lesson 1, pp. 88, 89 Lesson 2, pp. 92, 93 Lesson 3, p. 94	Assessment 4 for Book B, Part 1 (Chapters 11–14), is on pages 21–26 of Assessments. Interview Assessment is on page 27.

Chapter 14 Planning Guide

Lessons and Pacing	Activity	Component	Objectives and Math Focus
Lesson 1	**Combining Two Sets to Make 10, pp. 88–89**		• Combine two sets to find how many more to make 10.
DAY 1 Activities	1 Investigate	**Big Book B,** pp. 26–27	Count on to 10 using objects in a picture.
	2 Apply	**Student Book B, Part 1,** pp. 36–37	Count on to 10 and write how many more are needed.
Lesson 2	**Numbers 10 to 20, pp. 90–93**		• Review rote counting 0 to 20. • Count up to 20. • Review number order.
DAY 1 Activities	1 Investigate	**Teacher's Edition B,** pp. 90–91	Relate the numbers 11–20 to their numerals. **Recall, Reinforce, and Review** Play a number guessing game.
DAY 2 Activities	2 Discover	**Teacher's Edition B,** p. 91	Count on starting with a number from 11 to 20.
	3 Apply	**Student Book B, Part 1,** pp. 38–40	Identify sets with 11–20 objects and trace the numerals.
	4 Apply	**Student Book B, Part 1,** pp. 41–43	Identify sets with 11–20 objects and write the numerals.
Lesson 3	**Counting On, pp. 94–96**		• Count back using a number line. • Count back to find the difference.
DAY 1 Activities	1 Investigate	**Big Book B,** pp. 28–29	Introduce number comparisons to 20.
	2 Apply	**Student Book B, Part 1,** pp. 44–45	Count on to 15; find how many more are needed. **Recall, Reinforce, and Review** Model and count on numbers from 10 to get 11, 12, and so on.
	3 Apply	**Student Book B, Part 1,** pp. 46–47	Find the total number of objects in two sets; find how many more are needed to make 15.

Vocabulary	Manipulatives/Materials	Class Organization	NTCM Focal Points & Process Standards
		Whole class	Join two sets when one is shown.
	• Number Line 0–10 (TR23)	Independent	• Communication • Representation • Problem solving
	• Teacher Numeral Cards 0–20	Whole class	Use numbers and numerals to represent quantities.
	• Connecting cubes (10 red and 10 yellow)	Whole class	• Communication • Representation
		Independent	
		Independent	
	• Teacher Numeral Cards 0–20 • Teacher Activity Cards 14.3a–e	Whole class	Compare and order sets of up to 20 objects.
	• Number Line 0–15 (TR29), 1 per child • Scissors, 1 per child • Adhesive tape, a few short strips per child	Independent	• Communication • Representation • Problem solving
	• Number Line 0–15 (TR29), 1 per child (from Activity 2)	Independent	

Lesson 1
Combining Two Sets to Make 10

LESSON OBJECTIVE

• Combine two sets to find how many more to make 10.

MATERIALS

• Number Line 0–10 (TR23)

DAY 1

Teacher's Edition B, pp. 88–89
Big Book B, pp. 26–27
Student Book B, Part 1,
pp. 36–37

Big Book B, pp. 26–27

DAY 1

ACTIVITY 1
Investigate

Math Focus: Count on to 10 using objects in a picture.
Resource: Big Book B, pp. 26–27
Classroom Setup: Whole class, in front of the Big Book

1. *Ask* children to sit so that everyone can see the Big Book.

2. *Ask* children to count the number of children at the table. (10)

3. Next, ask them to count the number of sandwiches. (8)

4. *Ask:*
   • Are there enough sandwiches here for all the children? (no)
   • How many more sandwiches are needed? (2)

5. *Repeat* steps 3 and 4 for the number of apples (6 apples there, 4 apples needed) and cups (9 cups there, 1 cup needed).

 6. While children engage in the activity, ask check questions such as:
   • Are you sure?
   • How do you know?

7. *Remind* children that the total number of objects needed will be greater than the number of objects on the table. Using the example above, 2 more sandwiches are needed to feed 10 children. The 10 sandwiches needed is a greater number than the 8 sandwiches shown.

8. *Ask* children to recall the number of objects already present, and then count on from this number to the number needed.

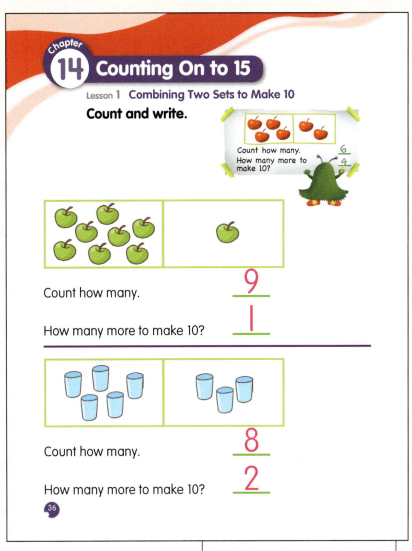

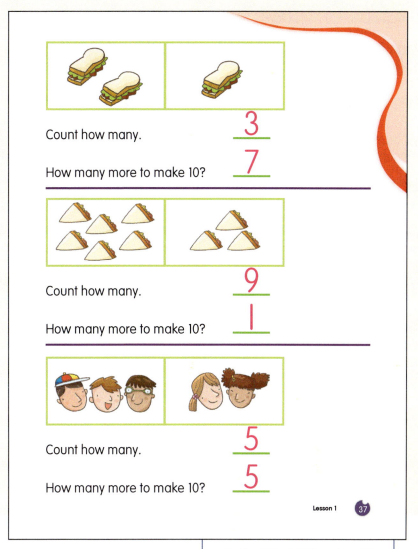

Student Book B, Part 1, p. 36

Student Book B, Part 1, p. 37

ACTIVITY 2
Apply

Math Focus: Count on to 10 and write how many more are needed.
Resource: Student Book B, Part 1, pp. 36–37
Classroom Setup: Children work independently.

1. *Encourage* children to return to their places and open their Student Books to page 36.

2. Children count the total number of objects in each exercise and write this number in the first answer blank.

3. Then, they count on from this number to 10 and write the answer in the next answer blank.

✔ 4. *Check* that children are counting on correctly to make 10.

Differentiated Instruction for Activity 2

Reinforcement

Classroom Setup: *Teacher with a child or two*

Encourage children to use their fingers to count.

Challenge

Materials: *Number Line 0–10 (TR23)*
Classroom Setup: *Teacher with a child or two*

Encourage children to use a number line to count, or to work out the answer mentally.

Lesson 2
Numbers 10 to 20

LESSON OBJECTIVES
• Review rote counting 0 to 20.
• Count up to 20.
• Review number order.

MATERIALS
• Teacher Numeral Cards 0–20
• Connecting cubes

DAY 1
Teacher's Edition B, pp. 90–91

DAY 2
Teacher's Edition B, pp. 91–93
Student Book B, Part 1,
pp. 38–43

DAY 1

ACTIVITY 1
Investigate

Math Focus: Relate the numbers 11–20 to their numerals.
Materials: Teacher Numeral Cards 0–20
Classroom Setup: Whole class

1. *Ask* children to recite the numbers 1 to 10.

2. *Hold up* numeral cards 0 to 10 randomly for children to identify.

3. *Invite* eleven children to the front of the class. Have each child hold one of the numeral cards 0 to 10 and ask them to make a number line.

4. *Ask:* Will the person holding the number that is 2 more than (4) take one step forward?
Repeat for other values.

   Best Practices If the wrong child steps forward, ask the children who are still in their seats if they could suggest a different answer.

5. *Ask* children to recite the numbers 1 to 20.

6. As children recite the numbers, hold up numeral cards 11 to 20.

7. *Invite* another ten children to the front of the class. Have each child hold one of the numeral cards 11 to 20 and ask them to stand behind the children holding numeral cards 1 to 10.

   Best Practices If there are insufficient children, have a few of them hold two consecutive numeral cards, one in each hand.

8. *Explain* to children that the two number lines are used in the same way to help with counting on and counting back.

9. *See* Recall, Reinforce, and Review idea on page 91.

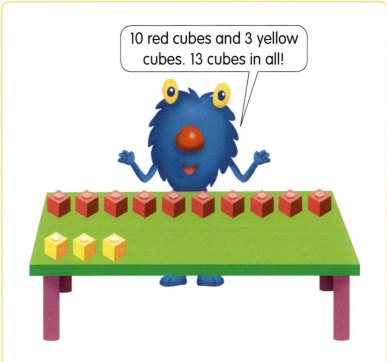

10 red cubes and 3 yellow cubes. 13 cubes in all!

ACTIVITY 2
Discover

Math Focus: Count on starting with a number from 11 to 20.
Materials: Connecting cubes (10 red and 10 yellow)
Classroom Setup: Whole class

1. *Invite* children to stand around a table.

2. *Make* a row of 10 red cubes.

3. *Ask:* How many red cubes are there? (10)

4. *Place* a yellow cube in front of the row of red cubes. Then, *ask:* How many cubes are there in all? (11)

5. *Repeat* step 4, increasing the number of yellow cubes by one each time, until there are 10 yellow cubes, making a total of 20 cubes.

6. *Explain* that when counting on to 20, they can start by counting on from 10.

7. *Take* away a small handful of the cubes and ask children to count the remaining cubes by counting on from 10.

Recall, Reinforce, and Review

Ask children what number you are thinking of and offer these clues: I am more than 10 and less than 15. When you add one more to me, I become 13. What number am I?

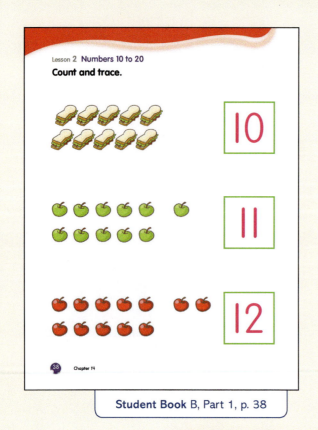

Student Book B, Part 1, p. 38

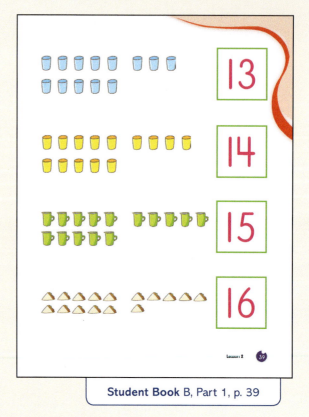

Student Book B, Part 1, p. 39

Count and trace.

(binoculars, 17)	17
(purple beads, 18)	18
(balloons, 19)	19
(pizza slices, 20)	20

Student Book B, Part 1, p. 40

ACTIVITY 3
Apply

Math Focus: Identify sets with 11–20 objects and trace the numerals.
Resource: Student Book B, Part 1, pp. 38–40
Classroom Setup: Children work independently.

1. *Encourage* children to return to their places and open their Student Books to page 38.

2. Children count the objects in each exercise, and trace over the total number for each set of objects in the adjacent box.

3. *Emphasize* that each set of objects to be counted has 10 in one group and a few more objects in the next group. They should start from the group of 10 and count on the additional objects to find the total.

✔ 4. *Check* that children are counting on from 10 by looking at the objects they point to as they count. If a child seems to be counting all objects, have him or her practice counting on to 20 from a number less than 10. Gradually increase the starting number until he or she can count on from 10.

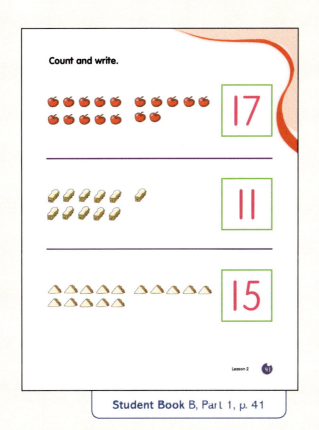

Student Book B, Part 1, p. 41

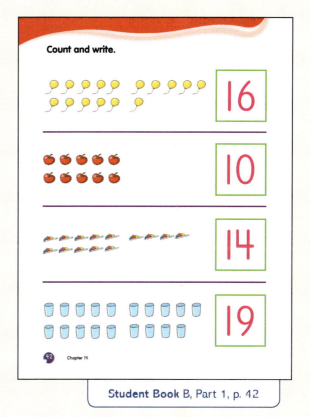

Student Book B, Part 1, p. 42

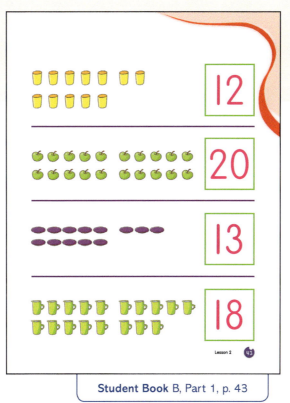

Student Book B, Part 1, p. 43

ACTIVITY 4
Apply

Math Focus: Identify sets with 11–20 objects and write the numerals.
Resource: Student Book B, Part 1, pp. 41–43
Classroom Setup: Children work independently.

1. Children count the objects in each exercise, and write the total number for each set of objects in the adjacent box.

2. *Emphasize* that each set of objects to be counted has 10 in one group, and a few more objects in the next group. They should start from the group of 10 and count on the additional objects to find the total.

✓ 3. *Check* that children are counting on from 10 by looking at the objects they point to as they count.

Lesson 3
Counting On

LESSON OBJECTIVES
• Count back using a number line.
• Count back to find the difference.

MATERIALS
• Teacher Numeral Cards 0–20
• Teacher Activity Cards 14.3a–e
• Number Line 0–15 (TR29)
• Scissors
• Adhesive tape

DAY 1

Teacher's Edition B, pp. 94–96
Big Book B, pp. 28–29
Student Book B, Part 1,
pp. 44–47

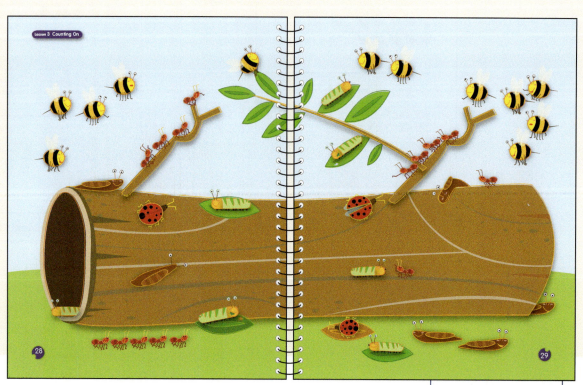

Big Book B, pp. 28–29

DAY 1

ACTIVITY 1
Investigate

Math Focus: Introduce number comparisons to 20.
Resource: Big Book B, pp. 28–29
Materials: Teacher Numeral Cards 0–20
  Teacher Activity Cards 14.3a–e
Classroom Setup: Whole class, in front of the Big Book

1. Before the lesson, attach the numeral cards, in order, to the board to form a number line. Also, attach Activity Cards 14.3a–e in a row to the board.

   Best Practices Attach Activity Cards 14.3a–e to the side of the numeral cards.

2. *Ask* children to sit so that everyone can see the Big Book.

3. *Ask* children to count the number of bees. (12)

4. *Write* this number under Activity Card 14.3a on the board.

5. *Repeat* steps 3 and 4 for the ants (15), slugs (6), ladybugs (3), and caterpillars (7).

6. Have children look at the number line on the board and show where each of the numbers for these creatures are. *Ask:*
   • Are there more (bees) than (slugs)?
   • Are there fewer (ladybugs) than (ants)?

 7. While children engage in the activity, ask check questions such as:
   • How do you know? Are you sure?
   • How does the number line help to show this?

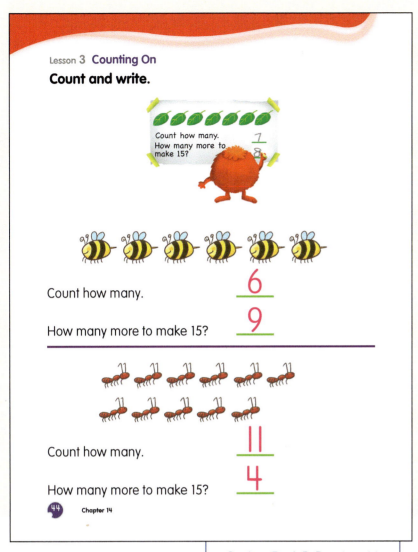

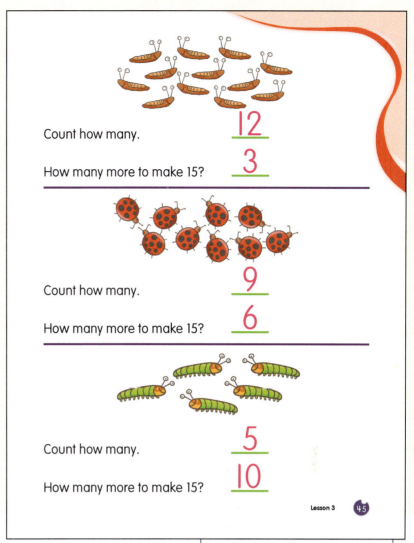

Student Book B, Part 1, p. 44

Student Book B, Part 1, p. 45

ACTIVITY 2
Apply

Math Focus: Count on to 15; find how many more are needed.
Resource: Student Book B, Part 1, pp. 44–45
Materials: Number Line 0–15 (TR29), 1 per child
  Scissors, 1 per child
  Adhesive tape, a few short strips per child
Classroom Setup: Children work independently.

1. *Encourage* children to return to their places and open their Student Books to page 44.

2. *Distribute* materials to the children.

3. Have children cut out their number lines.

4. Children count the bugs and write the total number in the first answer blank.

Best Practices Remind children that they can count by twos when there are many objects to count.

5. Next, ask them to use the number line to count on to 15 from the total number of bugs for each exercise, and write this number in the second answer blank.

6. *Model* the procedure using a number line. Remind children that using a number line is similar to putting the number in their heads and counting on. Explain that when they use a number line, they point to the first number and count on from this first number until the second number is reached to find the difference.

Best Practices Have children put their number lines in their Student Books for future activities.

Recall, Reinforce, and Review

Have two children stand together, one showing 10 fingers and the other showing (2) fingers. Have children model and count on the numbers from 10, so 10 and 1 more make 11. 10 and 1, 2 more make 12, and so on.

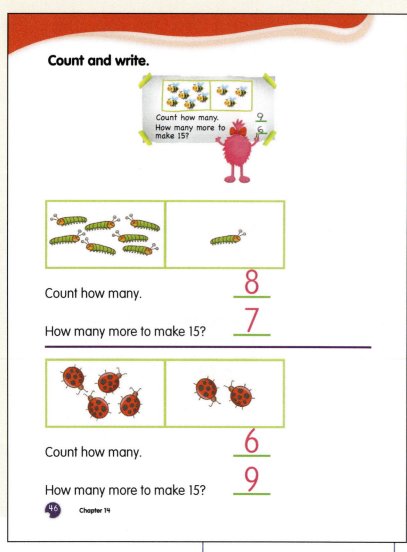

Count and write.

Count how many. 9

How many more to make 15? 6

Count how many. __8__

How many more to make 15? __7__

Count how many. __6__

How many more to make 15? __9__

 46   Chapter 14

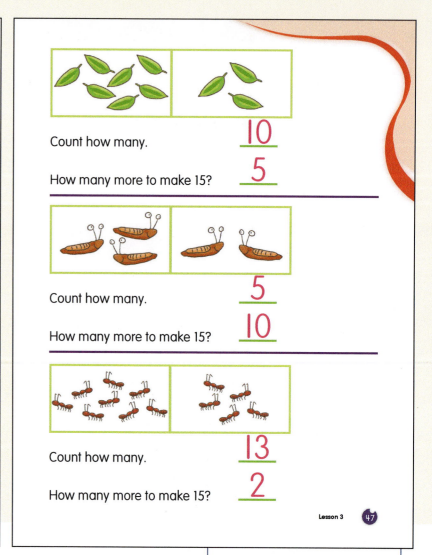

Count how many. __10__

How many more to make 15? __5__

Count how many. __5__

How many more to make 15? __10__

Count how many. __13__

How many more to make 15? __2__

Lesson 3   47

Student Book B, Part 1, p. 46

Student Book B, Part 1, p. 47

ACTIVITY 3
Apply

Math Focus: Find the total number of objects in two sets; find how many more are needed to make 15.
Resource: Student Book B, Part 1, pp. 46–47
Materials: Number Line 0–15 (TR29), 1 per child (from Activity 2)
Classroom Setup: Children work independently.

1. Children count the objects in the first box and remember the number in their heads.

   Best Practices Remind children that they can count by twos when there are many objects to count.

2. Next, ask them to count the objects in the second box, counting on from the number already in their heads and write the total number of objects in the first answer blank.

3. Next, ask them to use the number line to count on to 15 from the total number of objects for each exercise, and write this number in the second answer blank.

4. *Model* the steps using a number line. Remind children that using a number line is similar to putting the number in their heads and counting on. Explain that when they use a number line, they point to the first number and count on from this first number until the second number is reached.

Chapter Overview

Length and Height

Math Background

Measuring length has a variety of applications in the real world. Doctors measure children's heights to assess their growth. Architects use length and height to draw plans for buildings. One measurement concept that Kindergarten children should begin to understand is that the length will change depending on the size of the unit.

Measurement also connects ideas in the number strand with geometry concepts. As they progress through elementary school, children will learn that shapes have attributes that can be measured with numbers. For example, you can measure the length of the sides of squares and rectangles.

Vocabulary

long	longer	longest
short	shorter	shortest

tallest	shortest

Cross-Curricular Connections

Reading/Language Arts In this chapter, children describe length using the words *long*, *short*, and *tall*. Explain that these are describing words and that describing words are used to talk about objects. Ask children to name objects that are long, short, and tall. Then, point out different objects in the classroom and have children name other words that can be used to describe them.

Physical Education Put children in small groups to see how far they can jump. Have each group place a piece of masking tape on the floor. Each child stands behind the piece of tape and jumps as far as possible. Others in the group mark the landing with a piece of masking tape labeled with the child's name. After all group members have jumped, have children compare the length of the jumps and measure each using a non-standard unit.

Skills Trace

Grade K	Compare lengths using words such as long, longer, and longest.
Grade 1	Compare lengths using non-standard units. (Chap. 7)

EVERY DAY COUNTS® Calendar Math...

provides preview, review, and practice of skills and concepts taught in this program. April activities are shown here.

Preview writing number sentences. (Chapter 17)

Review patterns. (Chapter 13)

Practice using the language of comparing. (Lessons 2–4 in this chapter)

Chapter Resources

Manipulatives from the Manipulatives Kit

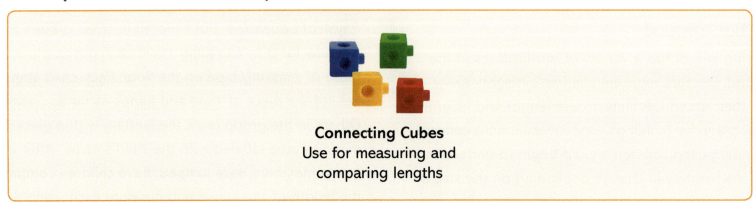

Connecting Cubes
Use for measuring and
comparing lengths

Technology Resources

- *Math in Focus*® eBooks
- *Math in Focus*® Teacher Resources CD
- Online Web Resources

Classroom/Household Items

- Paper clips
- Classroom objects, such as pencils, books, a stapler, and a tape dispenser
- Thick, white string
- Markers

Differentiation and Assessment

Differentiation for Special Populations (Resources in the Teacher's Edition)

	English Language Learners	Children Needing Reinforcement	Children Needing a Challenge
Lesson 1	Math Talk, Big Book B, pp. 30–31		
Lesson 2	Math Talk, Big Book B, pp. 32–33		
	Math Talk, Teacher's Edition B, p. 101		
Lesson 3	Math Talk, Teacher's Edition B, p. 102		
Lesson 5		Student Book B, Part 2, pp. 8–9	Student Book B, Part 2, pp. 8–9

Collect objects in the class whose main dimension is length, such as paint brushes, markers, crayons, and rulers. Put two objects next to each other and ask which is longer and which is shorter. Then, describe the comparison and have children repeat after you. For example, "The paint brush is longer than the pencil." or "The pencil is longer than the crayon and the crayon is shorter than the pencil."

Chapter 15 Assessments

On-Going Assessment	Formal Assessment
See the check questions in the Teacher's Edition on these pages	*Find Formal Assessment Blackline Masters in the Assessments book*
Teacher's Edition B	**Assessments Book**
Lesson 1, p. 99 Lesson 2, p. 101 Lesson 3, p. 103	Assessment 5 for Book B, Part 2, is on pages 28–34 of Assessments. Interview Assessment is on page 35.

Chapter 15 Planning Guide

Lessons and Pacing	Activity	Component	Objectives and Math Focus
Lesson 1	**'Long' and 'Short', pp. 98–99**		• Review *long*. • Review *short*.
DAY 1 Activities	1 Investigate	**Big Book B**, pp. 30–31	Identify long and short objects in a pair.
	2 Apply	**Student Book B, Part 2**, p. 2	Draw long and short tails.
Lesson 2	**Comparing Lengths, pp. 100–101**		• Review *longer, longest, shorter,* and *shortest*. • Compare lengths.
DAY 1 Activities	1 Investigate	**Big Book B**, pp. 32–33	Identify longer, shorter, longest, and shortest objects.
	2 Explore	**Teacher's Edition B**, p. 101	Compare lengths of paper clip snakes.
	3 Apply	**Student Book B, Part 2**, p. 3	Identify longest and shortest tails.
Lesson 3	**Comparing Lengths Using Non-standard Units, pp. 102–103**		• Use non-standard units to measure and compare lengths. • Understand that more units are needed to measure a longer object than a shorter object.
DAY 1 Activities	1 Explore	**Teacher's Edition B**, p. 102	Measure length using connecting cubes.
	2 Apply	**Student Book B, Part 2**, pp. 4–5	Measure and compare lengths using connecting cubes. **Recall, Reinforce, and Review** Choose connecting cube trains of various lengths and use learnt vocabulary to compare the lengths.
Lesson 4	**Comparing Heights Using Non-standard Units, pp. 104–105**		• Understand *tallest* and *shortest* in terms of height. • Use non-standard units to measure and compare heights. • Understand that more units are needed to measure a taller object than a shorter object.
DAY 1 Activities	1 Investigate	**Big Book B**, pp. 34–35	Introduce *tallest* and *shortest*.
	2 Apply	**Student Book B, Part 2**, pp. 6–7	Compare heights using pictures of connecting cubes.

Vocabulary	Manipulatives/Materials	Class Organization	NTCM Focal Points & Process Standards
long, short		Whole class Independent	Compare lengths directly. • Communication
longer, longest, shorter, shortest	• Paper clips, 30 per group	Whole class Small groups Independent	Compare lengths directly and by using non-standard units. • Communication • Connections
	• Connecting cubes, 20 per group • Classroom objects, such as pencils, books, and a stapler • Connecting cubes, 10 per child	Small groups Independent	Compare lengths by using non-standard units. • Communication • Connections
tallest, shortest	• Thick, white string, 3 long pieces • Markers, 3 different colors	Whole class Independent	Compare lengths by comparing each to another object. • Communication • Representation • Connections

Chapter 15 Planning Guide

Lessons and Pacing	Activity	Component	Objectives and Math Focus
Lesson 5	**Finding Differences in Length Using Non-standard Units,** p. 106		• Find differences in lengths using non-standard units.
DAY 1 Activities	1 Apply	**Student Book B, Part 2,** pp. 8–9	Count on to find the difference between two lengths.

Vocabulary	Manipulatives/Materials	Class Organization	NTCM Focal Points & Process Standards
	• Paper clips • Pairs of classroom objects, such as a stapler and tape dispenser	Independent	Compare sets to compare lengths. • Communication • Representation • Connections • Problem solving

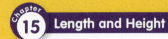

Lesson 1
'Long' and 'Short'

LESSON OBJECTIVES
- Review *long*.
- Review *short*.

Vocabulary
long
short

DAY 1

Teacher's Edition B, pp. 98–99
Big Book B, pp. 30–31
Student Book B, Part 2, p. 2

Big Book B, pp. 30–31

DAY 1

ACTIVITY 1
Investigate

Math Focus: Identify long and short objects in a pair.
Resource: Big Book B, pp. 30–31
Classroom Setup: Whole class, in front of the Big Book

1. **Ask** children to sit so that everyone can see the Big Book.

2. Next, ask what children notice about the girls' hair. (One girl has long hair and the other girl has short hair.)

3. **Ask:** What else can you see in the picture that is long and short? (mice tails, coats, umbrellas, girls' dresses, handbag straps, jump ropes, trains, pencils, and rulers)

4. **Math Talk** Elicit the words *long* and *short* from children as they describe what they notice.

Student Book B, Part 2, p. 2

ACTIVITY 2
Apply

Math Focus: Draw long and short tails.
Resource: Student Book B, Part 2, p. 2
Classroom Setup: Children work independently.

1. *Encourage* children to return to their places and open their Student Books to page 2.

2. Children draw a long tail on the first mouse and a short tail on the second mouse.

 3. As children engage in the activity, ask check questions such as:
   • Why have you drawn this tail here?
   • Will this tail fit on the other mouse instead? Why? or Why not?

Lesson 2
Comparing Lengths

LESSON OBJECTIVES
• Review *longer, longest, shorter,* and *shortest.*
• Compare lengths.

MATERIALS
• Paper clips

Vocabulary

longer

longest

shorter

shortest

DAY 1

Teacher's Edition B, pp. 100–101
Big Book B, pp. 32–33
Student Book B, Part 2, p. 3

Lesson 2 Comparing Lengths

32

33

Big Book B, pp. 32–33

DAY 1

ACTIVITY 1
Investigate

Math Focus: Identify longer, shorter, longest, and shortest objects.
Resource: Big Book B, pp. 32–33
Classroom Setup: Whole class, in front of the Big Book

1. *Ask* children to sit so that everyone can see the Big Book.

2. *Point* to the frog with the shortest tongue, and ask children why it is different from the frog with the next shortest tongue. (It has a *shorter* tongue. The other frog has a *longer* tongue.)

3. *Point* to all three frogs in turn and *say:*
   • This frog has the *shortest* tongue.
   • This frog has the *longest* tongue.
   • This frog's tongue is *shorter* than that frog's tongue.
   • This frog's tongue is *longer* than that frog's tongue.

4. *Repeat* steps 2 and 3 for the lengths of the tadpoles and fish, encouraging children to make length comparisons whenever possible.

5. **Math Talk** Elicit the words *longer, longest, shorter,* and *shortest* from children as they describe the animals.

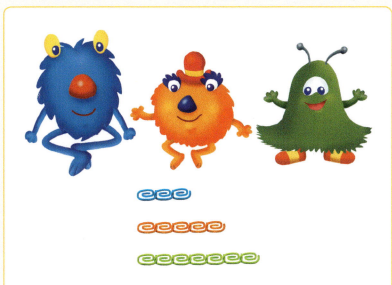

ACTIVITY 2
Explore

Math focus: Compare lengths of paper clip snakes.
Materials: Paper clips, 30 per group
Classroom Setup: Children work in small groups.

1. *Encourage* children to return to their places.

2. *Distribute* materials to the children.

3. *Ask* each child to form a paper clip snake by joining the ends of some paper clips. Give children about three minutes to complete the task.

4. *Ask* children to lay the snakes that their group made side by side and compare their lengths.

5. *Ask:*
   • Who made the longest snake?
   • Who made the shortest snake?

6. **Math Talk** Elicit answers using the words *longest* and *shortest*, such as:
   • (Child A) made the longest snake.
   • (Child B) made the shortest snake.

7. *Ask:*
   • Whose snake is longer than (Child C)'s snake?
   • Whose snake is shorter than (Child D)'s snake?

8. **Math Talk** Elicit answers using the words *longer* and *shorter*, such as:
   • (Child E)'s snake is longer than (Child C)'s snake.
   • (Child F)'s snake is shorter than (Child D)'s snake.

Best Practices Remind children to compare the lengths of snakes by lining them up side by side from the same starting point.

**Make an X on the kite with the longest tail.
Circle the kite with the shortest tail.**

Student Book B, Part 2, p. 3

ACTIVITY 3
Apply

Math Focus: Identify longest and shortest tails.
Resource: Student Book B, Part 2, p. 3
Classroom Setup: Children work independently.

1. Children make an X on the kite with the longest tail, and circle the kite with the shortest tail.

2. When children finish the activity, ask check questions such as:
   • Why did you make an X on this kite?
   • Why did you circle this kite? Are you sure?
   • Why did you make only one X? Could there be two longest tails?

Lesson 3
Comparing Lengths Using Non-standard Units

LESSON OBJECTIVES
- Use non-standard units to measure and compare lengths.
- Understand that more units are needed to measure a longer object than a shorter object.

MATERIALS
- Connecting cubes
- Classroom objects, such as pencils, books, and a stapler

DAY 1

Teacher's Edition B, pp. 102–103
Student Book B, Part 2, pp. 4–5

DAY 1

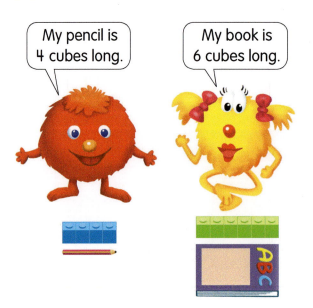

ACTIVITY 1
Explore

Math Focus: Measure length using connecting cubes.
Materials: Connecting cubes, 20 per group
Classroom objects, such as pencils, books, and a stapler
Classroom Setup: Children work in small groups.

1. *Measure* the length of a child's desk using connecting cubes. Have children count the number of cubes used.

   Best Practices Choose something shorter to measure if the desk is more than 20 cubes (approximately 15 inches) long.

2. *Say:* The desk is (15) cubes long.

3. *Distribute* materials to the children.

4. *Repeat* steps 1 and 2 with children using cubes to measure the lengths of other things in the classroom such as pencils, books, and a stapler.

5. **Math Talk** Elicit sentences such as:
   - My pencil is 4 cubes long.
   - My book is 6 cubes long.

6. You may want children to record their results on paper or the board, by drawing each item and writing the number of cubes below it.

   Best Practices The measurement of the lengths of some objects may not involve an exact number of cubes. Always round measurements up to the nearest cube. For example, if a backpack is more than 12 and a half cubes long, write the length as 13 cubes.

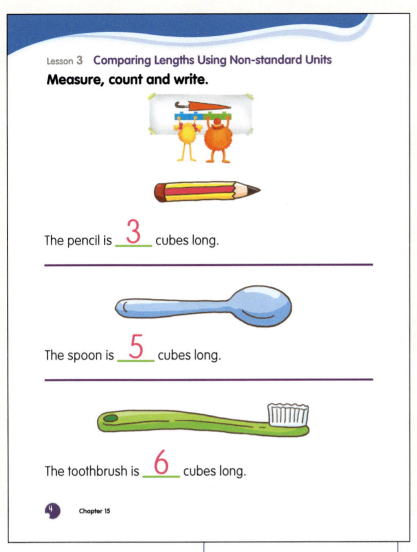

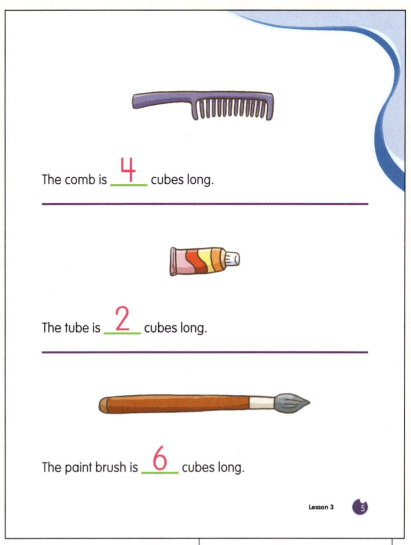

Student Book B, Part 2, p. 4

Student Book B, Part 2, p. 5

ACTIVITY 2
Apply

Math Focus: Measure and compare lengths using connecting cubes.
Resource: Student Book B, Part 2, pp. 4–5
Materials: Connecting cubes, 10 per child
Classroom Setup: Children work independently.

1. *Distribute* materials to the children.

2. Children use the connecting cubes to measure the length of the object in each exercise.

3. Then, in the answer blank, they write the number of cubes used to measure each length.

✔4. When children finish the activity, ask check questions such as:
   • Which is longer, the toothbrush or the pencil?
   • How do you know? (The longer object needs more cubes to measure it. The shorter objects needs fewer cubes to measure it.)
   • Which objects are the same length? How do you know?

Recall, Reinforce, and Review

Make trains of connecting cubes of various lengths up to 10 cubes. Ask a child to choose one train and find one train shorter than and longer than this one. Ask the child to then state the comparisons by using words such as shorter and longer.

Lesson 4
Comparing Heights Using Non-standard Units

LESSON OBJECTIVES

- Understand *tallest* and *shortest* in terms of height.
- Use non-standard units to measure and compare heights.
- Understand that more units are needed to measure a taller object than a shorter object.

MATERIALS

- Thick, white string
- Markers

Vocabulary

tallest

shortest

DAY 1

Teacher's Edition B, pp. 104–105
Big Book B, pp. 34–35
Student Book B, Part 2, pp. 6–7

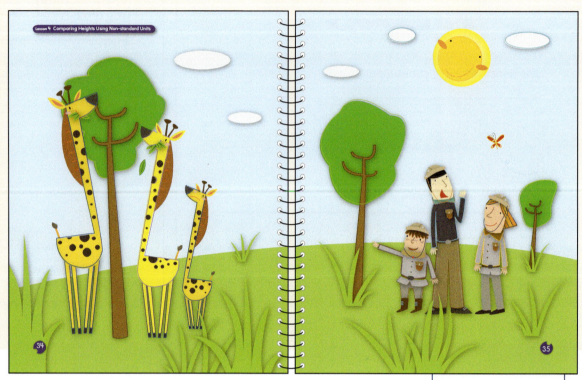

Big Book B, pp. 34–35

DAY 1

ACTIVITY 1
Investigate

Math Focus: Introduce *tallest* and *shortest*.
Resource: Big Book B, pp. 34–35
Materials: Thick, white string, 3 long pieces
   Markers, 3 different colors
Classroom Setup: Whole class, in front of the Big Book

1. **Ask** children to sit so that everyone can see the Big Book.
2. **Ask:**
   - Which giraffe is the tallest? (The one on the left.)
   - Which giraffe is the shortest? (The one on the right.)
   - How can you check that you are correct? (By noticing the difference in height as the giraffes stand side by side, or by measuring their heights.)
3. **Show** children how to compare the heights of the giraffes by using a piece of string. With the bottom of the string aligned with the base of each giraffe, mark the height of each giraffe on the string with a marker. Use a different colored marker for each giraffe.

   Best Practices You may want to tape the bottom end of the string in place while you mark it.

4. After measuring the three giraffes with the same piece of string, show children the difference in markings on the string. Explain that the highest marking represents the tallest giraffe and the lowest marking represents the shortest giraffe.
5. **Repeat** steps 3 and 4 for the heights of the trees and the rangers.

Lesson 4   Comparing Heights Using Non-standard Units

Count and write. Make an X on the taller vase.

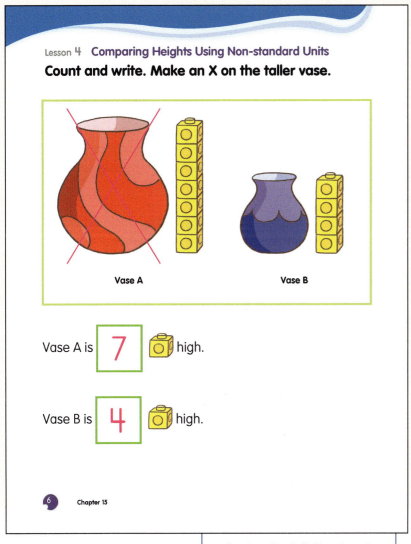

Vase A is **7** high.

Vase B is **4** high.

6   Chapter 15

Student Book B, Part 2, p. 6

Count and write. Circle the shorter flower.

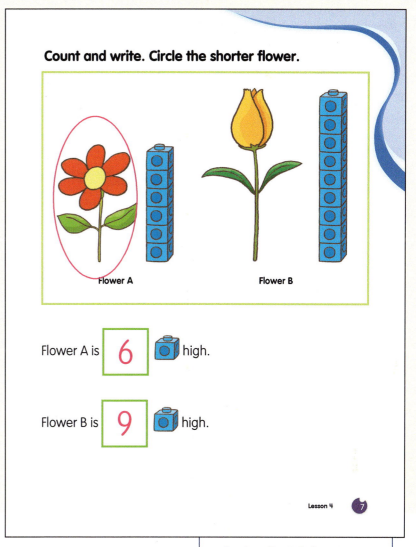

Flower A is **6** high.

Flower B is **9** high.

Lesson 4 7

Student Book B, Part 2, p. 7

ACTIVITY 2
Apply

Math Focus: Compare heights using pictures of connecting cubes.
Resource: Student Book B, Part 2, pp. 6–7
Classroom Setup: Children work independently.

1. *Encourage* children to return to their places and open their Student Books to page 6.

2. Children measure the heights of the objects in each exercise by counting the number of connecting cubes beside each vase or flower.

3. Then, they write this number in the box.

4. Next, have children compare the heights of both objects on the page.

5. *Ask* them to make an X on the taller vase and circle the shorter flower.

Lesson 5
Finding Differences in Length Using Non-standard Units

LESSON OBJECTIVE
- Find differences in lengths using non-standard units.

MATERIALS
- Paper clips
- Classroom objects, such as a stapler and tape dispenser

DAY 1

Teacher's Edition B, p. 106
Student Book B, Part 2, pp. 8–9

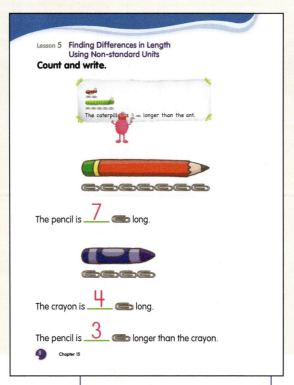

Student Book B, Part 2, p. 8

Student Book B, Part 2, p. 9

DAY 1

ACTIVITY 1
Apply

Math Focus: Count on to find the difference between two lengths.
Resource: Student Book B, Part 2, pp. 8–9
Classroom Setup: Children work independently.

1. Children count the number of paper clips used to measure the length of objects. Then, they write the answers in the answer blanks.

2. *Ask* them to find the difference in length between the two objects by counting how many more paper clips one object needs than the other object.

Differentiated Instruction for Activity 1

Reinforcement

Classroom Setup: *Teacher with a child or two*

Ask children to match up the paper clips used for measuring each object in the Student Book one-to-one and see how many are left after matching.

Challenge

Materials: *Paper clips*
   Pairs of classroom objects, such as a stapler and tape dispenser
Classroom Setup: *Teacher with a child or two*

Ask children to measure two classroom objects and then find the difference in the lengths.

Chapter Overview

Classifying and Sorting

Math Background

When children learn to sort and classify objects by different attributes, they are developing skills that will help them with other mathematical strands. Sorting and classifying skills help children to identify patterns and describe geometric objects. Children also use sorting and classifying skills when analyzing data.

Teachers should provide children with many opportunities to sort and classify classroom objects by size, color, shape, and any other attribute they can see. As children are involved in these activities, it is important to ask them to explain their thinking and describe the criteria they use to make their choices.

Vocabulary

| sort | arrange systematically in groups |

Cross-Curricular Connections

Reading/Language Arts Comparing and contrasting is an important reading comprehension skill. Use chapter concepts to have children practice using comparison language. Point out two objects in the classroom and ask children to tell how they are alike and different. Pick objects that are similar and different in shape, size, and color. Help children with vocabulary and sentence structure.

Science Children learn about attributes of objects in science. Point out that different objects are *hot/cold*, *fast/slow*, and *soft/hard*. Some objects float while others sink. Write these categories on the board and invite children to name objects that belong with each. Record their responses. You may want to conduct an experiment with a variety of objects to discover which ones float and which ones sink.

Skills Trace

Grade K	Sort and classify objects by two or three attributes.
Grade 1	Use the attributes of objects in a set to create patterns. (Chaps. 1, 5, 12, and 16)

EVERY DAY COUNTS®
Calendar Math...

provides preview, review, and practice of skills and concepts taught in this program. April activities are shown here.

Preview concepts with capacity. (Chapter 19)

Review language of comparing. (Chapter 15)

Practice recognizing spheres.
(Lesson 1 in this chapter)

Chapter Resources

Manipulatives from the Manipulatives Kit

Connecting Cubes
Use for grouping by attribute
and sorting activities

Counters
Use for grouping by attribute
and sorting activities

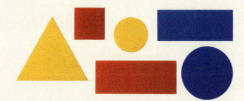

Attribute Blocks
Use for grouping by attribute

Technology Resources

- *Math in Focus*® eBooks
- *Math in Focus*® Teacher Resources CD
- Online Web Resources
- *Math in Focus*® Virtual Manipulatives
  for Lessons 1–3

Classroom/Household Items

- Paper clip
- Pencils
- Crayons
- White paper
- Colorful picture book
- Scissors

Differentiation and Assessment

Differentiation for Special Populations (Resources in the Teacher's Edition)

	English Language Learners	Children Needing Reinforcement	Children Needing a Challenge
Lesson 1	Math Talk, Teacher's Edition B, p. 110		
Lesson 2	Math Talk, Big Book B, pp. 38–39	Big Book B, pp. 38–39	Big Book B, pp. 38–39

Gather a group of red objects and another group of non-red objects. Ask children how you have sorted the objects. Now invite children to think of other ways the red objects could be sorted. Allow a volunteer to demonstrate each suggested sorting.

Chapter 16 Assessments

On-Going Assessment	Formal Assessment
See the check questions in the Teacher's Edition on these pages	*Find Formal Assessment Blackline Masters in the Assessments book*
Teacher's Edition B	**Assessments Book**
Lesson 1, pp. 109, 111	Assessment 5 for Book B, Part 2, is on pages 28–34 of Assessments. Interview Assessment is on page 35.

Chapter 16 Planning Guide

Lessons and Pacing	Activity	Component	Objectives and Math Focus
Lesson 1	**Classifying Things by One Attribute,** pp. 108–111		• Classify objects using one attribute (color, size, shape, special features). • Identify objects that do not belong to a set.
DAY 1 Activities	1 Investigate	**Big Book B,** pp. 36–37	Identify the attribute of a set.
	2 Apply	**Student Book B, Part 2,** pp. 10–13	Match objects to a set with the same attribute.
DAY 2 Activities	3 Discover	**Teacher's Edition B,** p. 110	Identify objects that do not belong to a set.
	4 Apply	**Student Book B, Part 2,** p. 14	Identify pictures of objects that do not belong to a set.
Lesson 2	**Classifying Things by Two Attributes,** pp. 112–114		• Classify objects according to two attributes. • Classify objects according to three attributes.
DAY 1 Activities	1 Investigate	**Big Book B,** pp. 38–39	Identify objects that have two given attributes.
	2 Explore	**Big Book B,** pp. 38–39	Identify objects that have three given attributes. **Recall, Reinforce, and Review** Say what is alike and what is different about a set of objects.
Lesson 3	**Sorting Things,** pp. 115–116		• Sort objects by one or two attributes (color, size, shape, and special features).
DAY 1 Activities	1 Explore	**Teacher's Edition B,** pp. 115–116	Sort objects by two attributes.

Vocabulary	Manipulatives/Materials	Class Organization	NTCM Focal Points & Process Standards
		Whole class Independent	Sort objects using one or more attributes.
	• Connecting cubes, 5 yellow and 5 blue • Paper clip • Counters, 3 blue • Pencils, 2 yellow • White crayon • Sheet of white paper • Colorful picture book	Whole class Independent	• Communication • Connections • Problem solving
	• Attribute blocks, 20 • Connecting cubes • Classroom objects, such pencils, crayons, and scissors	Whole class Whole class	Sort objects using one or more attributes. • Communication • Connections • Problem solving
sort	• Connecting cubes, 12 per group (3 red, 3 blue, 3 yellow, and 3 green) • Counters, 12 per group (3 red, 3 blue, 3 yellow, and 3 green) • Half sheets of paper, 8 per group	Small groups	Sort objects using one or more attributes. • Communication • Connections • Problem solving

Lesson 1
Classifying Things by One Attribute

LESSON OBJECTIVES
- Classify objects using one attribute (color, size, shape, special features).
- Identify objects that do not belong to a set.

MATERIALS
- Connecting cubes
- Paper clip
- Counters
- Pencils
- White crayon
- Sheet of white paper
- Colorful picture book

DAY 1

Teacher's Edition B, pp. 108–109
Big Book B, pp. 36–37
Student Book B, Part 2,
pp. 10–13

DAY 2

Teacher's Edition B, pp. 110–111
Student Book B, Part 2, p. 14

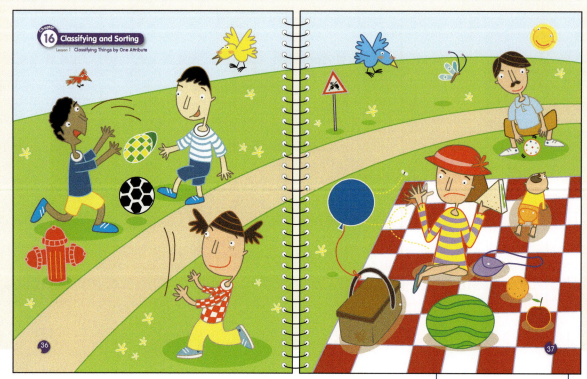

Big Book B, pp. 36–37

DAY 1

ACTIVITY 1
Investigate

Math Focus: Identify the attribute of a set.
Resource: Big Book B, pp. 36–37
Classroom Setup: Whole class, in front of the Big Book

1. *Ask* children to sit so that everyone can see the Big Book.

2. *Point* to pairs of objects in the picture and *ask:*
   - How are they the same?
   - Are there any other objects in this picture that are (name of attribute)?
   Some pairs of objects you might ask about include the following:
   - The lady's hat and the fire hydrant. (They have the same color: red. The small bird and the apple are also red.)
   - The balloon and the soccer ball. (They have the same round shape. The other ball, the orange, the sun, and many buttons and eyes are also round.)
   - The small red bird and the baby. (They are both small. There are no other small objects.)
   - The boy's striped T-shirt and the lady's dress. (They both have stripes. The watermelon is also striped.)

3. *Suggest* that children can sort the objects in the picture by putting them into groups according to color, shape, size, and other features such as stripes and checks.

4. *Guide* children to think about and list other objects in the picture that can form a group. Then, ask children to figure out why the objects make a group.

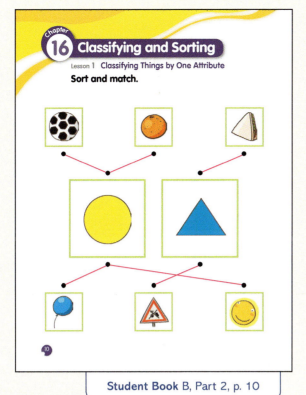

Student Book B, Part 2, p. 10

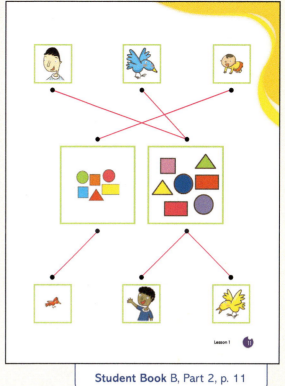

Student Book B, Part 2, p. 11

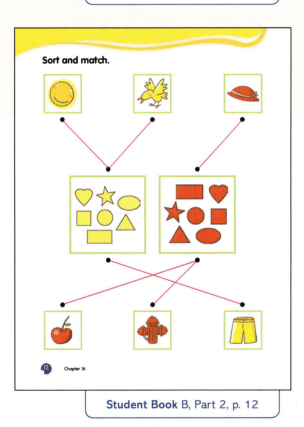

Student Book B, Part 2, p. 12

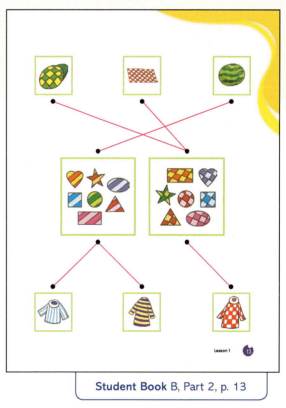

Student Book B, Part 2, p. 13

ACTIVITY 2
Apply

Math Focus: Match objects to a set with the same attribute.
Resource: Student Book B, Part 2, pp. 10–13
Classroom Setup: Children work independently.

1. **Encourage** children to return to their places and open their Student Books to page 10.

2. Children draw a line between each object and the group to which it belongs, based on shape, size, color, or other special features.

3. While children engage in the activity, ask check questions such as:
   • Why do you think this object belongs to this group?
   • Could it belong to the other group instead?
   • Why? or Why not?

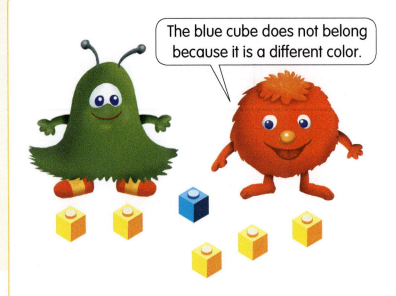

The blue cube does not belong because it is a different color.

ACTIVITY 3
Discover

Math Focus: Identify objects that do not belong to a set.
Materials: Connecting cubes, 5 yellow and 5 blue
   Paper clip
   Counters, 3 blue
   Pencils, 2 yellow
   White crayon
   Sheet of white paper
   Colorful picture book
Classroom Setup: Whole class

1. *Invite* children to stand around a table.

2. *Place* 5 yellow connecting cubes on the table. *Ask:* How are they the same? (They have the same size, shape, and color.)

3. *Place* a blue cube together with the yellow cubes. *Ask:*
   • Which cube does not belong? (The blue cube.)
   • Why? (It is a different color.)

4. *Remove* all the cubes from the table. Then, place 3 yellow cubes and 2 blue cubes on the table. Place a paper clip on the table with the cubes. *Ask:*
   • Which object does not belong? (The paper clip.)
   • Why? (It is a different shape.)

5. *Remove* all the objects from the table. Then, place 5 blue cubes, 3 blue counters, and 2 yellow pencils on the table. *Ask:*
   • Which does not belong? (The 2 yellow pencils.)
   • Why? (Because they are not blue.)

6. *Use* other combinations and ask children to pick out the object that does not belong. Include other objects that you find in the classroom, such as a white crayon, a sheet of white paper, and a colorful picture book. (The book does not belong because of its color. The crayon does not belong because of its shape.)

7. **Math Talk** Remind children to talk about the attributes of shape, size, color, and other special features as they point out what belongs to a group and what does not.

Make an X on the item that does not belong.

Student Book B, Part 2, p. 14

ACTIVITY 4
Apply

Math Focus: Identify pictures of objects that do not belong to a set.
Resource: Student Book B, Part 2, p. 14
Classroom Setup: Children work independently.

1. *Encourage* children to return to their places and open their Student Books to page 14.

2. For each exercise, children make an X on the object that does not belong to the set.

✔ 3. While children engage in the activity, ask check questions such as:
   • Why have you made an X here?
   • Could you make an X here instead?
   • Why? or Why not?

Best Practices All children may not always use the same attribute to form their groups. For example, in the third exercise, some children may cross out the bird because it is not a person, or some may cross out the older boy because he is not 'wearing' yellow. Accept any answer that children can justify.

Lesson 2
Classifying Things by Two Attributes

LESSON OBJECTIVES
- Classify objects according to two attributes.
- Classify objects according to three attributes.

MATERIALS
- Attribute blocks
- Connecting cubes
- Classroom objects, such as a pencil, a crayon and scissors

DAY 1

Teacher's Edition B, pp. 112–114
Big Book B, pp. 38–39

Big Book B, pp. 38–39

DAY 1

ACTIVITY 1
Investigate

Math Focus: Identify objects that have two given attributes.
Resource: Big Book B, pp. 38–39
Classroom Setup: Whole class, in front of the Big Book

1. *Ask* children to sit so that everyone can see the Big Book.

2. *Explain* that the attribute blocks in the picture are of different colors, shapes, and sizes. Point out other features such as stripes or dots on them.

3. *Ask* children to point to a block that is yellow and round.

4. Next, ask them to point to a block that is small and green.

5. Then, ask them to point to a block that is big and has other features, such as big and square, or big with dots.

6. *Repeat* steps 3 to 5, asking children to find two blocks with two of the same attributes. For example, ask if they can find two blocks that are both blue and triangular.

7. **Math Talk** Elicit the use of the words *same* and *different* when describing the attribute blocks.

8. *See* Differentiated Instruction idea on page 113.

Differentiated Instruction for Activity 1

Reinforcement

Materials: *Attribute blocks, 20*
Classroom Setup: *Teacher with a child or two*

Spread the attribute blocks out on a table and name two attributes, such as big and blue. Have the child select first all the blocks that are big. Then, from this set, have the child select the blue blocks.

Challenge

Classroom Setup: *Teacher with a child or two*

Point at 2 blocks with one attribute that is the same and one that is different and ask how the 2 blocks are different. (They are both yellow but not the same shape. or They are both squares but they are different colors.)

Big Book B, pp. 38–39

ACTIVITY 2
Explore

Math Focus: Identify objects that have three given attributes.
Resource: Big Book B, pp. 38–39
Classroom Setup: Continue with whole class setup as in Activity 1.

1. **Point** to the red circle at the bottom of page 38. **Say:** This is big, red, and round.

2. **Ask** children to point out another block that is big, red, and round. (The red circle at the top of page 39.)

3. **Repeat** steps 1 and 2 with three other combinations of attributes, such as small, blue, and dotted; big, round, and striped.

4. **Math Talk** Elicit the use of the words *same* and *different* when describing the attribute blocks.

Differentiated Instruction for Activity 2

Challenge

Classroom Setup: *Teacher with a child or two*

Point to 3 blocks, two of which have one similar attribute, such as color, and two that have another similar attribute, such as shape (but with different colors). For example, point to the yellow rectangle, blue rectangle and yellow square on page 39.

Ask how the 3 blocks are different. (Two have the same shape but are different colors. They are both rectangles, but one is yellow and the other is blue. Two have the same color but are different shapes. They are both yellow, but one is a square and the other is a rectangle.)

Recall, Reinforce, and Review

Gather a collection of classroom objects such as a pencil, a crayon, a connecting cube, and scissors. Ask children to say something about them that is alike, and something that is different. Repeat after removing or inserting a few objects to form a new set.

Lesson 3
Sorting Things

LESSON OBJECTIVE
• Sort objects by one or two attributes (color, size, shape, and special features).

MATERIALS
• Connecting cubes
• Counters
• Half sheets of paper

Vocabulary

sort

DAY **1**

Teacher's Edition B, pp. 115–116

DAY **1**

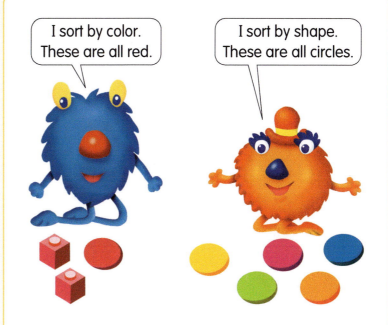

I sort by color. These are all red.

I sort by shape. These are all circles.

ACTIVITY 1
Explore

Math Focus: Sort objects by two attributes.

Materials: Connecting cubes, 12 per group (3 red, 3 blue, 3 yellow, and 3 green)
Counters, 12 per group (3 red, 3 blue, 3 yellow, and 3 green)
Half sheets of paper, 8 per group

Classroom Setup: Children work in small groups.

1. *Invite* children to stand around a table.

2. *Place* 3 red connecting cubes and two red counters on the table. Tell children that the objects are put together because they are all red.

   Best Practices Ensure that the cubes and counters are arranged randomly.

3. *Repeat* step 2 with blue cubes and counters, but this time, ask children to explain why the objects are grouped together.

4. *Show* children that within the blue objects, there are two groups. One group is made up of blue cubes and the other group is made up of blue counters. Place each group on a separate half sheet of paper to help distinguish the two groups.

5. *Explain* that they have the same color but are different shapes.

6. *Distribute* materials to the children.

7. *Ask* children to sort the objects by color and shape. Each set should be placed on its own half sheet of paper.

8. *Guide* children to see that each set of objects is sorted by two attributes – color and shape.

Notes

Chapter 17

Addition Stories

Math Background

One of the beginning skills in algebra is using symbols to represent mathematical situations. Children in Kindergarten begin to understand joining situations. They should be able to talk about the idea of equality and use the symbols + and = to write statements about equality.

Teachers need to make the point that mathematical situations can be represented in many ways. Addition can be shown with objects, pictures, models, numbers, and words. Children should be provided many opportunities to translate among the different representations.

Vocabulary

number sentence	a set of numerals and symbols that summarizes a number story

Cross-Curricular Connections

Reading/Language Arts In this chapter, children learn to write number sentences for pictures and situations. Explain that like numbers, words are combined to make sentences. A sentence tells a complete thought, and it begins with a capital letter and ends with a period. Ask children to look at the pictures in the Student Book and say a sentence that describes the pictures and number sentences. Correct any errors they make.

Social Studies Talk with children about what they like to do with their families. Ask where they like to go with their families and what activities they like to do. Make a list of some common activities and ask children to raise their hands for each that they do with their own family. Tally the results and work with children to write and describe number sentences that can be completed using the data.

Skills Trace

Grade K	Write addition sentences for joining situations.
Grade 1	Add numbers up to 100. (Chaps. 3, 7, 13, and 17)

**EVERY DAY COUNTS®
Calendar Math...**

provides preview, review, and practice of skills and concepts taught in this program. May/June activities are shown here.

Preview coin values. (Chapter 20)

Review patterns. (Chapter 13)

Practice problem solving skills. (Lesson 2)

Chapter Resources

Activity Cards

Also available on Teaching Resources CD.

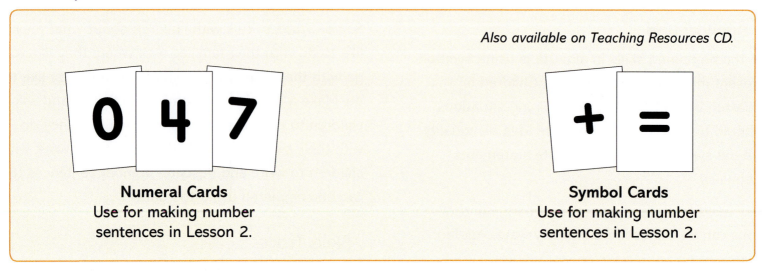

Numeral Cards
Use for making number
sentences in Lesson 2.

Symbol Cards
Use for making number
sentences in Lesson 2.

Manipulatives from the Manipulatives Kit

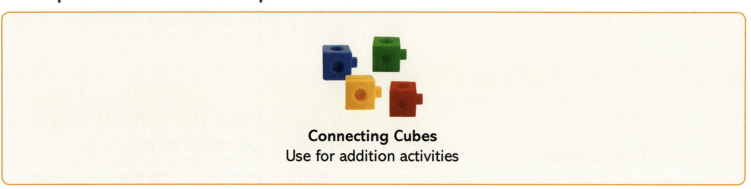

Connecting Cubes
Use for addition activities

Technology Resources

- *Math in Focus®* eBooks
- *Math in Focus®* Teacher Resources CD
- Online Web Resources
- *Math in Focus®* Virtual Manipulatives for Lessons 1 and 2

Differentiation and Assessment

Differentiation for Special Populations (Resources in the Teacher's Edition)

	English Language Learners	Children Needing Reinforcement	Children Needing a Challenge
Lesson 1		Teacher's Edition B, p. 118	Teacher's Edition B, p. 118
		Student Book B, Part 2, pp. 15–16	
Lesson 2	Math Talk, Big Book B, pp. 40–41	Big Book B, pp. 40–41	Big Book B, pp. 40–41
	Math Talk, Student Book B, Part 2, pp. 17–19	Student Book B, Part 2, pp. 17–19	Student Book B, Part 2, pp. 17–19

Make up addition stories and illustrate using connecting cubes. For example, James has 2 cats and gets 3 more. How many cats does he have in all? Show children how to form a number train from the story and how to represent it as the number sentence $2 + 3 = 5$. Repeat often. Keep the numbers small so that the emphasis is not on the answer but rather on constructing the number sentence.

Chapter 17 Assessments

On-Going Assessment	Formal Assessment
See the check questions in the Teacher's Edition on these pages	*Find Formal Assessment Blackline Masters in the Assessments book*
Teacher's Edition B	**Assessments Book**
Lesson 1, p. 119 Lesson 2, p. 123	Assessment 5 for Book B, Part 2, is on pages 28–34 of Assessments. Interview Assessment is on page 35.

Chapter 17 Planning Guide

Lessons and Pacing	Activity	Component	Objectives and Math Focus
Lesson 1	**Writing Addition Sentences, pp. 118–119**		• Understand addition as the joining of two sets. • Understand symbols + and = and *number sentence*. • Use symbols and numerals to write number sentences.
DAY 1 Activities	1 Discover	**Teacher's Edition B,** p. 118	Introduce *number sentence*.
	2 Apply	**Student Book B, Part 2,** pp. 15–16	Write addition sentences.
Lesson 2	**Showing Addition Stories with Numbers, pp. 120–124**		• Represent addition stories with small numbers.
DAY 1 Activities	1 Investigate	**Big Book B,** pp. 40–41	Make addition sentences that represent joining two sets.
	2 Explore	**Teacher's Edition B,** p. 121	Form addition stories and addition sentences. **Recall, Reinforce, and Review** Form number sentences from addition stories.
DAY 2 Activities	3 Apply	**Student Book B, Part 2,** pp. 17–19	Write a number sentence for a number story.

Vocabulary	Manipulatives/Materials	Class Organization	NTCM Focal Points & Process Standards
number sentence	• Connecting cubes, 20 per pair (10 blue and 10 green)	Pairs Independent	Count the number of items when joining two sets. • Communication • Representation • Connections • Problem solving
	• Teacher Numeral Cards 0–10 • Symbol Cards + and =	Whole class Whole class	Count the number of items when joining two sets. • Communication • Representation • Connections • Problem solving
		Independent	

Lesson 1
Writing Addition Sentences

LESSON OBJECTIVES
• Understand addition as the joining of two sets.
• Understand symbols + and =, and *number sentence.*
• Use symbols and numerals to write number sentences.

MATERIALS
• Connecting cubes

Vocabulary
number sentence

DAY **1**

Teacher's Edition B, pp. 118–119
Student Book B, Part 2, pp. 15–16

DAY **1**

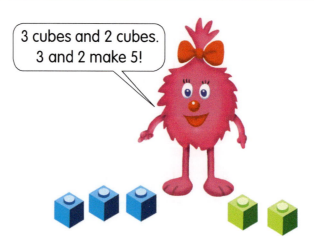

3 cubes and 2 cubes. 3 and 2 make 5!

ACTIVITY 1
Discover

Math Focus: Introduce *number sentence.*
Materials: Connecting cubes, 20 per pair (10 blue and 10 green)
Classroom Setup: Children work in pairs.

1. **Distribute** materials to the children.
2. **Ask** children to raise 2 fingers. Then, ask them to raise 2 more fingers. **Ask:** How many fingers are raised in all? (4)
3. **Repeat** with other number values totaling up to 10.
4. **Ask** children to take 3 blue cubes and 2 green cubes from their sets. **Ask:** How many cubes did you take in all? (5)
5. **Write** *3 and 2 make 5* on the board.
6. **Tell** children that there is another way of writing *3 and 2 make 5* using symbols.
7. Under *3 and 2 make 5*, write *3 + 2 = 5.* Align the numbers so that the sentences look like this:

$$3 \text{ and } 2 \text{ make } 5$$
$$3 \; + \; 2 \; = \; 5$$

   Explain that the '+' symbol means *and* and the '=' symbol means *make.*
8. Then, explain that *3 + 2 = 5* is a *number sentence.*
9. **Repeat** with other number values that together make up to 10.

Differentiated Instruction for Activity 1

Reinforcement

Materials: *Connecting cubes, 5 blue and 5 green*
Classroom Setup: *Teacher with a child or two*
Use smaller numbers totaling not more than 6.

Challenge

Materials: *Connecting cubes, 10 blue and 10 green*
Classroom Setup: *Teacher with a child or two*
Use greater numbers totaling up to 20.

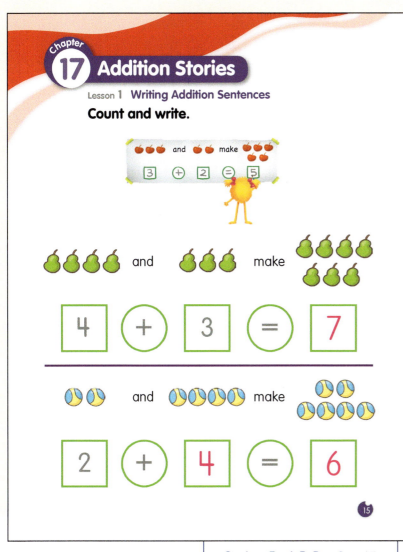

Student Book B, Part 2, p. 15

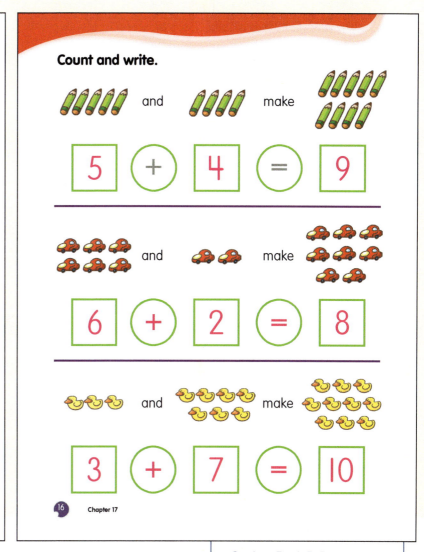

Student Book B, Part 2, p. 16

ACTIVITY 2
Apply

Math Focus: Write addition sentences.
Resource: Student Book B, Part 2, pp. 15–16
Classroom Setup: Children work independently.

1. *Point* out the example written by the furry. Help children understand they are to write numerals in the boxes and symbols in the circles.

2. Children write the number sentences that correspond to the addition illustrations in each exercise.

3. *Encourage* children to complete the number sentences by counting up.

4. When children finish the activity, ask check questions such as:
   • How do you say your number sentence?
   • Have you written all the parts to your number sentence?
   • How do you know the two numbers make your answer?

Lesson 2
Showing Addition Stories with Numbers

LESSON OBJECTIVE
- Represent addition stories with small numbers.

MATERIALS
- Teacher Numeral Cards 0–10
- Symbol Cards + and =

DAY 1

Teacher's Edition B, pp. 120–121
Big Book B, pp. 40–41

DAY 2

Teacher's Edition B, pp. 122–124
Student Book B, Part 2,
pp. 17–19

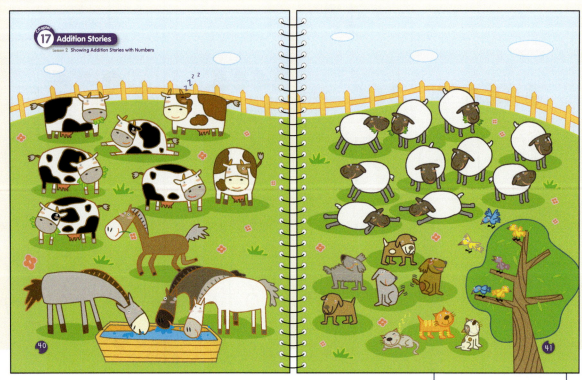

Big Book B, pp. 40–41

DAY 1

ACTIVITY 1
Investigate

Math Focus: Make addition sentences that represent joining two sets.
Resource: Big Book B, pp. 40–41
Classroom Setup: Whole class, in front of the Big Book

1. *Ask* children to sit so that everyone can see the Big Book.

2. *Ask* children questions in the form of number stories. For example, *say:* There are 5 cows with black patches and 2 cows with brown patches. How many cows are there in all? (7)

3. Math Talk Encourage children to answer in the form of a number sentence: 5 and 2 make 7.

4. *Write* the number sentence $5 + 2 = 7$ on the board.

5. *Repeat* steps 2 to 4 for another animal.

Differentiated Instruction for Activity 1

Reinforcement

Classroom Setup: *Teacher with a child or two*

Make number sentences using the smaller groups of animals, such as the cats.

ACTIVITY 2
Explore

Math Focus: Form addition stories and addition sentences.
Resource: Big Book B, pp. 40–41
Materials: Teacher Numeral Cards 0–10
Symbol Cards + and =
Classroom Setup: Continue with whole class setup as in
Activity 1.

1. With children still in front of the Big Book,
distribute the cards to 13 children.

2. *Ask* the remaining children to think of another
number story.

3. *Invite* children with the numerals from the story to
stand in an area near the Big Book.

4. *Ask:* What other cards do we need to make a
number sentence for this story?

5. *Invite* children with these cards to join the others
near the Big Book.

6. *Ask* another child to arrange the children with the
cards to form the addition sentence. Repeat the
number story and check that the number sentence
is correct.

7. *Repeat* steps 2 to 6 a few times, redistributing the
cards occasionally.

Differentiated Instruction for Activity 2

Challenge

Classroom Setup: *Teacher with a child or two*

*Challenge the child to think of a number story that includes 0. It
may be difficult for them to think of something that is not there.*

Recall, Reinforce, and Review

Tell children addition stories using small numbers, such as: I had 3
goldfish. I got 1 goldfish. Now I have 4 goldfish. Ask children how
they would write the number sentence.

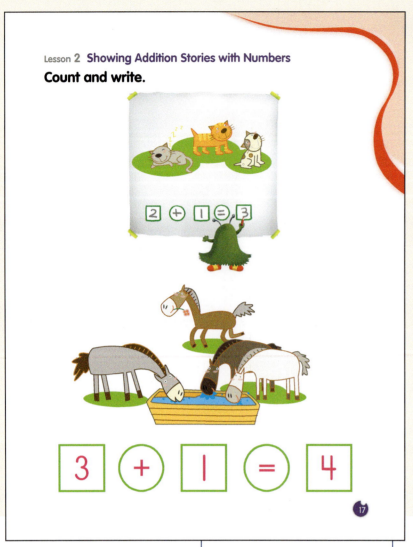

Student Book B, Part 2, p. 17

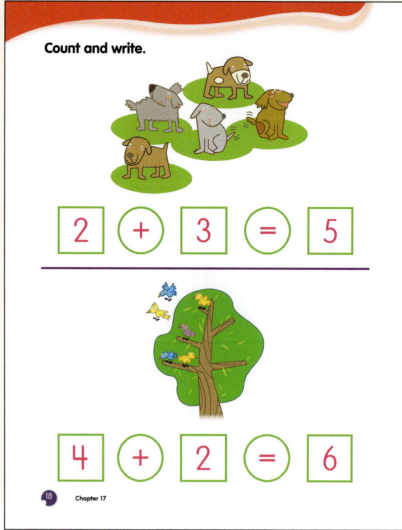

Student Book B, Part 2, p. 18

DAY 2

ACTIVITY 3
Apply 👤

Math Focus: Write a number sentence for a number story.
Resource: Student Book B, Part 2, pp. 17–19
Classroom Setup: Children work independently.

1. **Direct** children's attention to the green furry at the top of page 17.

2. **Tell** children that 2 cats are awake and 1 cat is asleep. **Ask:** How many cats are there in all? (3)

3. **Math Talk** Encourage children to answer in the form of a number sentence: 2 and 1 make 3.

4. **Tell** them that the green furry is writing the number sentence using the '+' symbol and the '=' symbol.

5. For each exercise, tell children the following number stories:
   • 3 horses are drinking water. 1 horse is not drinking water. How many horses are there in all?
   • 2 dogs are grey. 3 dogs are brown. How many dogs are there in all?
   • 4 birds are in the tree. 2 birds are flying away. How many birds are there in all?

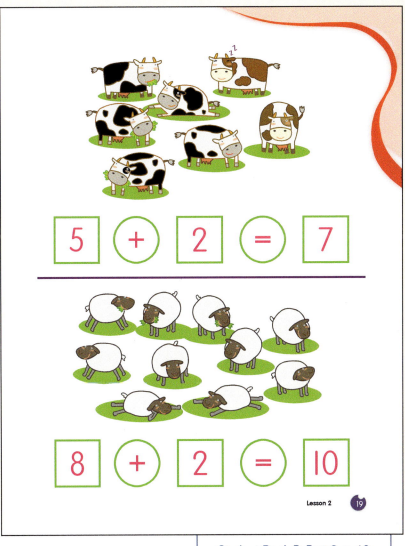

$$5 \,+\, 2 \,=\, 7$$

$$8 \,+\, 2 \,=\, 10$$

Lesson 2 19

Student Book B, Part 2, p. 19

- 5 cows have black patches. 2 cows have brown patches. How many cows are there in all?
- 8 sheep are standing. 2 sheep are lying down. How many sheep are there in all?

6. Children write number sentences to represent the number story for each exercise.

✓ 7. While children engage in the activity, ask check questions such as:
- How do you say your number sentence?
- Have you written all the parts to your number sentence?
- How do you know the two numbers make your answer?

8. *Encourage* children to complete the number sentences by counting on.

Reinforcement

Classroom Setup: *Teacher with a child or two*

Encourage children to count on using their fingers.

Challenge

Classroom Setup: *Teacher with a child or two*

Ask children if there are other ways to group the dogs, cows and sheep. Then, ask them to write a number sentence for each grouping they suggest. Some possible answers include:
- *2 dogs are wagging their tails and 3 are not.*
- *3 cows are eating grass and 4 are not.*
- *6 cows are standing and 1 is lying down.*
- *6 cows are awake and 1 is asleep.*
- *3 sheep are eating grass and 7 are not.*

Notes

Math Background

Problem solving is inherent in young children because they are naturally curious and are at a stage of discovering new ideas daily. As they learn new mathematics concepts, children should put them to use with the problem solving strategies that they have been developing.

Story problems are a common context for applying subtraction ideas. Kindergartners should be able to understand simple take-away and comparison subtraction problems. As the story problems are presented, children use manipulatives and models to make sense of the situations. The problem situations should also be connected to written numerals in number sentences. Together, these activities connect and develop basic concepts in the number, algebra, and problem solving strands.

Vocabulary

| take away | subtract from |
| left | remaining |

Cross-Curricular Connections

Reading/Language Arts Have children create their own story problems to practice oral language. Put children in pairs or small groups. Present a variety of take-away and comparison subtraction problems using classroom objects or the children themselves. Ask each group to create story problems for the situations, and invite them to share their stories.

Physical Education Play a modified version of *Red Rover*. Put the children into two or three groups, depending upon the total number in the class. Give directions such as the following: *Red rover, red rover, Group 1 send two players over (to Group 2)*. Members of Group 1 send over two players and say a subtraction sentence that shows how many players they started with, how many went away, and how many are left.

Skills Trace

Grade K	Write subtraction sentences for take-away situations.
	Compare two numbers using one-to-one correspondence and write the number sentence.
Grade 1	Subtract numbers to 100. (Chaps. 4, 8, 10, and 17)

EVERY DAY COUNTS® Calendar Math...

provides preview, review, and practice of skills and concepts taught in this program. May/June activities are shown here.

Preview coin values. (Chapter 20)

Review identifying circles. (Chapter 16)

Practice problem solving skills. (Lessons 1 and 2 in this chapter)

Chapter Resources

Activity Cards

Also available on Teaching Resources CD.

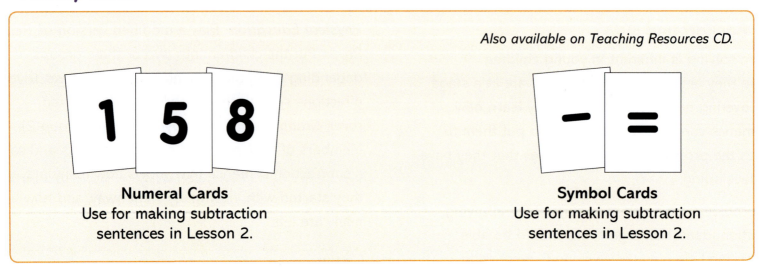

Numeral Cards
Use for making subtraction
sentences in Lesson 2.

Symbol Cards
Use for making subtraction
sentences in Lesson 2.

Manipulatives from the Manipulatives Kit

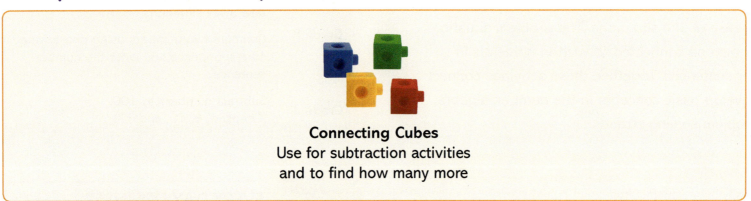

Connecting Cubes
Use for subtraction activities
and to find how many more

Technology Resources

- *Math in Focus®* eBooks
- *Math in Focus®* Teacher Resources CD
- Online Web Resources
- *Math in Focus®* Virtual Manipulatives for Lessons 1–3

Differentiation and Assessment

Differentiation for Special Populations (Resources in the Teacher's Edition)

	English Language Learners	Children Needing Reinforcement	Children Needing a Challenge
Lesson 1		Student Book B, Part 2, pp. 20–21	
Lesson 2	Math Talk, Big Book B, pp. 42–43	Big Book B, pp. 42–43	Big Book B, pp. 42–43
	Math Talk, Student Book B, Part 2, pp. 22–24	Student Book B, Part 2, pp. 22–24	
Lesson 3		Student Book B, Part 2, pp. 25–29	

Make up subtraction stories and illustrate using connecting cubes. For example, there are 7 fish swimming together, and 3 fish go the other way. How many fish are swimming together now? Show the number sentence: 7 − 3 = 4. Repeat using other stories and numbers. Encourage children to make up their own stories and write the number sentences.

Chapter 18 Assessments

On-Going Assessment	Formal Assessment
See the check questions in the Teacher's Edition on these pages	*Find Formal Assessment Blackline Masters in the Assessments book*
Teacher's Edition B	**Assessments Book**
Lesson 1, p. 127 Lesson 2, p. 131 Lesson 3, pp. 134, 135	Assessment 5 for Book B, Part 2, is on pages 28–34 of Assessments. Interview Assessment is on page 35.

Chapter 18 Planning Guide

Lessons and Pacing	Activity	Component	Objectives and Math Focus
Lesson 1	**Writing Subtraction Sentences,** pp. 126–127		• Understand simple subtraction. • Understand the minus '–' symbol. • Use symbols and numerals to write number sentences.
DAY 1 Activities	1 Explore	**Teacher's Edition B,** p. 126	Introduce *take away* and *left*.
	2 Apply	**Student Book B, Part 2,** pp. 20–21	Write number sentences for take-away situations.
Lesson 2	**Showing Subtraction Stories with Numbers,** pp. 128–131		• Represent subtraction stories with small numbers.
DAY 1 Activities	1 Investigate	**Big Book B,** pp. 42–43	Make subtraction sentences to represent take-away situations.
	2 Explore	**Teacher's Edition B,** p. 129 **Big Book B,** pp. 42–43	Form subtraction sentences from take-away situations.
DAY 2 Activities	3 Apply	**Student Book B, Part 2,** pp. 22–24	Write number sentences for take-away situations.
Lesson 3	**Comparing Sets,** pp. 132–136		• Review *how many more*. • Compare two sets and show the number sentence to answer *how many more?*
DAY 1 Activities	1 Investigate	**Teacher's Edition B,** p. 132	Find how many more objects are in one set than in another.
	2 Apply	**Student Book B, Part 2,** pp. 25–27	Compare two sets of aligned objects; write subtraction sentences.
	3 Apply	**Student Book B, Part 2,** pp. 28–29	Compare two sets of randomly placed objects; write subtraction sentences.

Vocabulary	Manipulatives/Materials	Class Organization	NTCM Focal Points & Process Standards
take away, left	• Connecting cubes, 10 per child	Whole class Independent	Model joining and separating sets. • Communication • Representation • Connections • Problem solving
	• Teacher Numeral Cards 0–10 • Symbol Cards – and =	Whole class Whole class Independent	Model joining and separating sets. • Communication • Representation • Connections • Problem solving
	• Connecting cubes, 20 (10 of Color A and 10 of Color B)	Whole class Independent Independent	Model joining and separating sets. • Communication • Representation • Connections • Problem solving

Lesson 1
Writing Subtraction Sentences

LESSON OBJECTIVES
- Understand simple subtraction.
- Understand the minus '–' symbol.
- Use symbols and numerals to write number sentences.

MATERIALS
- Connecting cubes

Vocabulary
take away

left

DAY 1

Teacher's Edition B, pp. 126–127
Student Book B, Part 2, pp. 20–21

DAY 1

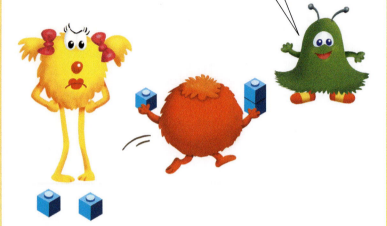

She had 5 cubes. He took away 3 cubes. 5 take away 3 is 2.

ACTIVITY 1
Explore

Math Focus: Introduce *take away* and *left*.
Materials: Connecting cubes, 10 per child
Classroom Setup: Whole class

1. **Distribute** materials to the children.

2. **Ask** children to raise 5 fingers. Then, have them put down 3 fingers. **Ask:** How many fingers are left? (2)

3. **Repeat** with other number values up to 10.

4. Have children take 5 connecting cubes from their sets and then remove 3 cubes. **Ask:** How many cubes are left? (2)

5. **Write** *5 take away 3 is 2* on the board.

6. **Tell** children that there is another way of writing *5 take away 3 is 2* using symbols.

7. Under *5 take away 3 is 2*, write *5 – 3 = 2*. Align the numbers so that the sentences look like this:

   5 take away 3 is 2

   5   –   3 = 2

   Tell children that the '–' symbol means *take away* and the '=' symbol means *is*.

8. Then, tell children that *5 – 3 = 2* is a *number sentence*.

9. **Repeat** with other number values up to 10.

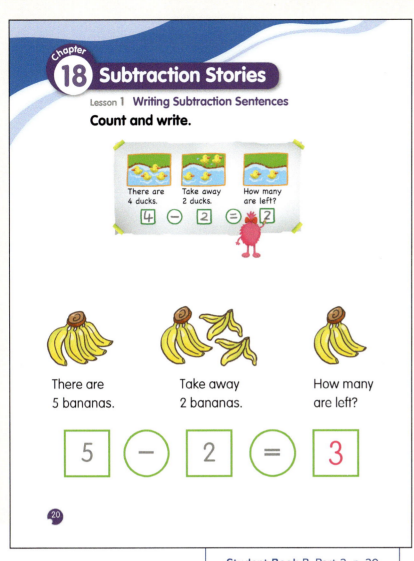

Student Book B, Part 2, p. 20

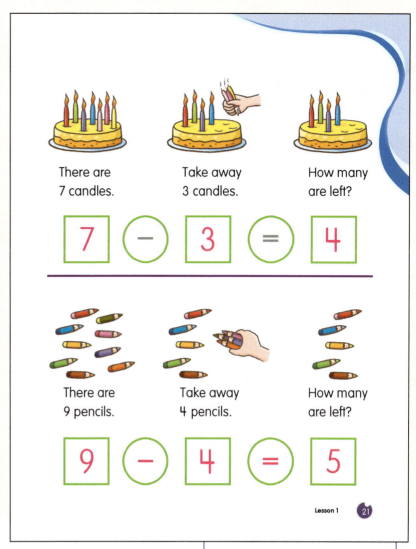

Student Book B, Part 2, p. 21

ACTIVITY 2
Apply

Math Focus: Write number sentences for take-away situations.
Resource: Student Book B, Part 2, pp. 20–21
Classroom Setup: Children work independently.

1. *Point* out the example written by the furry. Have children notice that they are to write numerals in the boxes and symbols in the circles.

2. Children write the number sentences that correspond to the subtraction illustration in each exercise.

3. *Encourage* children to complete the number sentences by counting back.

4. While children engage in the activity, ask check questions such as:
   • Which number tells how many in all?
   • Which number shows how many are being taken away?
   • Which number shows how many are left?
   • How do you know this is the correct number?
     Are you sure?

Differentiated Instruction for Activity 2

Reinforcement

Classroom Setup: *Teacher with a child or two*

Encourage children to count back using their fingers.

Lesson 2
Showing Subtraction Stories with Numbers

LESSON OBJECTIVE
• Represent subtraction stories with small numbers.

MATERIALS
• Teacher Numeral Cards 0–10
• Symbol Cards – and =

DAY 1

Teacher's Edition B, pp. 128–129
Big Book B, pp. 42–43

DAY 2

Teacher's Edition B, pp. 130–131
Student Book B, Part 2, pp. 22–24

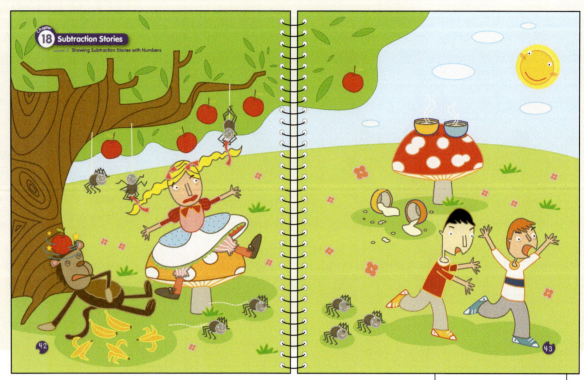

Big Book B, pp. 42–43

DAY 1

ACTIVITY 1
Investigate

Math Focus: Make subtraction sentences to represent take-away situations.
Resource: Big Book B, pp. 42–43
Classroom Setup: Whole class, in front of the Big Book

1. *Ask* children to sit so that everyone can see the Big Book.

2. *Ask* questions in the form of number stories, such as:
   • How many children can you see in the picture? (3)
   • How many children are running away? (2)
   • How many children are left behind? (1)

3. **Math Talk** Encourage children to answer in the form of a number sentence: 3 take away 2 is 1.

4. *Write* the number sentence $3 - 2 = 1$ on the board.

5. Repeat steps 2 to 4 using the bananas or apples.

Differentiated Instruction for Activity 1

Reinforcement

Classroom Setup: *Teacher with a child or two*

Make number sentences using the smaller groups of objects, such as the children or the bowls.

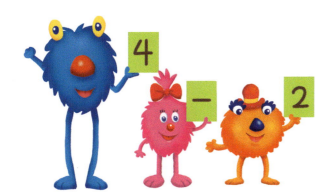

ACTIVITY 2
Explore

Math Focus: Form subtraction sentences from take-away situations.

Resource: Big Book B, pp. 42–43

Materials: Teacher Numeral Cards 0–10

Symbol Cards – and =

Classroom Setup: Continue with whole class setup as in Activity 1.

1. With children still in front of the Big Book, distribute the cards to 13 children.

2. *Ask* the remaining children to think of another take-away situation they can find in the picture.

3. *Invite* children with the numerals from the situation to stand in an area near the Big Book.

4. *Ask:* What other cards do we need to make a number sentence for this story?

5. *Invite* children with these cards to join the others near the Big Book.

6. *Ask* another child to arrange the children with the cards to form the subtraction sentence. Repeat the number story and check that the number sentence is correct.

7. *Repeat* steps 2 to 6 a few times, redistributing the cards occasionally.

Differentiated Instruction for Activity 2

Challenge

Classroom Setup: *Teacher with a child or two*

Challenge the child to think of a situation in the picture with 0 (nothing) taken away.

Lesson 2 Showing Subtraction Stories with Numbers

Count and write.

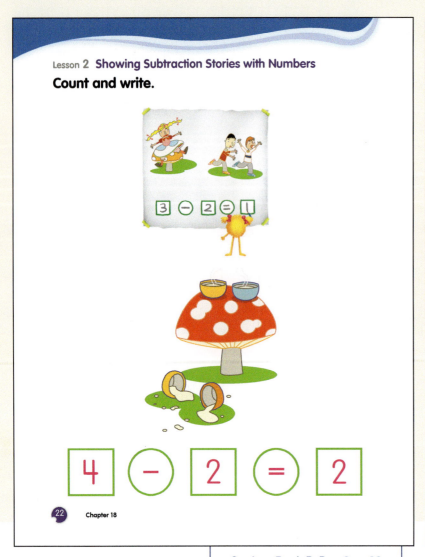

4 − 2 = 2

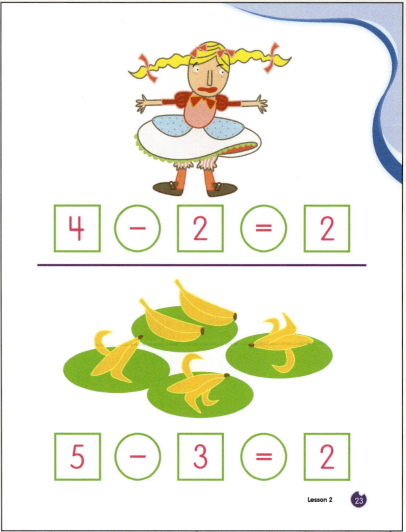

5 − 3 = 2

Student Book B, Part 2, p. 22

Student Book B, Part 2, p. 23

DAY 2

ACTIVITY 3
Apply

Math Focus: Write number sentences for take-away situations.
Resource: Student Book B, Part 2, pp. 22–24
Classroom Setup: Children work independently.

1. *Direct* children's attention to the yellow furry at the top of page 22.

2. *Tell* children that there are 3 children, but 2 children are running away. *Ask:* How many children are left behind? (1)

3. **Math Talk** Encourage children to answer in the form of a number sentence: 3 take away 2 is 1.

4. *Explain* that the yellow furry is writing the number sentence using the '−' symbol and the '=' symbol.

5. For each exercise, tell children the following number stories:
   • There are 4 bowls of soup. 2 bowls of soup have spilt. How many bowls of soup are left?
   • The girl has 4 ribbons in her hair. 2 ribbons have been untied. How many tied ribbons are left?
   • There are 5 bananas. 3 bananas have been eaten. How many bananas are left?

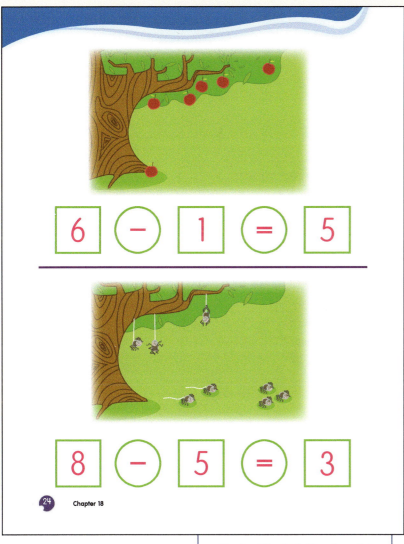

- There are 6 apples. 1 apple fell to the ground. How many apples are left on the tree?
- There are 8 spiders. 5 spiders are crawling away. How many spiders are left in the tree?

6. Children write number sentences to represent the number story for each exercise.

7. *Encourage* children to complete the sentences by counting back.

✓ 8. While children engage in the activity, ask check questions such as:
- Which number shows how many in all?
- Which number shows how many are being taken away?
- Which number shows how many are left?
- How do you know this is the correct number? Are you sure?

Lesson 3
Comparing Sets

LESSON OBJECTIVES
- Review *how many more.*
- Compare two sets and show the number sentence to answer *how many more?*

MATERIALS
- Connecting cubes

DAY 1

Teacher's Edition B, pp. 132–136
Student Book B, Part 2,
pp. 25–29

DAY 1

There are 2 more red cubes than yellow cubes.

ACTIVITY 1
Investigate

Math Focus: Find how many more objects there are in one set than in another.

Materials: Connecting cubes, 20 (10 of Color A and 10 of Color B)

Classroom Setup: Whole class

1. *Invite* children to gather around a table.

2. *Place* 5 (red) connecting cubes in a row. *Ask:* How many (red) cubes are there? (5)

3. *Place* 3 (yellow) cubes in a row. *Ask:* How many (yellow) cubes are there? (3)

4. *Place* both rows of cubes on the table and ensure they are aligned on the left. *Ask:* How many more (red) cubes are there than (yellow) cubes? (2)

Best Practices Point out to children that when the two rows are lined up, they only need to count the extra cubes. The extra will show them how many more cubes one row has than the other.

5. *Repeat* steps 2 to 4 with other numbers. The number of each color of cubes should not exceed 10.

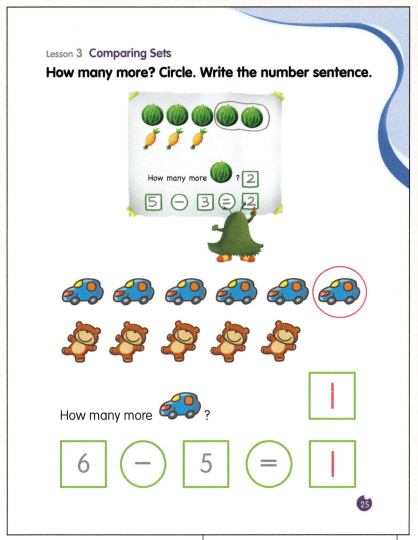

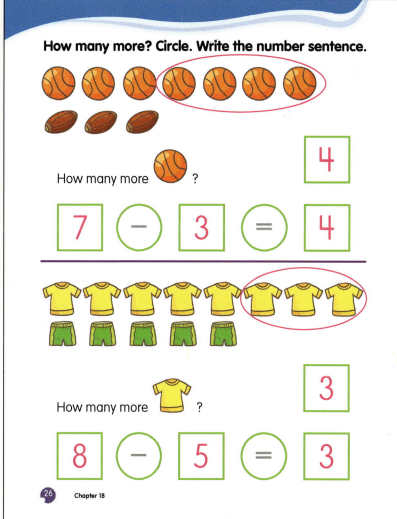

Student Book B, Part 2, p. 25

Student Book B, Part 2, p. 26

ACTIVITY 2
Apply

Math Focus: Compare two sets of aligned objects; write subtraction sentences.

Resource: Student Book B, Part 2, pp. 25–27

Classroom Setup: Children work independently.

1. *Encourage* children to return to their places and open their Student Books to page 25.

2. Children count both rows of objects and write how many more objects one row has than the other.

Best Practices Point out that you can find out by counting the extra objects, since both rows of objects are aligned.

3. Children write a number sentence to describe how many more one row of objects has than the other.

(continued on page 134)

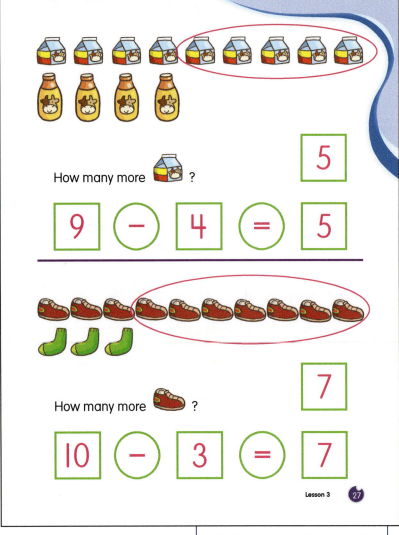

How many more 🥛 ?

5

9 − 4 = 5

How many more 👟 ?

7

10 − 3 = 7

Lesson 3 27

Student Book B, Part 2, p. 27

✓ 4. While children engage in the activity, ask check questions such as:
- Which number shows how many are in the bigger set?
- Which number shows how many are in the smaller set?
- Which number shows how many more?
- How do you know this is the correct number?

Differentiated Instruction for Activity 2

Reinforcement

Classroom Setup: *Teacher with a child or two*

Ask children to compare the sets in one-to-one correspondence, and cross out these objects to find the difference between the sets.

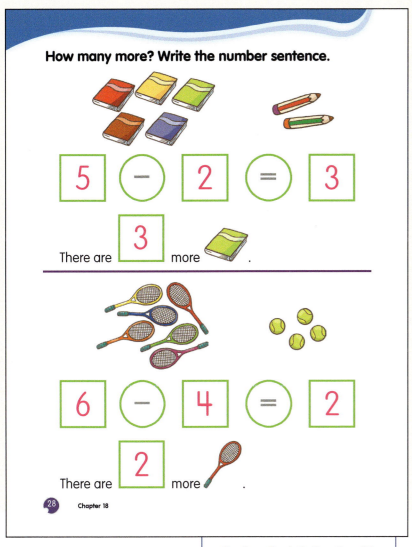

How many more? Write the number sentence.

5 − 2 = 3

There are 3 more 📗 .

6 − 4 = 2

There are 2 more 🎾 .

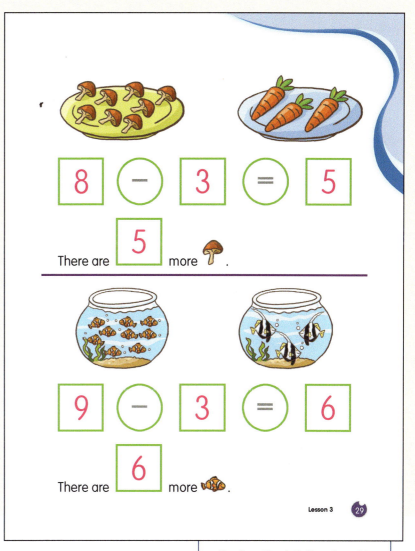

8 − 3 = 5

There are 5 more 🍄 .

9 − 3 = 6

There are 6 more 🐠 .

Student Book B, Part 2, p. 28
Student Book B, Part 2, p. 29

ACTIVITY 3
Apply 👤

Math Focus: Compare two sets of randomly placed objects; write subtraction sentences.

Resource: Student Book B, Part 2, pp. 28–29

Classroom Setup: Children work independently.

1. Children count the number of objects in each set and write the answer in the boxes. Then, they complete the number sentences.

2. Children then write how many more one set has than the other.

✔ 3. While children engage in the activity, ask check questions such as:
   • Which number shows how many there are in the bigger set?
   • Which number shows how many there are in the smaller set?
   • Which number shows how many more?
   • How do you know this is the correct number?

Differentiated Instruction for Activity 3

Reinforcement

Classroom Setup: *Teacher with a child or two*

Ask children to compare the sets in one-to-one correspondence, and cross out these objects to find the difference between the sets.

Notes

Chapter 19

Chapter Overview

Measurement

Math Background

In Kindergarten, measurement activities teach important life skills while laying a foundation for more complex concepts and processes that are developed in later grades. In the early years, measurement techniques are informal and are mainly based on the child's insight. At this level, the basis of measurement instruction is on comparing objects and situations.

Teachers should introduce and demonstrate the use of measurement tools and techniques by engaging children in physical activities, such as comparing the weights of two objects on a balance. The use of non-standard units in measurement allows students to begin to think about the effect of the size of the units on the final measure.

Vocabulary

heavy	of considerable weight
heavier	of greater weight
light	of little weight
lighter	of less weight
holds more	contains a bigger quantity
holds less	contains a smaller quantity
hold the same amount	contain an equal quantity
more time	a longer duration
less time	a shorter duration
bigger	larger
smaller	tinier

Cross-Curricular Connections

Reading/Language Arts Discuss with children comparison language. Explain that sometimes the *–er* ending is added to words to compare. Give examples from the chapter: *bigger, smaller, heavier, lighter.* Tell children that the words *more* and *less* are also used, as in *more time, less time, holds more, holds less.*

Encourage children to use these words to compare classroom objects and situations.

Social Studies Talk about different jobs and some of the activities that these jobs require. For example, an artist creates a painting and a chef cooks a meal. Elicit several jobs and activities from children, and add to the list as necessary. Encourage children to make statements to compare the amount of time that the different activities take. For example, making a painting takes more time than cooking a meal.

Skills Trace

Grade K	Compare objects of different weights, capacities, and areas.
	Compare duration of events.
Grade 1	Weigh objects using non-standard units. (Chap. 10)
	Tell time to the half hour. (Chap. 15)

**EVERY DAY COUNTS®
Calendar Math...**

provides preview, review, and practice of skills and concepts taught in this program. March activities are shown here.

Preview coin values. (Chapter 20)

Review subtraction as comparing. (Chapter 18)

Practice using non-standard units of weight. (Lesson 1 in this chapter)

Chapter Resources

Manipulatives from the Manipulatives Kit

Balance Bucket
Use for comparing weights

Connecting Cubes
Use for weighing objects,
comparing capacities, and
comparing areas

Technology Resources

- *Math in Focus*® eBooks
- *Math in Focus*® Teacher Resources CD
- Online Web Resources
- *Math in Focus*® Virtual Manipulatives
  for Lesson 1

Classroom/Household Items

- Classroom objects, such as pencils, books, rolls of tape, and erasers
- Empty ice cream tub
- Plastic cups
- Colored pencils
- Envelopes

Differentiation and Assessment

Differentiation for Special Populations (Resources in the Teacher's Edition)

	English Language Learners	Children Needing Reinforcement	Children Needing a Challenge
Lesson 1	Math Talk, Teacher's Edition B, p. 138		Teacher's Edition B, p. 140
Lesson 3	Math Talk, Big Book B, pp. 44–45	Big Book B, pp. 44–45	Big Book B, pp. 44–45

Help children understand that weight cannot always be judged by size. Use two small boxes, with one noticeably smaller than the other. Leave the larger one empty and fill the smaller one with dried beans or rice. Have children identify the heavier one both by hefting the two and by using the balance scale.

Chapter 19 Assessments

On-Going Assessment	Formal Assessment
See the check questions in the Teacher's Edition on these pages	*Find Formal Assessment Blackline Masters in the Assessments book*
Teacher's Edition B	**Assessments Book**
Lesson 1, p. 141 Lesson 3, p. 146 Lesson 4, p. 148	Assessment 5 for Book B, Part 2, is on pages 28–34 of Assessments. Interview Assessment is on page 35.

Chapter 19 Planning Guide

Lessons and Pacing	Activity	Component	Objectives and Math Focus
Lesson 1	**Comparing Weights Using Non-standard Units,** pp. 138–141		• Review *heavy, heavier, light,* and *lighter*. • Compare weights using non-standard units.
DAY 1 Activities	1 Explore	**Teacher's Edition B,** p. 138	Use a balance scale to identify heavier and lighter objects.
	2 Apply	**Student Book B, Part 2,** pp. 30–31	Identify heavier or lighter objects shown on a balance scale.
DAY 2 Activities	3 Investigate	**Teacher's Edition B,** p. 140	Weigh objects using a non-standard unit of weight.
	4 Apply	**Student Book B, Part 2,** pp. 32–33	Identify heavier and lighter objects from their weight in non-standard units.
Lesson 2	**Comparing Capacities,** pp. 142–143		• Compare containers according to capacity. • Use the terms *holds more, holds less,* and *hold the same amount*.
DAY 1 Activities	1 Investigate	**Teacher's Edition B,** p. 142	Introduce *holds more, holds less,* and *hold the same amount*.
	2 Apply	**Student Book B, Part 2,** pp. 34–36	Identify which containers hold more, hold less, or hold the same amount.
Lesson 3	**Comparing Events in Time,** pp. 144–146		• Compare events according to duration.
DAY 1 Activities	1 Investigate	**Big Book B,** pp. 44–45	Introduce *more time* and *less time*.
	2 Apply	**Student Book B, Part 2,** pp. 37–38	Identify which activities take more time or less time.
Lesson 4	**Comparing Areas Using Non-standard Units,** pp. 147–148		• Compare areas of flat surfaces using non-standard units.
DAY 1 Activities	1 Investigate	**Teacher's Edition B,** p. 147	Build awareness of area as a way to compare the size of two objects.
	2 Apply	**Student Book B, Part 2,** pp. 39–40	Identify bigger and smaller surfaces from the number of tiles that cover them.

Vocabulary	Manipulatives/Materials	Class Organization	NTCM Focal Points & Process Standards
heavy, heavier, light, lighter	• Balance scale • Classroom objects, such as pencils, books, rolls of tape, and erasers	Whole class Independent	Compare objects using measurable attributes, such as weight. • Communication • Representation
	• Balance scale • Connecting cubes, 20 • Classroom objects, such as pencils, erasers, and rolls of tape • Objects with similar weight	Small groups Independent	• Connections • Problem solving • Reasoning / Proof
holds more, holds less, hold the same amount	• An empty ice cream tub (about a 1- or 2-quart size) • Plastic cups, 2 (1 of Color A and 1 of Color B) • Connecting cubes, 20–30 • Colored pencils, 1 per child	Whole class Independent	Compare objects using measurable attributes, such as capacity. • Communication • Representation • Connections
more time, less time		Whole class Independent	The Focal Points do not address time. • Communication • Connections
bigger, smaller	• A large book • A small book • Connecting cubes, 40–50 • Grey Tiles (TR30) • Envelopes, 1 per child	Whole class Independent	Compare objects using measurable attributes, such as area. • Communication • Representation • Connections • Problem solving • Reasoning / Proof

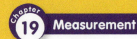

Lesson 1
Comparing Weights Using Non-standard Units

LESSON OBJECTIVES
- Review *heavy*, *heavier*, *light*, and *lighter*.
- Compare weights using non-standard units.

MATERIALS
- Balance scale
- Classroom objects, such as pencils, books, rolls of tape, and erasers
- Connecting cubes

Vocabulary

heavy

heavier

light

lighter

DAY 1

Teacher's Edition B, pp. 138–139
Student Book B, Part 2, pp. 30–31

DAY 2

Teacher's Edition B, pp. 140–141
Student Book B, Part 2, pp. 32–33

DAY 1

ACTIVITY 1
Explore

Math Focus: Use a balance scale to identify heavier and lighter objects.
Materials: Balance scale
Classroom objects, such as pencils, books, rolls of tape, and erasers
Classroom Setup: Whole class

1. *Hold up* a pencil. *Ask:*
   - Is this heavy?

2. Then, while still holding up the pencil, hold up a small book. *Ask:*
   - Which do you think is heavier?
   - How can you find out?

3. *Invite* a child to hold an object in each hand and tell the class which is heavier.

4. *Say:* There is another way to find out which object is heavier.

5. *Place* one object in each pan of the balance scale. Explain that the pan which is lower contains the heavier object.

6. **Math Talk** Elicit sentences such as: The book is *heavier* than the pencil.

7. *Repeat* steps 1 to 6 using a roll of tape and an eraser. Ask questions and elicit answers using the words *light* and *lighter*. Then, repeat using other classroom objects.

Best Practices Do not use identical objects with equal weights. Equal weight objects will be taught later. However, you may want to compare objects that, when carried, feel about the same weight, such as a pencil and an eraser. The balance scale will then give the answer when children are unsure.

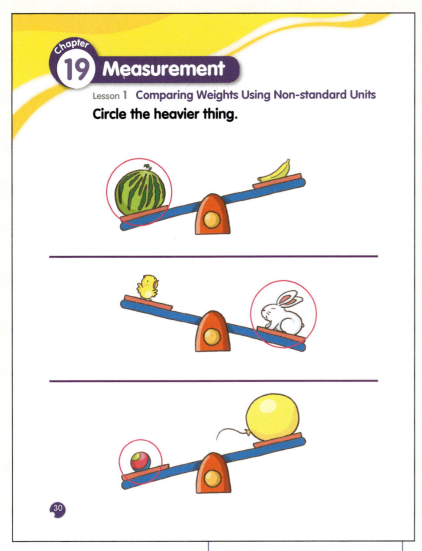

Student Book B, Part 2, p. 30

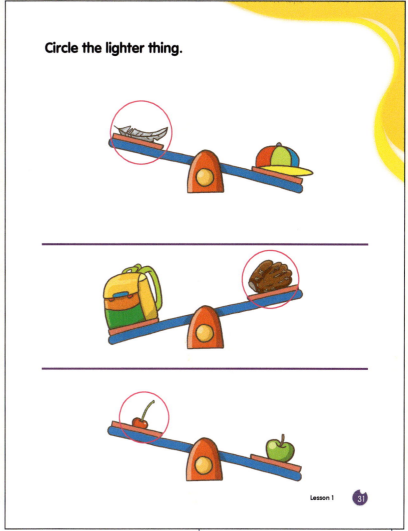

Student Book B, Part 2, p. 31

ACTIVITY 2
Apply

Math Focus: Identify heavier or lighter objects shown on a balance scale.

Resource: Student Book B, Part 2, pp. 30–31

Classroom Setup: Children work independently.

1. Children circle the heavier object in each exercise on page 30.

2. Children circle the lighter object in each exercise on page 31.

Best Practices Remind children not to use the size of an object to determine if it is heavier or lighter. Remind them to look at the way the balance is tipped.

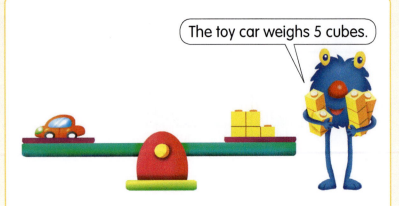

The toy car weighs 5 cubes.

ACTIVITY 3
Investigate

Math Focus: Weigh objects using a non-standard unit of weight.

Materials: Balance scale
Connecting cubes, 20
Classroom objects, such as pencils, erasers, and rolls of tape

Classroom Setup: Children work in small groups at the math center with teacher direction.

1. *Model* the activity for children.

2. *Place* a (roll of tape) on one end of the balance. On the other end of the balance, keep adding connecting cubes until the balance is as close to horizontal as possible.

3. *Explain* that when the balance is horizontal, this means that the (roll of tape) and the cubes weigh the same.

4. *Count* the number of cubes needed to balance the weight of the (roll of tape).

5. *Say:* The (roll of tape) weighs (12) cubes.

6. *Invite* groups to work at the math center to balance objects, such as pencils and erasers, with cubes.

Differentiated Instruction for Activity 3

Challenge

Materials: *Balance scale*
Connecting cubes, 20
Objects with similar weight

Classroom Setup: *Teacher with a child or two*

Ask children to find how many cubes will balance Object A. Then, ask them to find another object (Object B) to balance the same number of cubes. Explain that this means that Object A is as heavy as Object B.

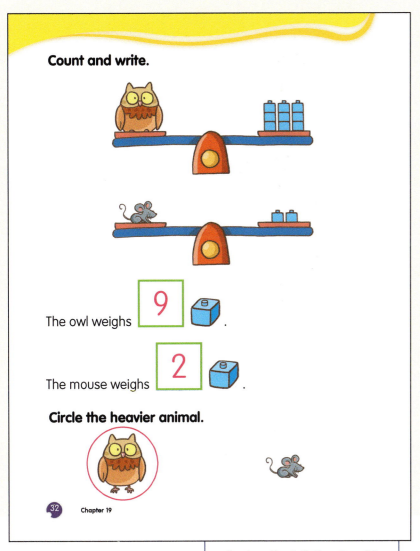

Count and write.

The owl weighs 9 <image of blue cube> .

The mouse weighs 2 .

Circle the heavier animal.

Student Book B, Part 2, p. 32

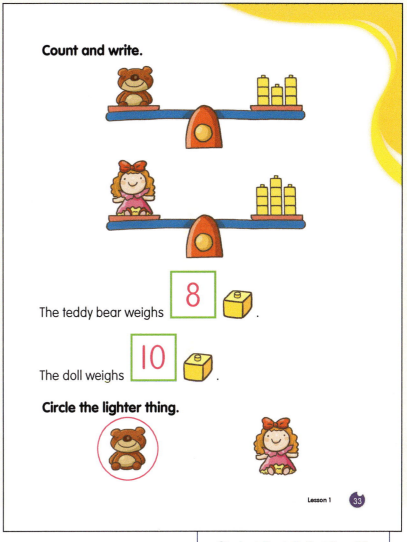

Count and write.

The teddy bear weighs 8 <image of yellow cube> .

The doll weighs 10 <image of yellow cube> .

Circle the lighter thing.

Student Book B, Part 2, p. 33

ACTIVITY 4
Apply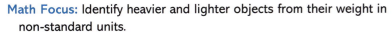

Math Focus: Identify heavier and lighter objects from their weight in non-standard units.

Resource: Student Book B, Part 2, pp. 32–33

Classroom Setup: Children work independently.

1. *Encourage* children to return to their places and open their Student Books to page 32.

2. Children count the number of connecting cubes that balances each object. The heavier object will have more cubes balancing it and the lighter object will have fewer cubes.

3. Children write the weight of each object (in terms of the number of cubes balancing it) in the appropriate box.

4. Then, they circle the heavier animal on page 32 and the lighter toy on page 33.

✓5. While children engage in the activity, ask check questions such as:
   • How many cubes does each object weigh?
   • How does this help you find the heavier/lighter object?
   • Are you sure this object is heavier/lighter?
   • Is the bigger object always heavier?
   • Is the smaller object always lighter?

Lesson 2
Comparing Capacities

LESSON OBJECTIVES
- Compare containers according to capacity.
- Use the terms *holds more*, *holds less*, and *hold the same amount*.

MATERIALS
- Empty ice cream tub
- Plastic cups
- Connecting cubes
- Colored pencils

Vocabulary

holds more

holds less

hold the same amount

DAY 1

Teacher's Edition B, pp. 142–143
Student Book B, Part 2,
pp. 34–36

DAY 1

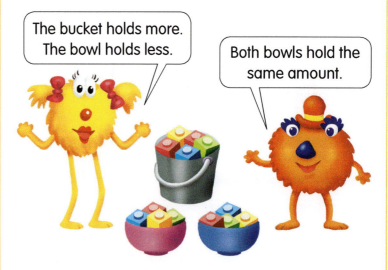

ACTIVITY 1
Investigate

Math Focus: Introduce *holds more*, *holds less*, and *hold the same amount*.

Materials: An empty ice cream tub (about a 1- or 2-quart size)
Plastic cups, 2 (1 of Color A and 1 of Color B)
Connecting cubes, 20–30

Classroom Setup: Whole class

1. *Fill* the tub and both cups to the brim with connecting cubes.

   Best Practices Be sure that both cups hold the same number of cubes.

2. *Invite* children to stand around a table.

3. *Show* them the filled tub and one of the filled cups.

4. *Ask:*
   - Which container do you think holds more cubes? (the tub)
   - Which container do you think holds fewer cubes? (the cup)
   - How can you find out? (Count the number of cubes.)

5. *Empty* the cubes one by one from the tub. Have children count the cubes one by one as you empty the tub.

6. *Say:* The tub holds (15) cubes.

7. *Repeat* step 5 for the cup. *Say:* The cup holds (5) cubes.

8. *Say:* The tub holds (15) cubes. The cup holds (5) cubes. So, the tub *holds more* and the cup *holds less*.

9. *Show* children the second filled cup.

10. *Repeat* step 5. *Say:* This cup also holds (5) cubes.

11. *Say:* The (red) cup holds (5) cubes. The (yellow) cup also holds (5) cubes. So, both cups *hold the same amount*.

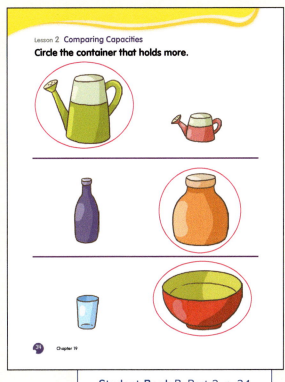

Student Book B, Part 2, p. 34

Student Book B, Part 2, p. 35

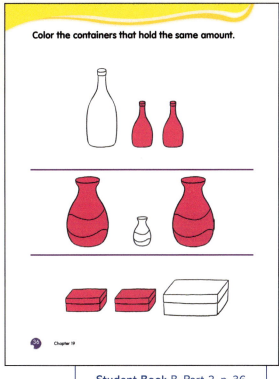

Student Book B, Part 2, p. 36

ACTIVITY 2
Apply

Math Focus: Identify which containers hold more, hold less, or hold the same amount.
Resource: Student Book B, Part 2, pp. 34–36
Materials: Colored pencils, 1 per child
Classroom Setup: Children work independently.

1. *Encourage* children to return to their places and open their Student Books to page 34.

2. *Distribute* materials to the children.

3. Children circle the container that holds more for each exercise on page 34.

4. Children circle the container that holds less for each exercise on page 35.

5. Children color the containers that hold the same amount for each exercise on page 36.

Lesson 3
Comparing Events in Time

LESSON OBJECTIVE
• Compare events according to duration.

Vocabulary

more time

less time

DAY 1

Teacher's Edition B, pp. 144–146
Big Book B, pp. 44–45
Student Book B, Part 2,
pp. 37–38

Big Book B, pp. 44–45

DAY 1

ACTIVITY 1
Investigate

Math Focus: Introduce *more time* and *less time*.
Resource: Big Book B, pp. 44–45
Classroom Setup: Whole class, in front of the Big Book

1. *Ask* children to sit so that everyone can see the Big Book

2. *Explain* that the pictures show what a boy named Tommy does on a Sunday. Discuss each picture frame with children.
   • Picture 1: Tommy brushes his teeth.
   • Picture 2: Tommy combs his hair.
   • Picture 3: Tommy has his breakfast.
   • Picture 4: Tommy changes into his soccer uniform.
   • Picture 5: Tommy plays soccer.
   • Picture 6: Tommy has a shower.
   • Picture 7: Tommy has his lunch.
   • Picture 8: Tommy reads a story book.
   • Picture 9: Tommy bikes to the park with his father and sister.
   • Picture 10: Tommy has a drink at the water fountain while his father and sister fly a kite.
   • Picture 11: Tommy pushes his bicycle home because it has a flat tire.
   • Picture 12: Tommy goes to bed.

3. **Compare** the duration of events. Ask questions such as: Which takes *more time*? Combing your hair or eating your breakfast? (eating breakfast)

Best Practices Point to the pictures as you ask each question. Ask children to explain their choices.

4. **Math Talk** Ask children for their own examples of an activity that would take more time than another. Elicit answers such as: Brushing my teeth takes *more time* than squeezing toothpaste onto my toothbrush.

5. **Ask** questions such as: Which takes *less time*? Biking to the park or pushing a bicycle home from the park? (biking to the park)

Best Practices Point to the pictures as you ask each question. Ask children to explain their choices.

6. **Math Talk** Ask children for their own examples of an activity that would take less time than another. Elicit answers such as: Drinking a glass of water takes *less time* than having lunch.

Differentiated Instruction for Activity 1

Reinforcement

Classroom Setup: *Teacher with a child or two*

Ask questions with broad differences in time, such as putting on soccer shoes or playing a soccer game.

Challenge

Classroom Setup: *Teacher with a child or two*

Ask questions that require a finer sense of time duration, such as eating breakfast or eating dinner. Have children justify these answers, since answers will vary.

Lesson 3 Comparing Events in Time

Which takes more time? Circle.

37

Student Book B, Part 2, p. 37

Which takes less time? Circle.

38   Chapter 19

Student Book B, Part 2, p. 38

ACTIVITY 2
Apply 👤

Math Focus: Identify which activities take more time or less time.
Resource: Student Book B, Part 2, pp. 37–38
Classroom Setup: Children work independently.

1. *Encourage* children to return to their places and open their Student Books to page 37.

2. Children circle the picture that takes more time for each exercise on page 37.

3. Children circle the picture that takes less time for each exercise on page 38.

✓4. While children engage in the activity, ask check questions such as:
   • Why did you circle this activity?
   • Are you sure it takes you more (less) time than the other activity?

   Best Practices Accept any answer that children can reasonably justify. For example, a child who has had a bad experience with a zipper may think of zipping as being more time-consuming than buttoning.

Lesson 4
Comparing Areas Using Non-standard Units

LESSON OBJECTIVE
• Compare areas of flat surfaces using non-standard units.

MATERIALS
• A large book
• A small book
• Connecting cubes
• Grey Tiles (TR30)
• Envelopes

Vocabulary
bigger

smaller

DAY 1

Teacher's Edition B, pp. 147–148
Student Book B, Part 2,
pp. 39–40

DAY 1

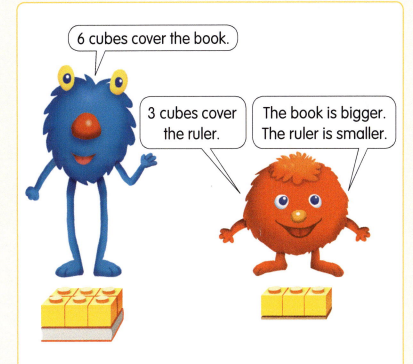

6 cubes cover the book.

3 cubes cover the ruler.

The book is bigger. The ruler is smaller.

ACTIVITY 1
Investigate

Math Focus: Build awareness of area as a way to compare the size of two objects.

Materials: A large book
A small book
Connecting cubes, 40–50

Classroom Setup: Whole class

1. *Show* children the two books. *Ask:*
   • Which is bigger?
   • How do you know?
   • Which is smaller?
   • How do you know?

2. *Suggest* that a useful way to compare the size of the books would be to see how many connecting cubes will cover each book.

3. *Place* the books on a table and place enough cubes to cover their top surfaces. The cubes should form an array that covers the book as much as possible. Count each cube as you place it on a book.

4. *Write* your findings on the board. For example:
   • (18) cubes cover Book A.
   • (12) cubes cover Book B.

5. *Explain* that since Book A requires more cubes to cover its surface, it has a *bigger* surface. Since Book B requires fewer cubes to cover its surface, it has a *smaller* surface.

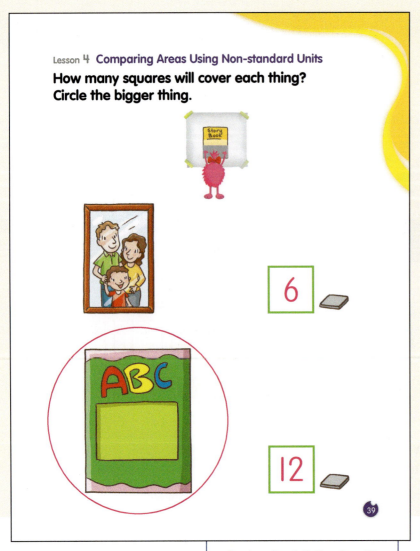

Lesson 4 **Comparing Areas Using Non-standard Units**

How many squares will cover each thing? Circle the bigger thing.

6

12

Student Book B, Part 2, p. 39

How many squares will cover each thing? Circle the smaller thing.

15

9

Student Book B, Part 2, p. 40

ACTIVITY 2
Apply

Math Focus: Identify bigger and smaller surfaces from the number of tiles that cover them.

Resource: Student Book B, Part 2, pp. 39–40

Materials: Grey Tiles (TR30)
Envelopes, 1 per child

Classroom Setup: Children work independently.

1. *Make* sufficient copies of Grey Tiles (TR30) to ensure that each child receives 20 grey tiles.

> **Best Practices** Tagboard tiles, if available, will be easier for children to work with.

2. *Cut* out the small grey tiles and place each child's allotment in an envelope.

3. *Distribute* envelopes to the children.

4. For each exercise, children use the grey tiles to cover each object completely without gaps or overlaps.

5. Then, they count the number of grey tiles they used to cover the object and write this number in the box.

6. Then, they circle the bigger object on page 39 and the smaller object on page 40.

 7. While children engage in the activity, ask check questions such as:
   • Have you covered all of this object?
   • Are any of your tiles covering up part of another tile?
   • How do you know this object is bigger/smaller? Are you sure?

Math Background

Using money is a real-world application of concepts taught in the numbers and operations strand of mathematics. In the early years, children learn that coins have a value, measured in a unit called cents, and that those values relate to our numeration system. Many Kindergarten children will be able to count combinations of coins up to about 10 cents. Doing so, they apply the counting on strategy. Eventually young children learn to count by fives and tens, which is then applied to counting groups of dimes and nickels. Of course, any activity that includes the use of coins is teaching important life skills.

Vocabulary

penny	a 1-cent coin
nickel	a 5-cent coin
dime	a 10-cent coin
quarter	a 25-cent coin
cent	a monetary unit equal to one hundredth of a dollar
change	money returned as the balance of the amount paid for something

Cross-Curricular Connections

Reading/Language Arts Children listen to a rhyme about coins in the first lesson. Ask children to name as many words as they can that rhyme with coin vocabulary. Some examples follow: penny (any, many), nickel (pickle, tickle), dime (chime, lime, mime, prime, rhyme, time), quarter (porter, shorter), cent (bent, dent, gent, lent, meant, rent, sent, tent, vent, went). Encourage children to create rhyming phrases or sentences with the words.

Social Studies Discuss with children that people work to earn money. Have children name different jobs. Then, talk about classroom jobs that children do, such as put away materials and clean the desks. Make a list of classroom jobs and assign each a different value, up to 10 cents. After children perform a classroom job, ask them to show in coins the amount that they have 'earned'. Have them show more than one combination of coins, if possible.

Skills Trace

	Identify penny, nickel, dime, and quarter.
Grade K	Understand how to use pennies, nickels, and dimes to purchase objects less than 10¢.
Grade 1	Understand how to use money (coins and bills) to purchase objects less than $10. (Chap. 19)

EVERY DAY COUNTS® Calendar Math...

provides preview, review, and practice of skills and concepts taught in this program. May/June activities are shown here.

Preview counting. (Grade 1, Chapter 1)

Review problem solving. (Chapter 18)

Practice counting coins.
(Lesson 2 in this chapter)

Chapter Resources

Activity Cards

Also available on Teaching Resources CD.

Teacher Activity Cards
Use for identifying coins in Lesson 1.

Manipulatives from the Manipulatives Kit

Plastic Coins
Use for identifying coins
and addition activities

Technology Resources

- *Math in Focus* eBooks
- *Math in Focus* Teacher Resources CD
- Online Web Resources
- *Math in Focus* Virtual Manipulatives
  for Lessons 1–3

Classroom/Household Items

- State-specific quarters
  (optional)
- Colored pencils

Differentiation and Assessment

Differentiation for Special Populations (Resources in the Teacher's Edition)

	English Language Learners	Children Needing Reinforcement	Children Needing a Challenge
Lesson 1			Student Book B, Part 2, p. 41
Lesson 2		Student Book B, Part 2, pp. 42–43	Student Book B, Part 2, pp. 42–43
Lesson 3	Math Talk, Teacher's Edition B, p. 155		

Sort and classify coins by attributes, such as coins that are silver and coins that are not; small coins and big coins. Each time you sort, point to and name the coins.

Chapter 20 Assessments

On-Going Assessment	Formal Assessment
See the check questions in the Teacher's Edition on these pages	*Find Formal Assessment Blackline Masters in the Assessments book*
Teacher's Edition B	**Assessments Book**
Lesson 3, p. 156	Assessment 5 for Book B, Part 2, is on pages 28–34 of Assessments. Interview Assessment is on page 35.

Chapter 20 Planning Guide

Lessons and Pacing	Activity	Component	Objectives and Math Focus
Lesson 1	**Coin Values,** pp. 150–151		• Recognize penny, nickel, dime, and quarter. • Know the value of a penny, nickel, dime, and quarter.
DAY **1** Activities	1 Investigate	**Teacher's Edition B,** p. 150	Introduce *penny, nickel, dime, quarter,* and *cent.*
	2 Apply	**Student Book B, Part 2,** p. 41	Match coins to their values.
Lesson 2	**Counting Coins,** pp. 152–154		• Add coins up to 10¢. • Use 1¢ coins to buy up to three objects (up to 10¢).
DAY **1** Activities	1 Explore	**Big Book B,** p. 46	Add and subtract money amounts; introduce the concept of *change.*
	2 Apply	**Student Book B, Part 2,** pp. 42–43	Identify the number of pennies needed to make a purchase.
Lesson 3	**Different Coins, Same Value,** pp. 155–156		• Recognize different combinations of coins that make 10¢.
DAY **1** Activities	1 Explore	**Teacher's Edition B,** p. 155 **Big Book B,** p. 46	Find combinations of coins needed to buy objects.
	2 Apply	**Student Book B, Part 2,** pp. 44–45	Identify the coins needed to make a purchase. **Recall, Reinforce, and Review** Order a set of coins by size and by value.

Vocabulary	Manipulatives/Materials	Class Organization	NTCM Focal Points & Process Standards
penny, nickel, dime, quarter, cent	• *Coins* rhyme (TR31) • Teacher Activity Cards 20.1a–d • Plastic coins, 4 per pair (1 penny, 1 nickel, 1 dime, and 1 quarter) • State-specific quarters (optional)	Whole class Independent	The Focal Points do not address money. • Communication • Representation • Connections
change	• Colored pencils, 1 per child • Plastic pennies, 10	Whole class Independent	Join and separate sets using coins. • Communication • Representation • Connections • Problem solving
	• Plastic coins, 13 per group (10 pennies, 2 nickels, and 1 dime) • Plastic coins (1 penny, 1 nickel, 1 dime, and 1 quarter)	Small groups Independent	Join and separate sets using coins. • Communication • Representation • Connections • Problem solving

Money

Lesson 1
Coin Values

LESSON OBJECTIVES
- Recognize penny, nickel, dime, and quarter.
- Know the value of a penny, nickel, dime, and quarter.

MATERIALS
- *Coins* rhyme (TR31)
- Teacher Activity Cards 20.1a–d
- Plastic coins
- State-specific quarters (optional)

Vocabulary

penny

nickel

dime

quarter

cent

> This is a penny. It is brown and worth 1 cent.

DAY 1

Teacher's Edition B, pp. 150–151
Student Book B, Part 2, p. 41

ACTIVITY 1
Investigate

Math Focus: Introduce *penny, nickel, dime, quarter,* and *cent.*
Materials: *Coins* rhyme (TR31)
   Teacher Activity Cards 20.1a–d
   Plastic coins, 4 per pair (1 penny, 1 nickel, 1 dime, and 1 quarter)
   State-specific quarters (optional)
Classroom Setup: Whole class

1. *Invite* children to sit at the front of the classroom.

2. *Recite* the *Coins* rhyme to children. As the rhyme is said, hold up cards 20.1a–d in the order the coins are mentioned in the rhyme.

3. *Set* the cards on the board's implement tray. Write 1¢, 5¢, 10¢, and 25¢ above the appropriate card.

4. *Distribute* coins to each pair of children.

5. *Tell* them that each coin has a different value and is worth a different number of cents.

6. *Describe* the coins to children. *Say:*
   - A penny has a picture of Abraham Lincoln on one side and the Lincoln Memorial in Washington, D.C., on the other side.
   - A nickel has a picture of Thomas Jefferson on one side and a picture of his home, Monticello, on the other side.
   - A dime has a picture of Franklin Delano Roosevelt on one side and on the other side, a torch with two tree branches.
   - Some quarters have a picture of George Washington on one side and on the other side, the presidential coat of arms (an eagle with outstretched wings).

   Best Practices You may want to discuss with and show children any state quarters you have available, especially the quarter for your state.

7. As each coin is described, ask children to recall its value in cents.

8. *Draw* children's attention to the values written on the board. Explain that the symbol ¢ means cents.

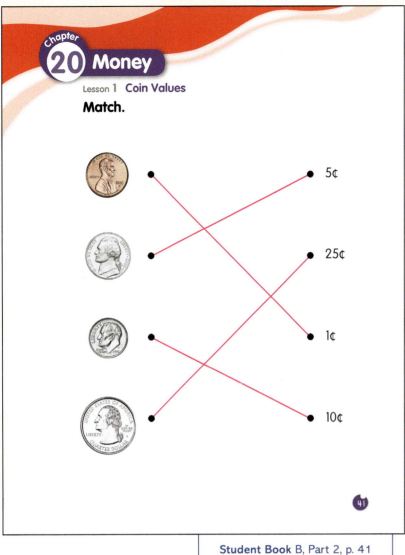

Lesson 1 **Coin Values**

Match.

5¢

25¢

1¢

10¢

41

Student Book B, Part 2, p. 41

ACTIVITY 2
Apply

Math Focus: Match coins to their values.
Resource: Student Book B, Part 2, p. 41
Classroom Setup: Children work independently.

1. *Encourage* children to return to their places and open their Student Books to page 41.

2. Children draw a line to match each coin to its corresponding value.

3. After children complete the activity, have them compare the size of the coins to their values. *Ask:*
   • Does the biggest coin have the most value? (Yes, the quarter is the biggest and has the most value.)
   • Does the smallest coin have the least value? (No, the dime is the smallest but has more value than the penny.)

Differentiated Instruction for Activity 2

Challenge

Classroom Setup: *Teacher with a child or two*

Suggest that children ask an adult if there are any other coins in the U.S., what they are called, and what their values are.

Lesson 2
Counting Coins

LESSON OBJECTIVES
- Add coins up to 10¢.
- Use 1¢ coins to buy up to three objects (up to 10¢).

MATERIALS
- Colored pencils
- Plastic coins

Vocabulary

change

DAY 1

Teacher's Edition B, pp. 152–154
Big Book B, p. 46
Student Book B, Part 2,
pp. 42–43

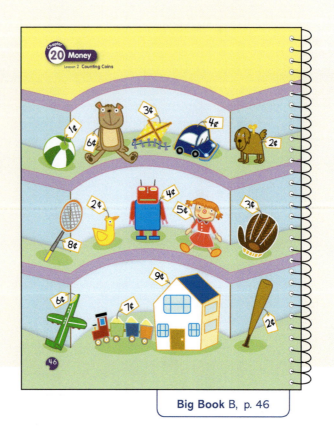

Big Book B, p. 46

DAY 1

ACTIVITY 1
Explore

Math Focus: Add and subtract money amounts; introduce the concept of *change*.
Resource: Big Book B, p. 46
Classroom Setup: Whole class, in front of the Big Book

1. **Ask** children to sit so that everyone can see the Big Book.

2. **Talk** about the picture of a toy shop showing toys with price tags.

3. **Ask:**
   - Which toy costs 1¢? (the ball)
   - Which toys cost 2¢? (the wind-up dog, the duck, and the baseball bat)
   - Which toys cost 3¢? (the kite and the baseball glove)
   - Which toys cost 4¢? (the car and the robot)
   - Which toy costs 5¢? (the doll)
   - Which toys cost 6¢? (the teddy bear and the aeroplane)
   - Which toy costs 7¢? (the train)
   - Which toy costs 8¢? (the racket)
   - Which toy costs 9¢? (the doll house)

4. **Ask:** How can you find out how many cents you need to buy the teddy bear and the duck?

5. **Write** on the board:

The teddy bear costs 6¢.

The duck costs 2¢.

What is the cost of both toys?

Then, write the number sentence with the help of the children:

6¢ + 2¢ = 8¢

The cost of both toys is 8¢.

6. **Ask:** How many cents do you need to buy the ball, the doll, and the kite? (9¢)

7. **Write** on the board:

The ball costs 1¢.

The doll costs 5¢.

The kite costs 3¢.

What is the cost of all three toys?

Then, write the number sentence with the help of the children:

1¢ + 5¢ + 3¢ = 9¢

The cost of the three toys is 9¢.

8. **Suggest** to children that they have only one dime. **Ask:**
   • What is the value of your dime? (10¢)
   • Do you have enough money to buy these three toys? (yes)
   • How can you find out?

9. **Ask:** If you give the cashier your dime, how much money would you get back? (1¢)

10. **Write** the following number sentence on the board:

   10¢ – 9¢ = 1¢

11. **Explain** that the amount you get back is called *change*.

12. **Explain** that you can add and subtract coin values in the same way you add and subtract numbers. You can write number stories and number sentences using coin values in the same way as well.

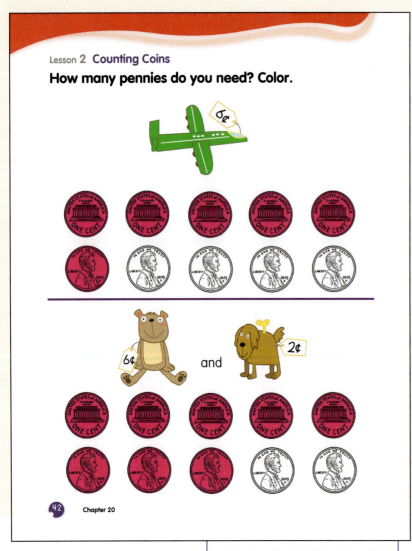

Lesson 2 **Counting Coins**

How many pennies do you need? Color.

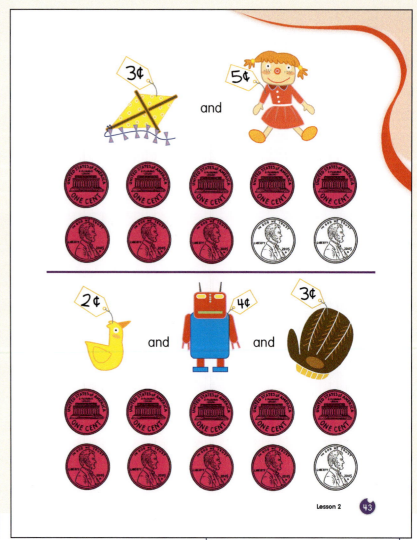

Student Book B, Part 2, p. 42

Student Book B, Part 2, p. 43

ACTIVITY 2
Apply

Math Focus: Identify the number of pennies needed to make a purchase.

Resource: Student Book B, Part 2, pp. 42–43

Materials: Colored pencils, 1 per child

Classroom Setup: Children work independently.

1. *Encourage* children to return to their places and open their Student Books to page 42.

2. *Distribute* materials to the children.

3. Children color the number of pennies required to purchase each toy or set of toys in each exercise.

Best Practices Remind children that each penny is worth 1 cent.

Differentiated Instruction for Activity 2

Reinforcement

Materials: *Plastic pennies, 10*

Classroom Setup: *Teacher with a child or two*

For exercises 2–4, have children count out the number of pennies for each toy and then combine the coins to find the total.

Challenge

Classroom Setup: *Teacher with a child or two*

Ask children how many pennies they would have left after paying for the toys with the 10 pennies shown. (4, 2, 2, and 1)

Lesson 3
Different Coins, Same Value

LESSON OBJECTIVE
• Recognize different combinations of coins that make 10¢.

MATERIALS
• Plastic coins

DAY 1
Teacher's Edition B, pp. 155–156
Big Book B, p. 46
Student Book B, Part 2, pp. 44–45

DAY 1

7 pennies make 7 cents.

1 nickel and 2 pennies also make 7 cents.

ACTIVITY 1
Explore

Math Focus: Find combinations of coins needed to buy objects.

Resource: Big Book B, p. 46

Materials: Plastic coins, 13 per group (10 pennies, 2 nickels, and 1 dime)

Classroom Setup: Children work in small groups.

1. *Distribute* materials to the children.

2. *Refer* to the picture on page 46 of Big Book B, and ask each group to select a toy.

3. *Tell* children to pretend that they are buying this toy. Ask them to select the coins to show how much the toy costs.

4. **Math Talk** Ask one child from each group to tell which toy and which coins they selected, and why.

5. *Repeat* steps 2 and 3, but this time, have each group select two toys.

6. *Guide* children to use other combinations of coins to show the cost of these toys.

7. **Math Talk** Ask a different child from each group what coin combinations they found to pay for their two toys.

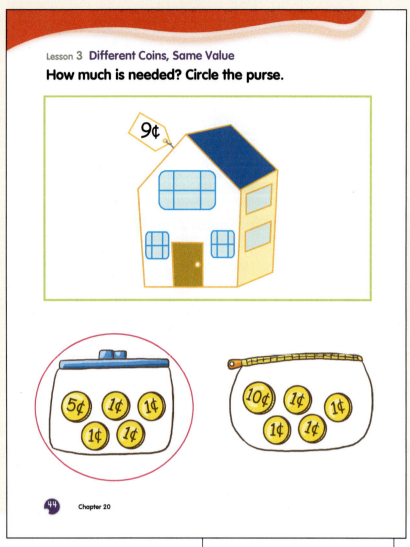

Student Book B, Part 2, p. 44

Student Book B, Part 2, p. 45

ACTIVITY 2
Apply

Math Focus: Identify the coins needed to make a purchase.
Resource: Student Book B, Part 2, pp. 44–45
Classroom Setup: Children work independently.

1. Children circle the purse on each page that represents the total amount needed to buy the toy(s) in each exercise.

✓ 2. While children engage in the activity, ask check questions such as:
   • How much money is in this purse?
   • Is it the same as the cost of the object(s)?
   • How do you know? Are you sure?

> **Recall, Reinforce, and Review**
>
> Ask children to order a set of coins (penny, nickel, dime, and quarter) by size, and then by value. Each time the order is complete, they should say the name of each coin as they touch it.

Professional Resources Bibliography

American Institutes for Research.® *What the United States Can Learn from Singapore's World-Class Mathematics System.* U. S. Department of Education Policy and Program Studies Services, 2005.

Chapin, Susan and Art Johnson. *Math Matters: Understanding the Math You Teach.* Math Solutions Publications, 2000.

Chapin, Susan, Catherine. O'Connor, and Nancy Canavan Anderson. *Classroom Discussions: Using Math Talk to Help Students Learn.* Math Solutions Publications, 2003.

Charles, Randall. *Teaching and Assessing of Mathematical Problem Solving.* Lawrence Earlbaum, 1989.

Copley, Juanita. *Mathematics in the Early Years,* National Council of Teachers of Mathematics, 1999.

Copley, Juanita. *The Young Child and Mathematics,* National Council of Teachers of Mathematics, 2000.

Gonzales, Patrick, Juan Carlos Guzmán, Lisette Partelow, Erin Pahlke, Leslie Jocelyn, David Kastberg, and Trevor Williams. *Highlights From the Trends in International Mathematics and Science Study: TIMSS 2003.* U.S. Department of Education, National Center for Education Statistics, 2004.

Hiebert, J., T. Carpenter, E. Fennema, K. Fuson, D. Wearne, H. Murray, A. Olivier, and P. Human. *Making Sense: Teaching and Learning Mathematics with Understanding.* Heinemann, 1997.

Fong, Dr. Ho Kheong. *The Essential Parents' Guide to Primary Maths.* Marshall Cavendish International, 2002.

Lee, Peng Yee, ed. *Teaching Primary School Mathematics: A Resource Guide.* Singapore Math Education Series, McGraw Hill Education, 2007.

Lee, Peng Yee, ed. *Teaching Secondary School Mathematics: A Resource Book.* Singapore Math Education Series, McGraw Hill Education, 2008

Ma, Liping. *Knowing and Teaching Elementary Mathematics.* Lawrence Earlbaum Associates, Inc., 1999. Martin et al. *TIMSS 2003 International Mathematics Report: Findings from IEA's Trends in International Mathematics and Science Study at the Eighth and Fourth-Grades.* Institute of Education Sciences, 2004.

National Council of Teachers of Mathematics. *Curriculum Focal Points for Prekindergarten through Grade 8 Mathematics,* 2006.

National Council of Teachers of Mathematics. *Principals and Standards for School Mathematics,* 2000.

National Mathematics Advisory Panel. *Foundations for Success.* U.S. Department of Education, 2008.

National Research Council. *Adding It Up: Helping Children Learn Mathematics.* Washington, D.C., National Academy Press, 2001

Ng Chye Huat, Juliana (Mrs.) and Mrs. Lim Kian Huat. *A Handbook for Mathematics Teachers in Primary Schools.* Marshall Cavendish International, 2003.

Polya, George. *How to Solve It.* Princeton University Press, 1945.

Richardson, Kathy. *Developing Number Concepts Books* (Grades K-3): *Counting, Comparing, and Pattern Book 1; Addition and Subtraction, Book 2; Place Value, Multiplication, and Division.* Dale Seymour Publications, 1998.

Stigler, James W. and James Hiebert. *The Teaching Gap: Best Ideas from the World's Teachers for Improving Education in the Classroom.* The Free Press, 1999.

Sullivan, Peter, and Pat Lilburn. *Good Questions for Math Teaching: Why Ask Them and What to Ask.* Math Solutions Publications, 1997.

Van de Walle, John A. *Elementary and Middle School Mathematics: Teaching Developmentally.* Allyn and Bacon, 2003.

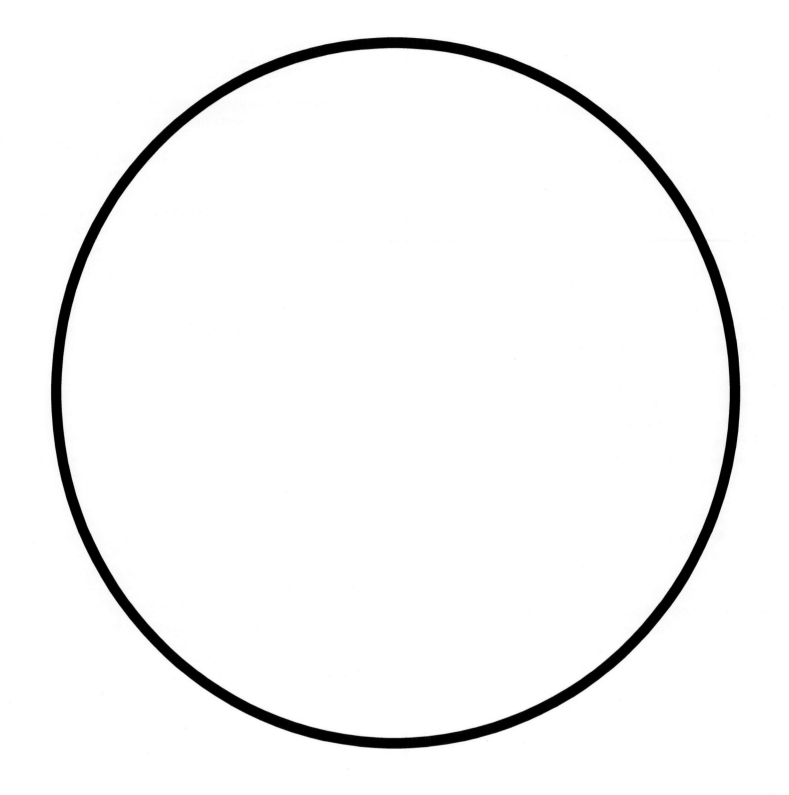

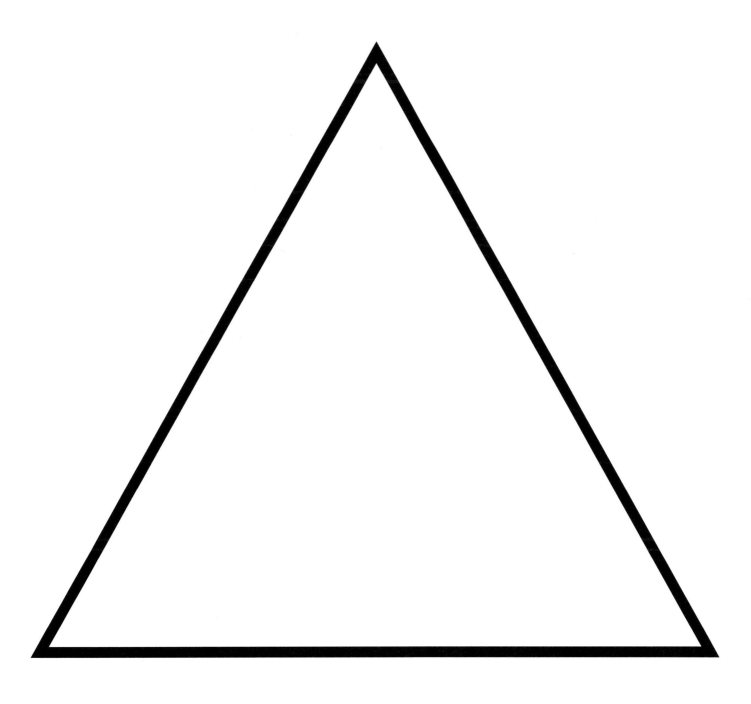

Triangle   **TR18**
Use with Teacher's Edition B, pp. 6, 9, and 14

Rectangle **TR20**
Use with Teacher's Edition B, pp. 6, 9, and 14

Number Line 1–10 **TR21**
Use with Big Book B, p. 10,
Teacher's Edition B, p. 33

Counting Claps

One, one,
All clap one.

Two, two,
All clap two.

Three, three,
All clap three.

Four, four,
All clap four.

Five, five,
All clap five.

Six, six,
All clap six.

Seven, seven,
All clap seven.

Eight, eight,
All clap eight.

Nine, nine,
All clap nine.

Ten, ten,
All clap ten.

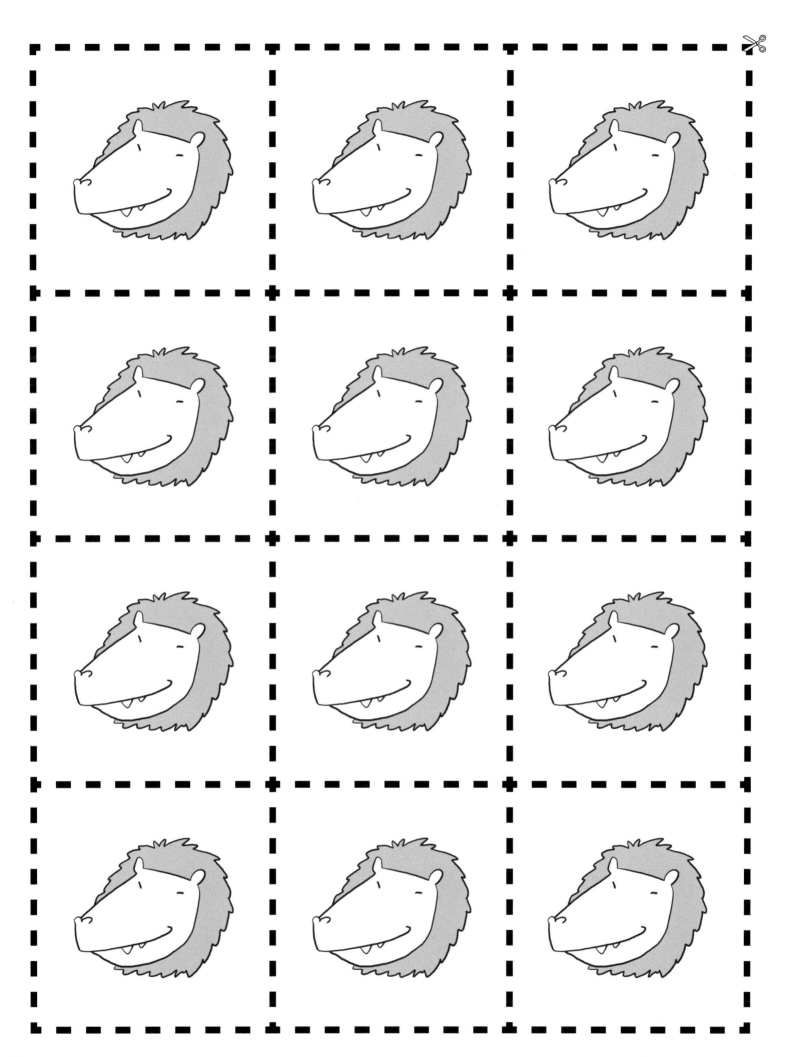

Lion Faces   TR24
Use with Teacher's Edition B, p. 60

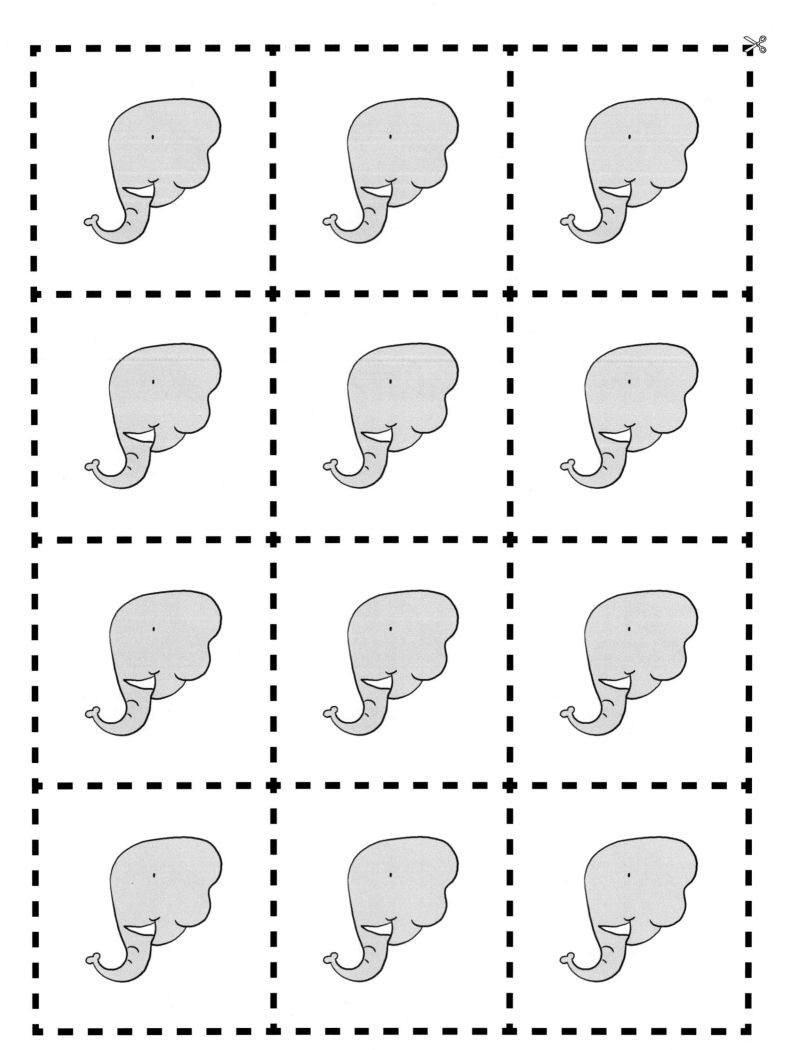

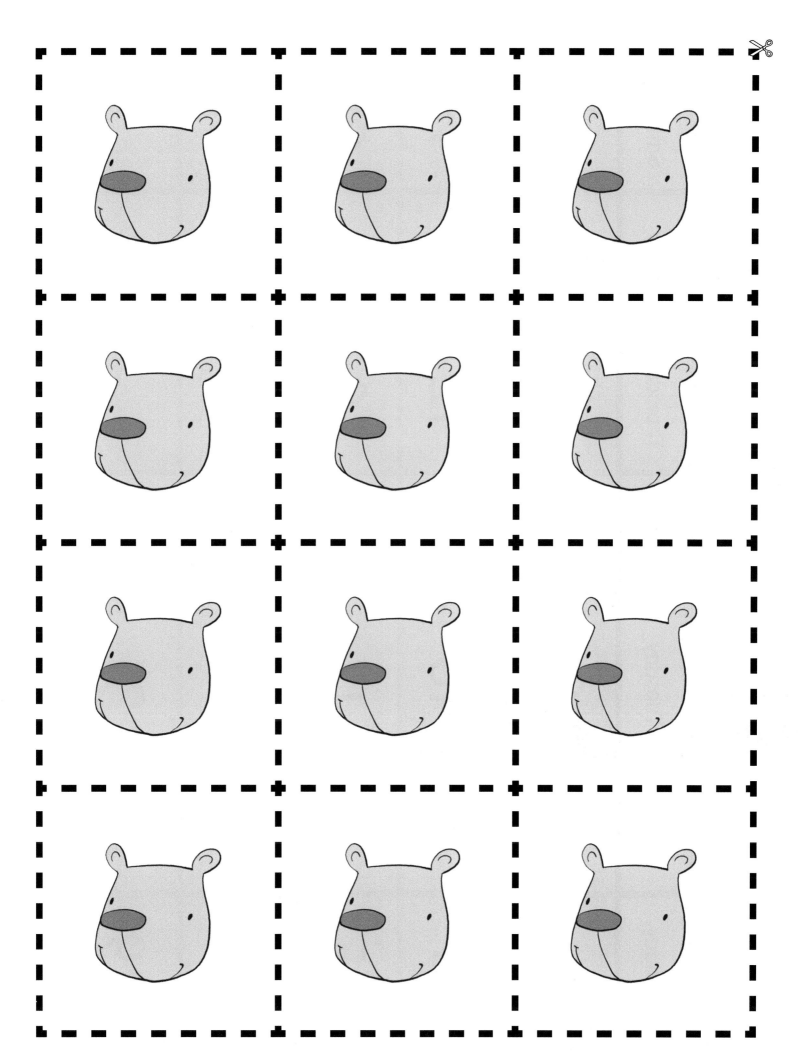

Bear Faces   **TR26**
Use with Teacher's Edition B, p. 60

Month: _____

Sunday	Monday	Tuesday	Wednesday	Thursday	Friday	Saturday
1	2	3	4	5	6	7
8	9	10	11	12	13	14
15	16	17	18	19	20	21
22	23	24	25	26	27	28
29	30	31				

Teacher Resource Page: T42

Calendar Page a   TR27a
Use with Big Book B, p. 15,
Teacher's Edition B, pp. 63 and 64

Month: _____

Sunday	Monday	Tuesday	Wednesday	Thursday	Friday	Saturday
	1	2	3	4	5	6
7	8	9	10	11	12	13
14	15	16	17	18	19	20
21	22	23	24	25	26	27
28	29	30	31			

Calendar Page b   TR27b
Use with Big Book B, p. 15,
Teacher's Edition B, pp. 63 and 64

Month: _____

Sunday	Monday	Tuesday	Wednesday	Thursday	Friday	Saturday
		1	2	3	4	5
6	7	8	9	10	11	12
13	14	15	16	17	18	19
20	21	22	23	24	25	26
27	28	29	30	31		

© 2009 Marshall Cavendish International (Singapore) Private Limited

Calendar Page c   **TR27c**
Use with Big Book B, p. 15,
Teacher's Edition B, pp. 63 and 64

Month: _____

Sunday	Monday	Tuesday	Wednesday	Thursday	Friday	Saturday
			1	2	3	4
5	6	7	8	9	10	11
12	13	14	15	16	17	18
19	20	21	22	23	24	25
26	27	28	29	30	31	

Calendar Page d   TR27d
Use with Big Book B, p. 15,
Teacher's Edition B, pp. 63 and 64

Month: _____

Sunday	Monday	Tuesday	Wednesday	Thursday	Friday	Saturday
				1	2	3
4	5	6	7	8	9	10
11	12	13	14	15	16	17
18	19	20	21	22	23	24
25	26	27	28	29	30	31

Teacher Resource Page: T46

© 2009 Marshall Cavendish International (Singapore) Private Limited

Calendar Page e   TR27e
Use with Big Book B, p. 15,
Teacher's Edition B, pp. 63 and 64

Month: _____

Sunday	Monday	Tuesday	Wednesday	Thursday	Friday	Saturday
31					1	2
3	4	5	6	7	8	9
10	11	12	13	14	15	16
17	18	19	20	21	22	23
24	25	26	27	28	29	30

Calendar Page f   TR27f
Use with Big Book B, p. 15,
Teacher's Edition B, pp. 63 and 64

Teacher Resource Page: T47

Month: _____

Sunday	Monday	Tuesday	Wednesday	Thursday	Friday	Saturday
30	31					1
2	3	4	5	6	7	8
9	10	11	12	13	14	15
16	17	18	19	20	21	22
23	24	25	26	27	28	29

Calendar Page g   TR27g
Use with Big Book B, p. 15,
Teacher's Edition B, pp. 63 and 64

Stick Figures   **TR28**
Use with Teacher's Edition B, pp. 66 and 67

| 0 | 1 | 2 | 3 | 4 | 5 | 6 | 7 | 8 | 9 | 10 | 11 | 12 | 13 | 14 | 15 |

Grey Tiles **TR30**
Use with Student Book B, Part 2, pp. 39–40

Coins

A penny is small and easily spent,
It's copper-colored brown and worth 1 cent.

A nickel is thicker and weighs a bit more
You can use this 5-cent piece to buy at the store.

A dime looks silver and is really small,
It's worth 10 cents and is the thinnest of them all.

A quarter is large and heavy and shiny,
It's worth 25 cents—that's a lot of money!

Index for Book A and Book B

Q

R

S

Notes

Notes

Math in Focus

Singapore Math
by Marshall Cavendish

Student Book
Kindergarten Ⓑ
Part 1

Author
Dr. Pamela Sharpe

U.S. Consultants
Andy Clark and Patsy F. Kanter

Marshall Cavendish
Education

**Houghton
Mifflin
Harcourt**

Published by Marshall Cavendish Education
Times Centre, 1 New Industrial Road, Singapore 536196
Customer Service Hotline: (65) 6213 9444
US Office Tel: (1-914) 332 8888 | Fax: (1-914) 332 8882
E-mail: tmesales@mceducation.com
Website: www.mceducation.com

Distributed by
Houghton Mifflin Harcourt
222 Berkeley Street
Boston, MA 02116
Tel: 617-351-5000
Website: www.hmheducation.com/mathinfocus

First published 2009

Math in Focus® Kindergarten B Part 1
ISBN 978-0-669-01635-2

Printed in Singapore

14 15 16   1401   19 18
4500697353   B C D E

Contents

Contents

Lesson 1 Solid Shapes

Match.

Lesson 2 Solid Shapes in Everyday Things

Pair.

Lesson 3 **Flat Shapes**

Draw.

Big circle

Small circle

Small square

Big square

5

Draw.

Small triangle

Big triangle

Big rectangle

Small rectangle

Color the squares red. Color the rectangles green. Color the circles yellow. Color the triangles blue.

Lesson 6 Shape Patterns

Complete the pattern.

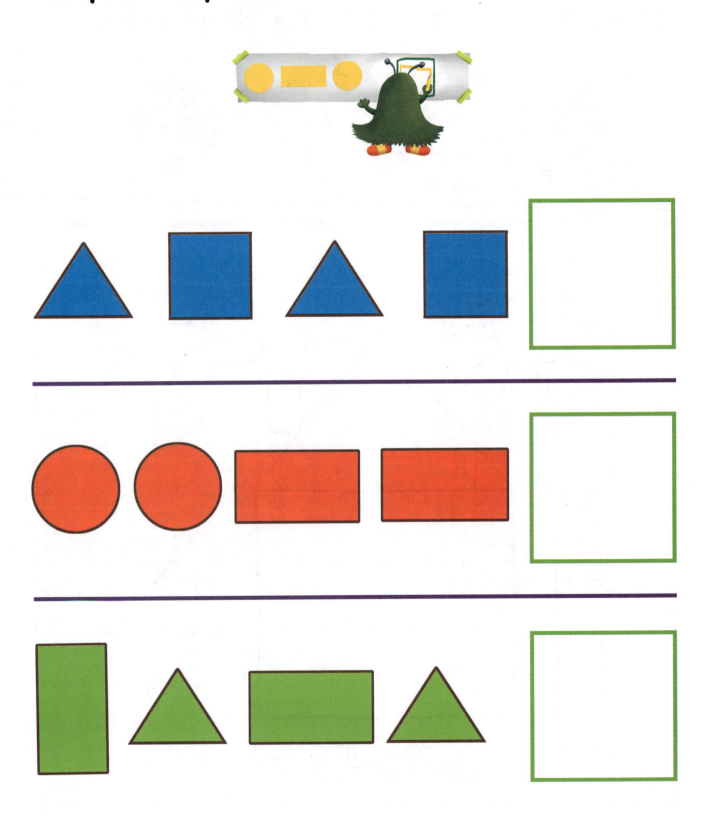

Counting by 2s and 5s

Lesson 1   Making Pairs

Pair.

Count and write.

 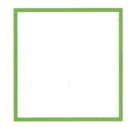　　　　

Lesson 3 **Counting by 5s**

Circle the groups of 5 ants.

Make the tally.

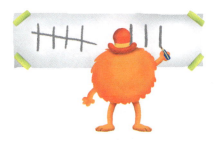

Lesson 4 Odd and Even Numbers

Count and write. Circle to show if the number is odd or even.

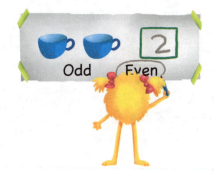

Odd   Even

Odd   Even

Odd   Even

Odd   Even

Odd   Even

Color the odd numbers red.
Color the even numbers green.

1	2	3	4
5	6	7	8
9	10	11	12
13	14	15	16
17	18	19	20

Lesson 5 Number Conservation

Pair.

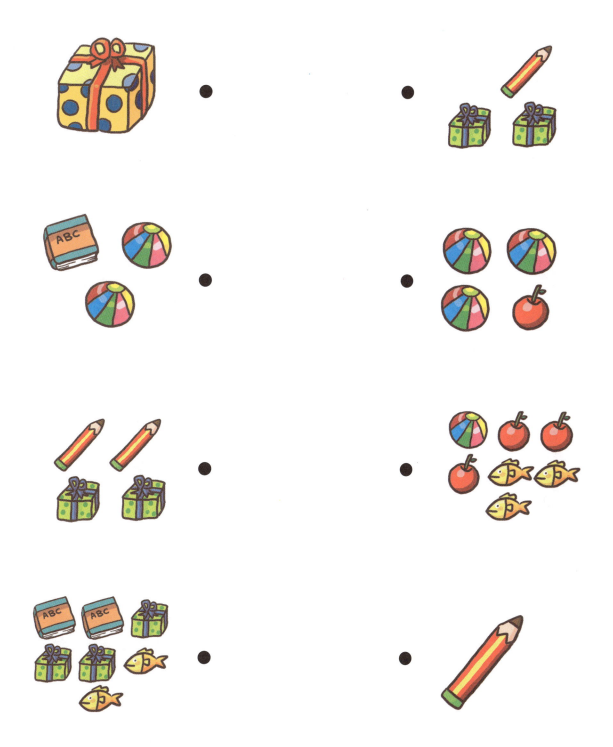

Comparing Sets

Lesson 1 Comparing Sets One-to-One

Count and write.

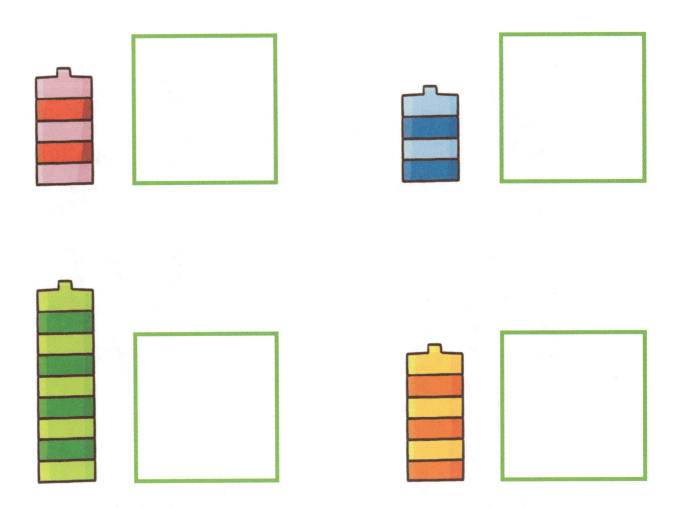

Count, circle, and write.

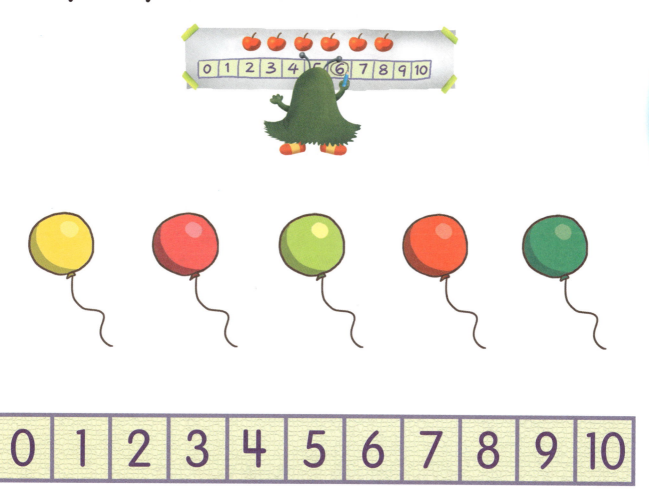

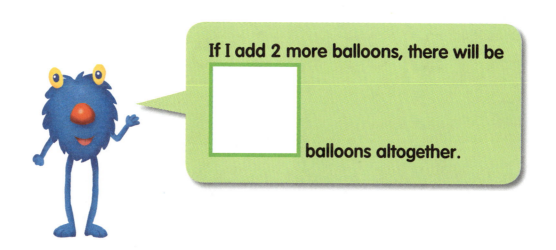

If I add 2 more balloons, there will be

☐

balloons altogether.

Count, circle, and write.

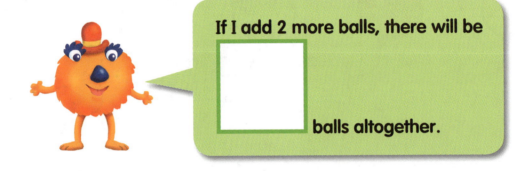

If I add 2 more balls, there will be
[ ] balls altogether.

If I add 2 more cups, there will be
[ ] cups altogether.

Lesson 3 Fewer and More

Color the extra cubes red.
Count and write how many more.

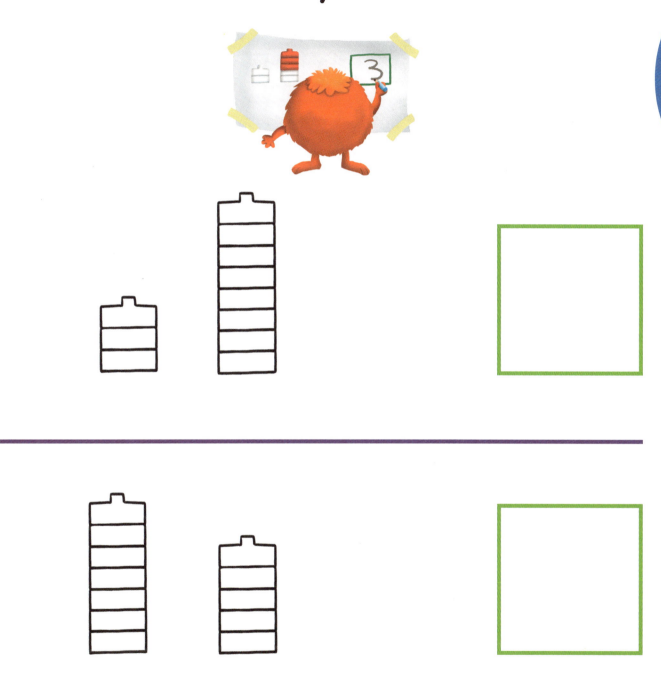

Draw, count, and write.

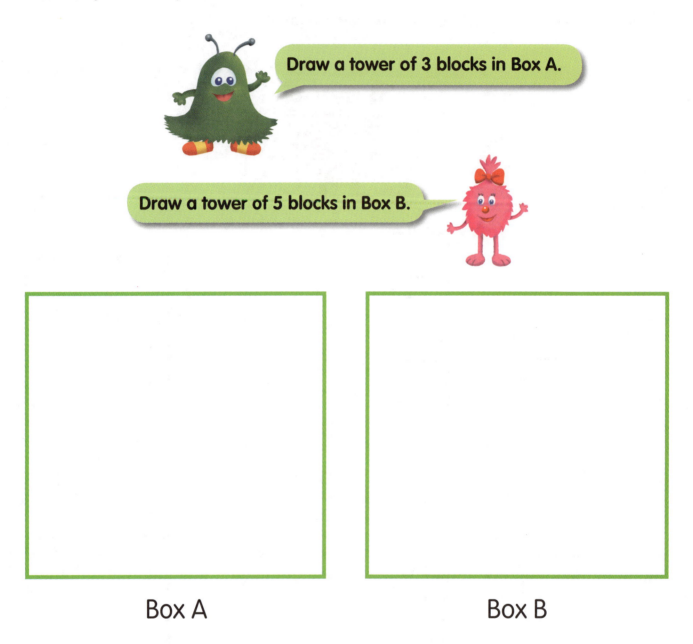

Draw a tower of 3 blocks in Box A.

Draw a tower of 5 blocks in Box B.

Box A

Box B

The tower in Box A has _____ fewer blocks than the

tower in Box B.

Count and circle.

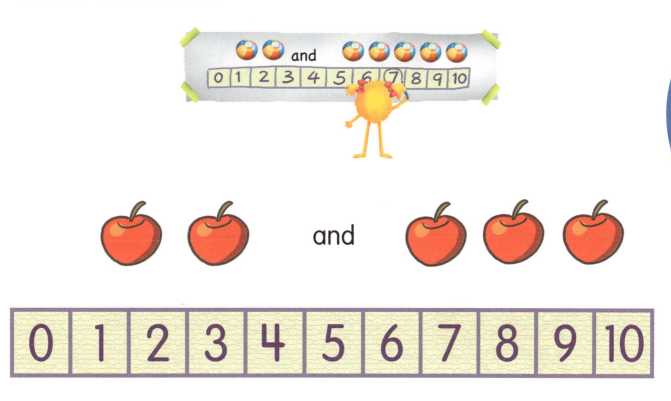

and

| 0 | 1 | 2 | 3 | 4 | 5 | 6 | 7 | 8 | 9 | 10 |

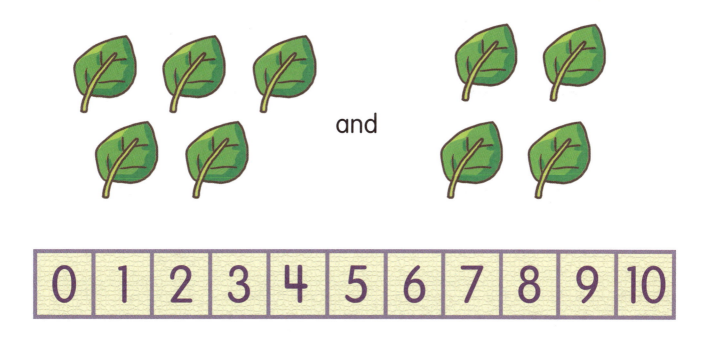

and

| 0 | 1 | 2 | 3 | 4 | 5 | 6 | 7 | 8 | 9 | 10 |

Count and circle.

 and

0	1	2	3	4	5	6	7	8	9	10

 and

0	1	2	3	4	5	6	7	8	9	10

 and

0	1	2	3	4	5	6	7	8	9	10

Lesson 7 Counting On Using Fingers

Count and write.

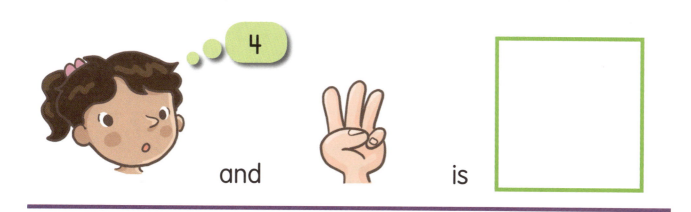

23

Count and write.

7 and [hand] is [ ]

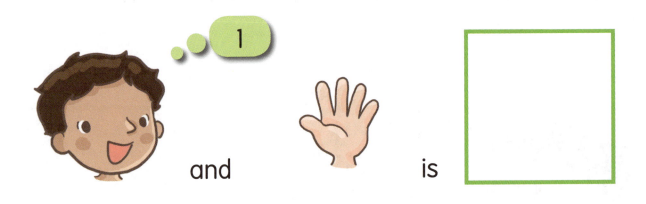

1 and [hand] is [ ]

9 and [hand] is [ ]

Chapter 10

Ordinal Numbers

Lesson 1 'First', 'Next', and 'Last'

Pair.

first •   •

next •   •

last •   •

Color the frames.

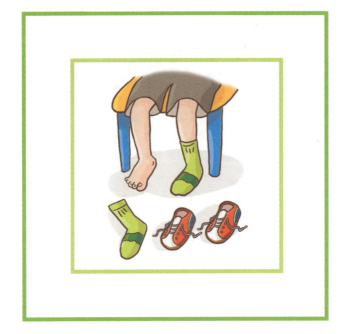

Color.

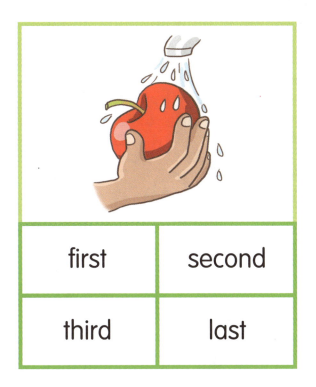

first	second
third	last

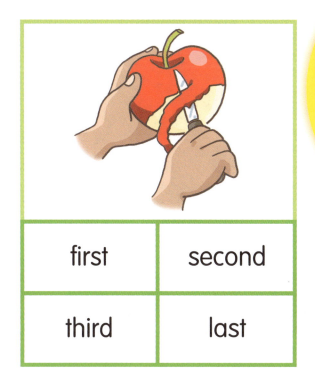

first	second
third	last

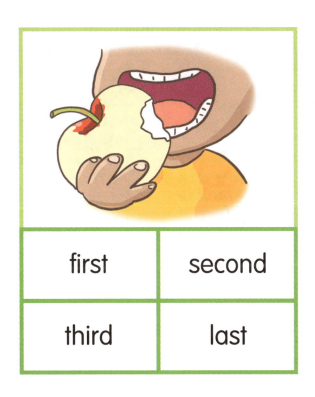

first	second
third	last

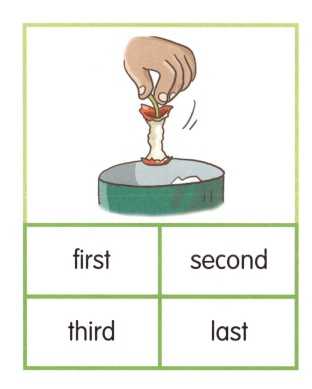

first	second
third	last

27

Color the child that comes before Baby Bear.
Circle the child that comes after Baby Bear.

Pair.

1ˢᵗ choice •

2ⁿᵈ choice •

3ʳᵈ choice •

Lesson 2 Months of the Year

Make an X on the month before August. Circle the month after February. Color the month between October and December.

1 **January**	2 **February**	3 **March**
4 **April**	5 **May**	6 **June**
7 **July**	8 **August**	9 **September**
10 **October**	11 **November**	12 **December**

Chapter 12

Counting On and Counting Back

Lesson 1 Counting On Using Fingers

How many more to make 10? Count and write.

How many more to make 10? Count and write.

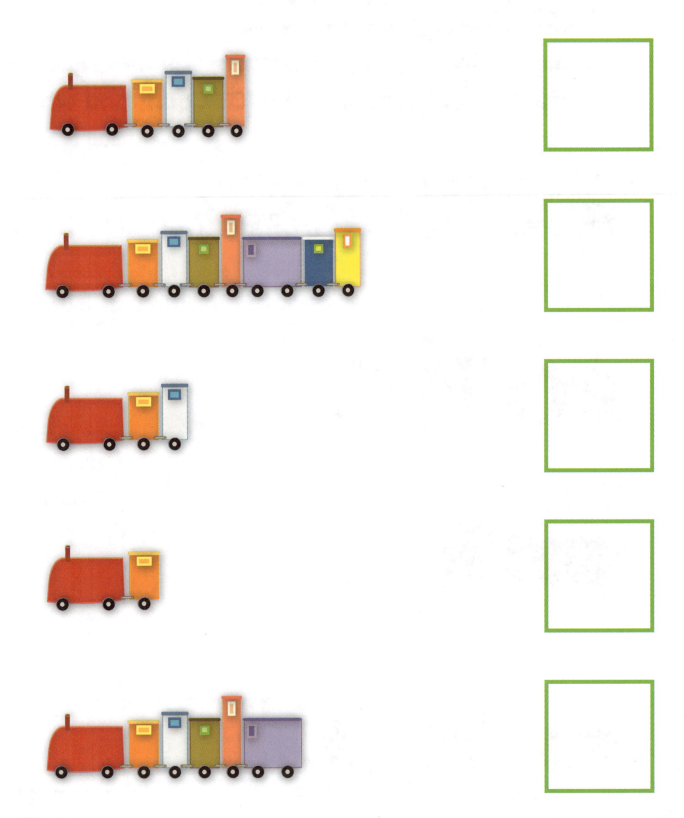

Lesson **1** **Repeating Shape Patterns**

The shapes follow a repeating pattern. Circle the shape that comes next.

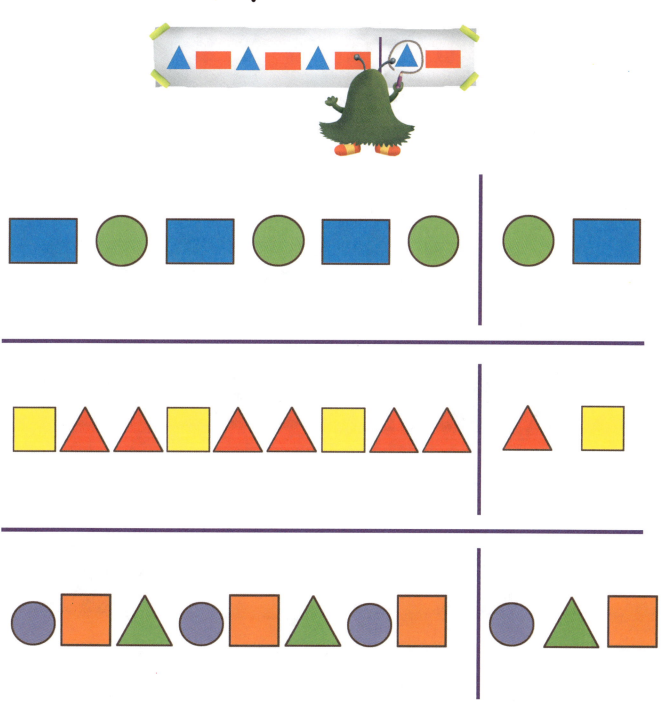

The shapes follow a repeating pattern.
Draw the missing shapes to complete the pattern.

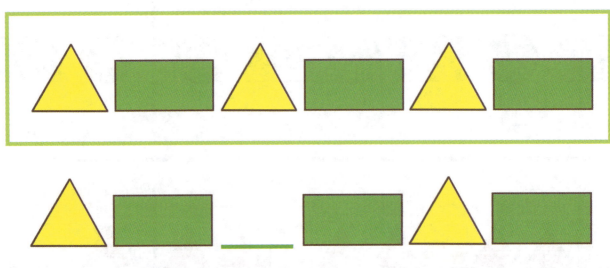

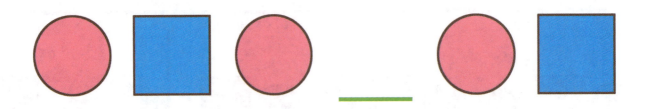

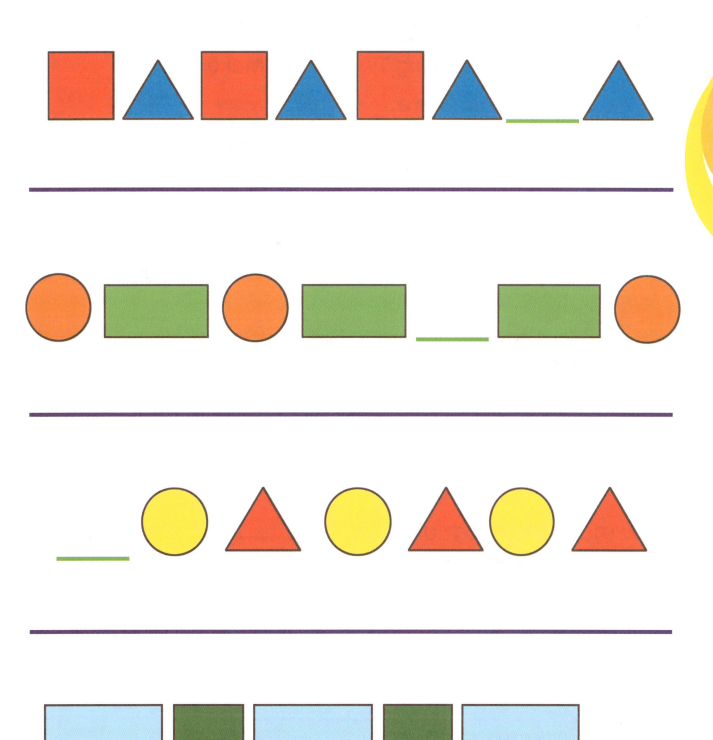

Lesson 1 Combining Two Sets to Make 10

Count and write.

Count how many.
How many more to
make 10?

6
4

Count how many.   _____

How many more to make 10?   _____

Count how many.   _____

How many more to make 10?   _____

Count how many. _____

How many more to make 10? _____

Count how many. _____

How many more to make 10? _____

Count how many. _____

How many more to make 10? _____

Lesson **2** **Numbers 10 to 20**

Count and trace.

Count and trace.

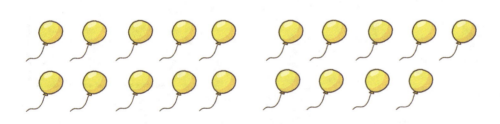 

Count and write.

Count and write.

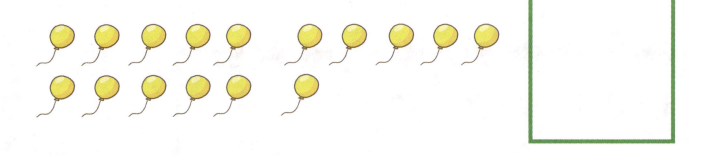

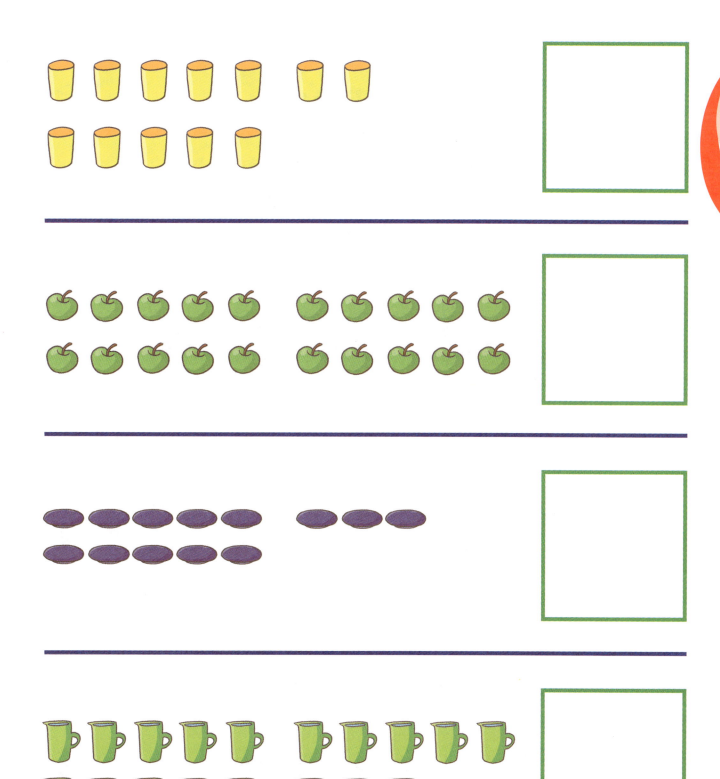

Lesson **3** **Counting On**

Count and write.

Count how many.
How many more to
make 15?

7
8

Count how many. _____

How many more to make 15? _____

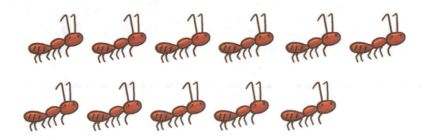

Count how many. _____

How many more to make 15? _____

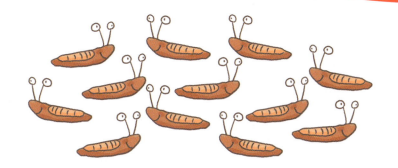

Count how many. _____

How many more to make 15? _____

Count how many. _____

How many more to make 15? _____

Count how many. _____

How many more to make 15? _____

Count and write.

Count how many.
How many more to make 15?

9
6

Count how many.   ————

How many more to make 15?   ————

Count how many.   ————

How many more to make 15?   ————

Count how many. _____

How many more to make 15? _____

Count how many. _____

How many more to make 15? _____

Count how many. _____

How many more to make 15? _____

Math in Focus®

Singapore Math®
by Marshall Cavendish®

Student Book
Kindergarten Ⓑ
Part 2

Author
Dr. Pamela Sharpe

U.S. Consultants
Andy Clark and Patsy F. Kanter

Marshall Cavendish
Education

**Houghton
Mifflin
Harcourt**

© 2009 Marshall Cavendish International (Singapore) Private Limited
© 2014 Marshall Cavendish Education Pte Ltd

Published by Marshall Cavendish Education
Times Centre, 1 New Industrial Road, Singapore 536196
Customer Service Hotline: (65) 6213 9688
US Office Tel: (1-914) 332 8888 | Fax: (1-914) 332 8882
E-mail: cs@mceducation.com
Website: www.mceducation.com

Distributed by
Houghton Mifflin Harcourt
222 Berkeley Street
Boston, MA 02116
Tel: 617-351-5000
Website: www.hmheducation.com/mathinfocus

First published 2009

Math in Focus® Kindergarten B Part 2
ISBN 978-0-669-01638-3

Printed in Singapore

| 14 | 15 | 16 | | 1401 | | 21 | 20 | 19 |
4500754264   B C D E

Contents

Lesson 1 'Long' and 'Short'

Draw a long tail.

Draw a short tail.

Make an X on the kite with the longest tail.
Circle the kite with the shortest tail.

3

Measure, count, and write.

The pencil is _____ cubes long.

The spoon is _____ cubes long.

The toothbrush is _____ cubes long.

The comb is _____ cubes long.

The tube is _____ cubes long.

The paint brush is _____ cubes long.

Count and write. Make an X on the taller vase.

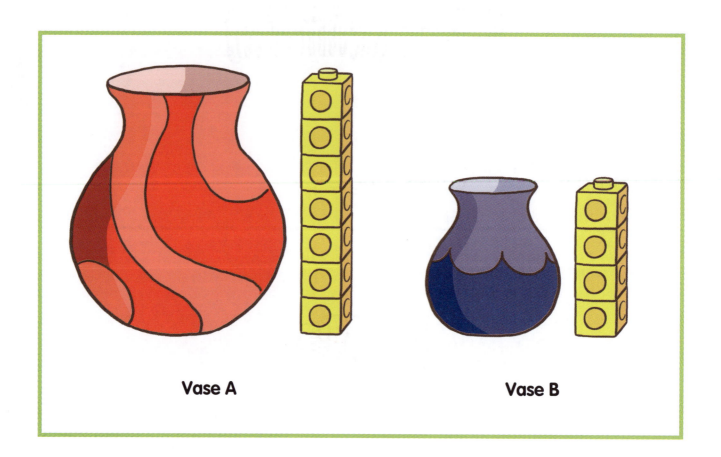

Vase A   Vase B

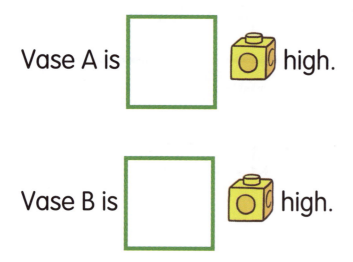

Vase A is [ ] high.

Vase B is [ ] high.

Count and write. Circle the shorter flower.

Flower A   Flower B

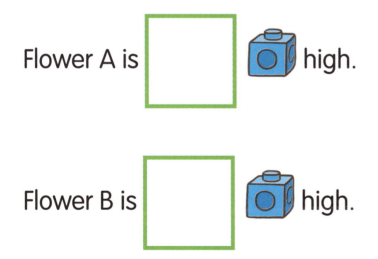

Flower A is ☐ 🔲 high.

Flower B is ☐ 🔲 high.

Lesson 5 **Finding Differences in Length Using Non-standard Units**

Count and write.

The caterpillar is 3 🖇 longer than the ant.

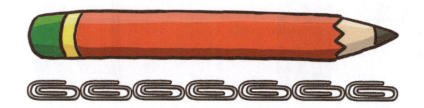

The pencil is _____ 🖇 long.

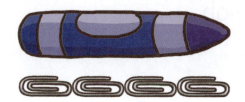

The crayon is _____ 🖇 long.

The pencil is _____ 🖇 longer than the crayon.

The leaf is _____ 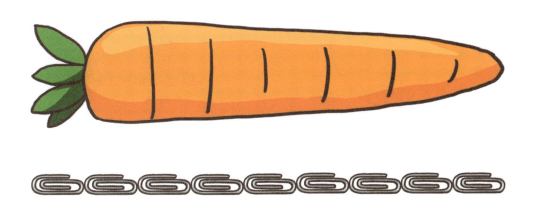 long.

The carrot is _____ 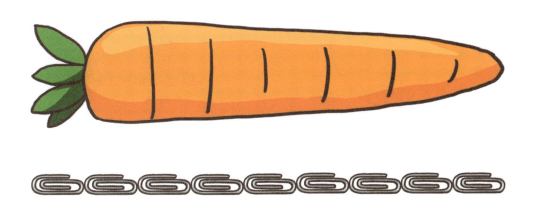 long.

The leaf is _____ shorter than the carrot.

Chapter 16 Classifying and Sorting

Lesson 1   Classifying Things by One Attribute

Sort and match.

•

•

•

•   •

•   •

•   •   •

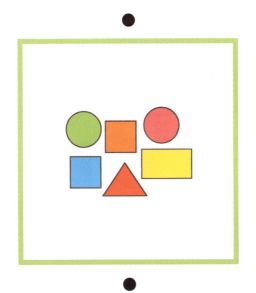

Sort and match.

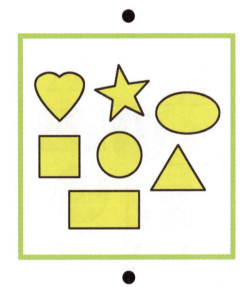

Make an X on the item that does not belong.

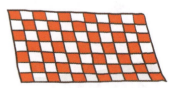

Lesson 1 Writing Addition Sentences

Count and write.

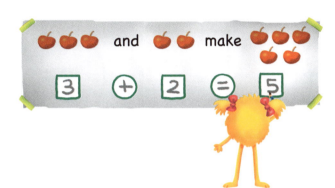

 and  make

| 4 | $+$ | 3 | $=$ | |

---

 and  make

| 2 | $+$ | | $=$ | |

Count and write.

 and  make

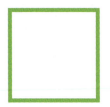 +  =

 and  make

 and  make

Lesson 2 Showing Addition Stories with Numbers
Count and write.

Count and write.

18 Subtraction Stories

Lesson 1 Writing Subtraction Sentences

Count and write.

There are 4 ducks. Take away 2 ducks. How many are left?

4 − 2 = 2

There are 5 bananas.

Take away 2 bananas.

How many are left?

5 − 2 = ☐

There are
7 candles.

Take away
3 candles.

How many
are left?

There are
9 pencils.

Take away
4 pencils.

How many
are left?

Count and write.

How many more? Circle. Write the number sentence.

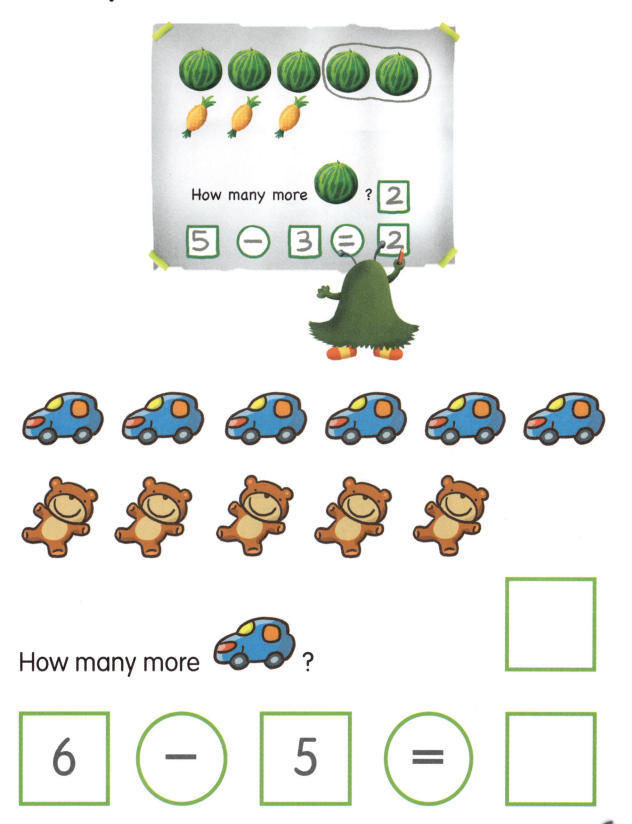

How many more 🚗 ?

6 − 5 = ☐

How many more? Circle. Write the number sentence.

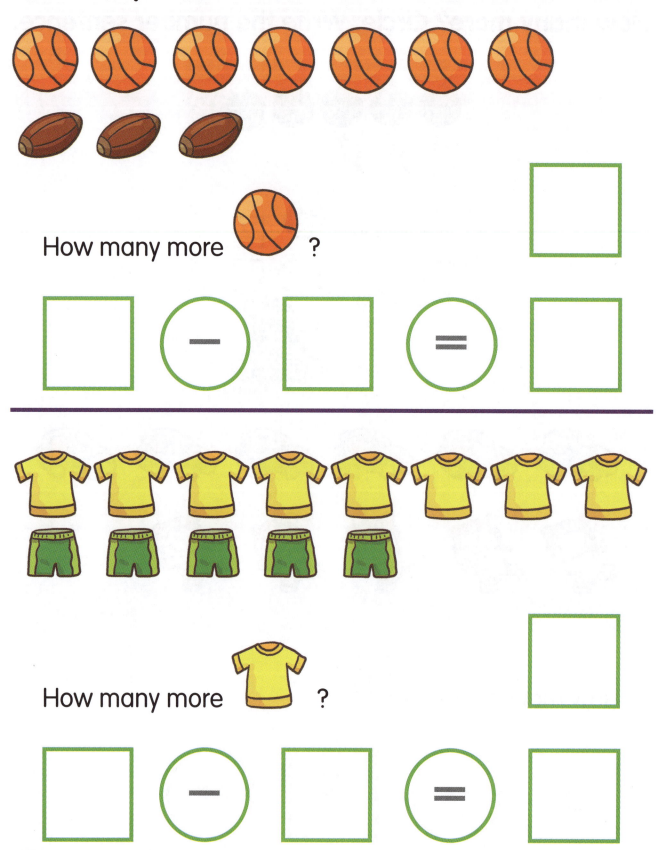

How many more 🏀 ?

☐ ⊖ ☐ ⊜ ☐

How many more 👕 ?

☐ ⊖ ☐ ⊜ ☐

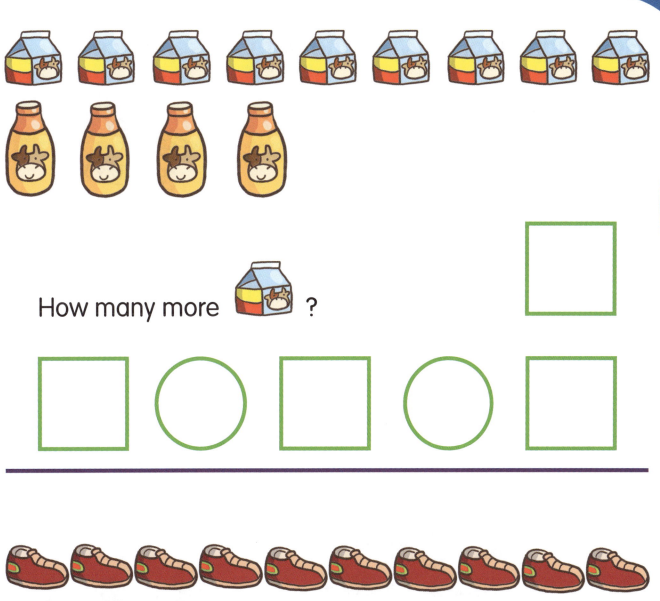

How many more  ?

How many more ?

How many more? Write the number sentence.

There are ☐ more 📗 .

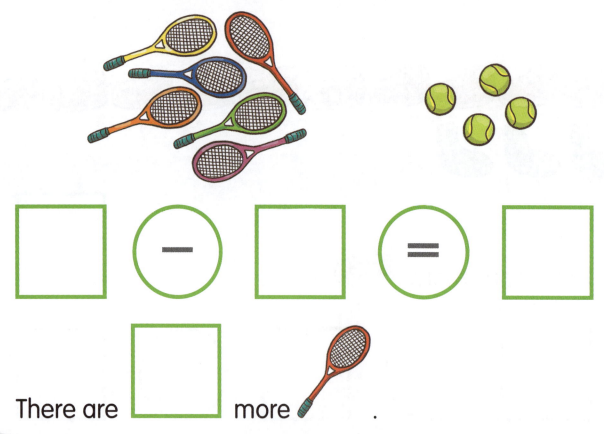

There are ☐ more 🎾 .

There are ☐ more 🍄 .

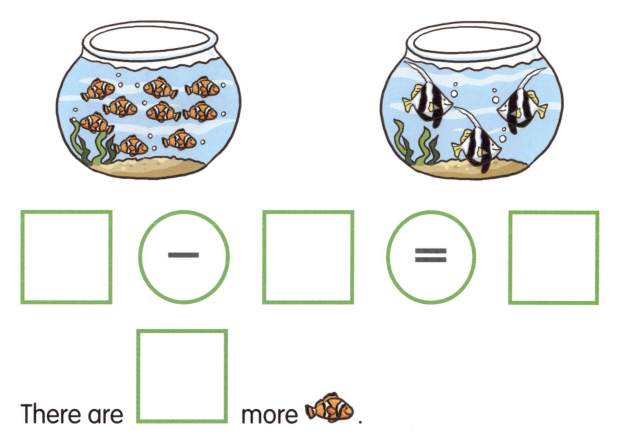

There are ☐ more 🐟 .

Lesson 1 Comparing Weights Using Non-standard Units

Circle the heavier thing.

Circle the lighter thing.

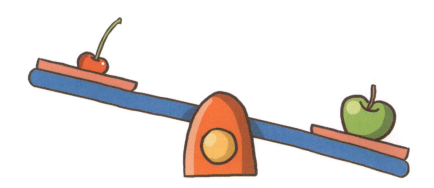

Count and write.

The owl weighs [ ] .

The mouse weighs [ ] .

Circle the heavier animal.

Count and write.

The teddy bear weighs  .

The doll weighs .

Circle the lighter thing.

Circle the container that holds more.

Circle the container that holds less.

Color the containers that hold the same amount.

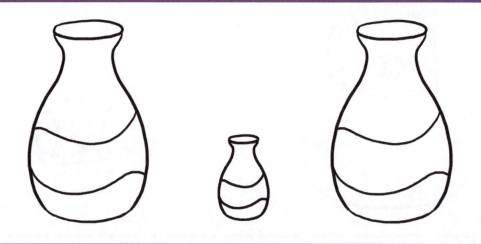

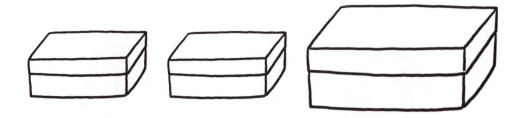

Which takes more time? Circle.

Which takes less time? Circle.

Lesson 4 Comparing Areas Using Non-standard Units

How many squares will cover each thing?
Circle the bigger thing.

How many squares will cover each thing? Circle the smaller thing.

Lesson 1 Coin Values

Match.

 ●   ● 5¢

 ●   ● 25¢

 ●   ● 1¢

 ●   ● 10¢

How many pennies do you need? Color.

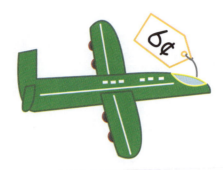

 and

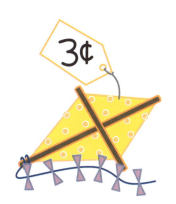 and

 and  and

How much is needed? Circle the purse.

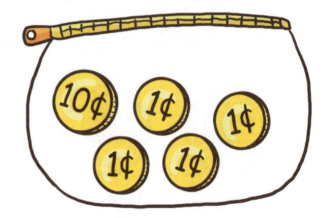

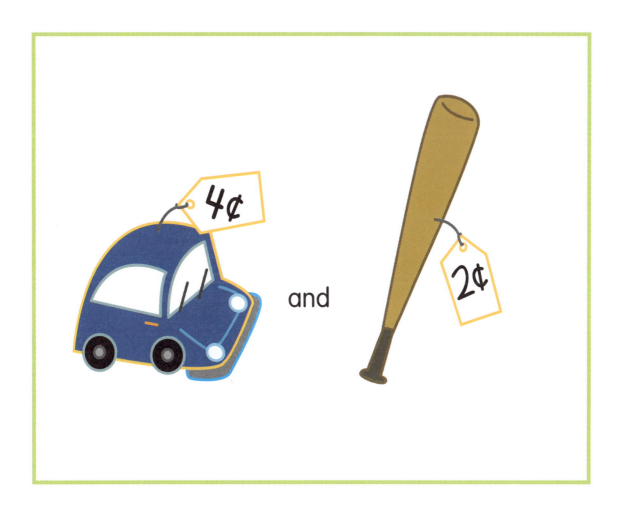

and

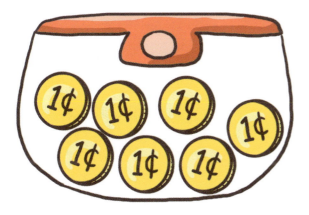

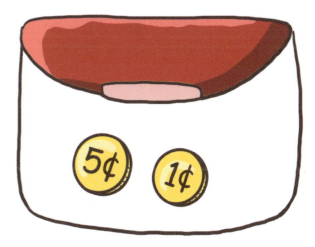